Sexuality, Women, and Tourism

This book is the first to focus on why and how foreign Western women engage in cross-border sexual and intimate relations as tourists traveling, or temporarily dwelling, in a Central American country. As an in-depth ethnographic account, the book traces the experiences of heterosexual North American and European women's transnational encounters, and examines new sexual and social practices arising from contemporary global tourism, shifting sexual cultures both at home and abroad, consumer culture, and women's increasing mobility. The book combines descriptions of women's travels and sexual relations across racial and class boundaries with feminism, postcolonial theory, and poststructuralist theories of gender and sexuality, to show how tourism as a wide range and set of desires serves as a central shaping force in the formation of women's sexual subjectivities in contemporary life in post-industrial capitalism. In doing so it offers new insights into how tourist women express heterosexuality shaped by gender, race, class, and identities.

This fascinating book, focusing on the structure of tourism and role of local culture and social organization in the shoring-up of desire, develops a unique contribution to the understanding of sex tourism. It will be of interest not only to tourism scholars, but also to those interested in sexuality, anthropology, sociology, cultural studies, women studies, gender studies, and geography.

Susan Frohlick is Associate Professor of Cultural Anthropology at the University of Manitoba, Canada.

Contemporary Geographies of Leisure, Tourism and Mobility

Series Editor: C. Michael Hall
Professor at the Department of Management,
College of Business and Economics, University of Canterbury,
Christchurch, New Zealand

The aim of this series is to explore and communicate the intersections and relationships between leisure, tourism and human mobility within the social sciences.

It will incorporate both traditional and new perspectives on leisure and tourism from contemporary geography, e.g. notions of identity, representation and culture, while also providing for perspectives from cognate areas such as anthropology, cultural studies, gastronomy and food studies, marketing, policy studies and political economy, regional and urban planning, and sociology, within the development of an integrated field of leisure and tourism studies.

Also, increasingly, tourism and leisure are regarded as steps in a continuum of human mobility. Inclusion of mobility in the series offers the prospect to examine the relationship between tourism and migration, the sojourner, educational travel, and second home and retirement travel phenomena.

The series comprises two strands:

Contemporary Geographies of Leisure, Tourism and Mobility aims to address the needs of students and academics, and the titles will be published in hardback and paperback. Titles include:

Routledge Studies in Contemporary Geographies of Leisure, Tourism and Mobility is a forum for innovative new research intended for research students and academics, and the titles will be available in hardback only. Titles include:

Sexuality, Women, and Tourism

Cross-border desires through contemporary travel

Susan Frohlick

LONDON AND NEW YORK

First published 2013
by Routledge
2 Park Square, Milton Park, Abingdon, Oxon OX14 4RN

Simultaneously published in the USA and Canada
by Routledge
711 Third Avenue, New York, NY 10017

*Routledge is an imprint of the Taylor & Francis Group, an informa
business*

British Library Cataloguing in Publication Data
A catalogue record for this book is available from the British Library

Library of Congress Cataloging in Publication Data
Frohlick, Susan.
Sexuality, women, and tourism: cross-border desires through
contemporary travel / Susan Frohlick.
   p. cm.
Includes bibliographical references and index.
1. Women travellers—Sexual behavior. 2. Heterosexual women—Travel.
3. Sex customs. 4. Cross-cultural orientation. 5. Tourism—Social aspects.
I. Title.
G156.5.W66F76 2012
306.7082—dc23
2012008504

ISBN: 978-0-415-67147-7 (hbk)
ISBN: 978-0-203-09816-5 (ebk)

Typeset in Times New Roman
by Book Now Ltd, London

MIX
Paper from
responsible sources
FSC
www.fsc.org   FSC® C004839

Printed and bound in Great Britain by the MPG Books Group

In memory of my grandmother, Vera Sierra Nevada Madden Wingen

Contents

List of figures

Acknowledgments

I approached the writing of this book with much trepidation and discovered instead the incredible satisfaction and joy that came from the support and collaboration I received along the way. Perhaps like most anthropologists, I cherish being in the field above all and, although it was often a tremendous struggle for me to stay at my desk here in Canada rather than return to the field, the relationships I formed during my fieldwork are what kept me at the computer long enough to write these pages. For each page I wrote, people I came to care deeply about were in some way present. Puerto Viejo is without a doubt a special place – and while the natural beauty of the ocean, jungle, and mountains is absolutely stunning, it is the people in the community who capture the hearts of so many foreigners, mine included. It is trite but true that sometimes we don't choose our field sites and instead they choose us. This book is the beginning of many contributions I hope to make to a wider project that gives pause to consider how peoples' lives are affected, in myriad ways, by this obsession, this cure-all, this Babylon, this hope, this connection, we call "tourism." I want to acknowledge, and give my heartfelt appreciation, to both the transient and long-time residents of Puerto Viejo alike for allowing me to make these first steps in the midst of your generosity and mutual curiosity and caring over the past seven years.

First and foremost I extend my greatest debt to people in Costa Rica who contributed their valuable time and knowledge to this project. I am grateful to the research participants whose willingness to share intimate details of their lives allowed me to gain a wide perspective, even though promises of anonymity prevent me from naming them. I am sorry that I could not include the stories of everyone I interviewed, but those who do not see themselves in the pages that follow should know that their stories have shaped the book. For those whose stories appear, I hope that I have gotten things at least partially right, while at the same time I recognize that my words have delimited the richness of your identities and lives. Thank you for allowing me the opportunity to try. In Puerto Viejo, so many people extended their friendliness and hospitality to me and my daughter. Our visits would simply have not been the same without the warmth and kindness from people I would like to single out: Maria, Sam, Susana, Shaun, Denise, Rachel, Vera, Rene, Boogie, and Dilan – their friendship has indelibly touched our lives. Moreover, without their input and expertise, my research would have been greatly diminished. Their patience too, while I have worked on this book that has taken so long to finish, has been greatly appreciated.

The research for this book was funded by a grant from the Social Sciences and Humanities Research Council of Canada (2004–2007). Institutional grants from the University of Manitoba provided support for conference travel. A Research Leave in 2010 from the Department of Anthropology at the University of Manitoba allowed me six months of devoted writing time, for which I am grateful.

This manuscript took shape as kernels of ideas first articulated in conference papers and talks before becoming book chapters, and I wish to acknowledge the expertise and generosity of those people who provided feedback on various versions. My writing group colleagues, Liz Millward and Sonia Bookman at the University of Manitoba, have been extremely gracious and astute readers for the entire manuscript. Our coffee "meetings" were much welcomed respite in what has been an especially hectic past two years. Their sage advice, reflected in many parts of the book, deserves much credit. During my Research Leave in 2009, Lynda Johnston at the University of Waikato and the Geography, Tourism, and Environmental Planning Department who hosted me as a Visiting Scholar provided me with space and time to talk about my research. The main ideas in Chapter 6 were developed out of a talk I gave there. Not only did Lynda and her partner open their beautiful home to Breck and me for several weeks during our stay in New Zealand, but Lynda has also been a supportive and incisive reader of much of my work, as well as an astounding writing partner! Ara Wilson at Duke University was instrumental in inspiring me to get moving on this book. The panel we organized together in 2008 for the American Anthropology Association meetings, "Erotic Mobilities: Gender, Affect, and Desire in Transactional Heterosexual Romance," brought together an incredible group of cultural anthropologists working in this area: Ana Dragojvolic, Akiko Takeyama, Anastasia Panagakos, Maria Törnqvist, and Bianca Robinson. Our conversations during, and following, the AAA meetings have enhanced my work. I am especially grateful for Ana's insights drawing from her own fieldwork in Bali. In 2009 on my return from New Zealand, I stopped over in Australia. At Ana's suggestion, I was fortunate to join a panel at the Australian Anthropological Meetings at Macquarie University in Sydney organized by Rosemary Wiss and Sverre Molland, "$exualities: Ethnographies of Sexual Commerce." I appreciated the opportunity to present material related to this book, and to think more explicitly about the role of money and exchange in the relationships formed specifically in Puerto Viejo, as well as more broadly. I also appreciated the conversations I had with Tom Selwyn when we participated in a panel together at the Emotional Geographies conference at the University of South Australia in 2010. His thoughts on the anthropology of pleasure have influenced my analysis and writing.

Once I began fleshing out the manuscript, several more colleagues, friends, and "research buddies" provided feedback on various chapters. Dawn Skorczewski, whose skillfulness in writing was immensely helpful to me in getting the manuscript underway, deserves a special mention. (Thanks to Ara Wilson for referring Dawn to me.) In addition to Liz Millward and Sonia Bookman, I extend my gratitude to Julia Harrison, Lynda Johnston, Megan Rivers-Moore, Shaun Sellers, Sam Wild-Chick, Rachel Thomas, Carlos Sandoval-García, Jessa Leinaweaver, Pamela Downe, Katherine Frank, Kris Maksymowicz, Ken Little, Stephen

Holden, Maria Perez, and anonymous reviewers. Many students in both undergraduate and graduate courses over the past few years have allowed me to discuss my work and engage in conversations with them about the issues raised in the book: Their wisdom has helped me hone my arguments. Although I have tried to incorporate many excellent suggestions from friends and colleagues into the book, any mistakes, errors, or omissions are entirely my own doing.

Student research assistants provided invaluable labor with transcribing of interviews and copyright permissions: I thank Kris Maksymowicz, Gabi Aguero, and Nitasha Ali for their proficient work. I took on the duties of Department Head in January 2010 when the manuscript still required much work. The generous support from our Associate Head, Stacie Burke, in enabling me some much needed time away to write last summer meant a great deal to me. I greatly appreciated Lynne Dalman's extraordinary administrative support as well. During the final stages of manuscript completion, Robert Phillips took over some teaching for me, which was a magnanimous gesture for which I am extremely (and forever) grateful. I was lucky to have received such exceptional editorial guidance from Emma Travis, the Tourism Editor at Routledge, at the outset of this project. Editorial assistance from Faye Leerink and her successor, Carol Barber, has also been exceptional. I appreciate the sensitivity they have shown to me concerning the many demands placed on me in my efforts to meet "the deadline," which they have compassionately extended more than once. Maureen Allen has been a wonderful copyeditor.

On the home front, I would like to acknowledge my parents, Bill and June Frohlick, for their unwavering encouragement. Across the provinces, it always uplifted me to hear their voices and best wishes for "the book writing." They demonstrated such love and understanding when I had to forego summer holidays with them to work on the manuscript instead. I dedicate this book to my maternal grandmother, Vera Wingen, for the stories she told about her travels to Hawaii and Yosemite, California as a young tourist in the 1920s left a lasting impression on me. Jane Frohlick, my sister, accompanied me on my first research trip to Costa Rica, and I am grateful for her companionship and keen observations and insights when I first visited Puerto Viejo. She has continued to ask me relevant questions long after our first visit together. Nancy Frohlick has encouraged me at every step of the project, as always, and I especially appreciate how she opened her home to Breck last summer in such a generous and loving way while I tended to my writing.

Finally, it is Alex and Breck to whom I extend a special acknowledgement: It is their vibrancy and love that sustained and energized me during such a lengthy process. Alex, my son, took care of our home and pets in Winnipeg while I was back and forth to Costa Rica over the past seven years, and has tried hard to keep the music down while I write on the top floor of the house. Breck has been the best travel companion I could ever imagine – curious, insightful, adaptable, witty, and fun loving. She made my time in Costa Rica especially joyful. Both have lent their support in immeasurable ways and both have grown a lot in the time it has taken for me to finish what has seemed to them like an impossibly demanding task. My writing is always and absolutely dedicated to them.

Introduction

Desire is an opening, not a closure, a relationship, not a thing. It is not within us, but without.

(Lancaster 2003: 266)

People say to me, "You're making this so complicated. Isn't this just women wanting to fuck men?" Precisely, I think. But the anthropological question is through what social structures and contexts does such "fucking" happen? Heterosexual sexualities don't "just happen."

(Fieldnotes, August 11, 2006)

Foreign women and local men in Caribbean Costa Rica

Riding my bicycle past the soccer field on the way back to my guesthouse, situated in the back of the town, I spot a light-skinned woman with auburn hair sitting on the grass. Her bike is leaning against a fence post. I see the ubiquitous plastic water bottle and beach towel in the basket. The woman's skin is sunburnt. It is obvious to me that she is a recently arrived tourist. I look beyond her to the group of men chasing the ball, all in various sorts of dress, from full soccer gear to shorts only and bare feet. I wonder which one she is with.

She is the only foreigner watching the informal game where local men band together in the late afternoon, as they often do, to play the nation's favorite sport. Children ride their bikes up and down the gravel street parallel to the field adjacent to the bright green elementary school. Mothers, or possibly older siblings, call after them, "*Venga, venga.*" A few townspeople mill around outside the nearby Baptist church. Dogs, and the occasional horse, wander on and off the field.

I see her a few times again later that week with the same man, a local resident. I spot them together at the liquor store, walking down the main street, and standing side-by-side outside the reggae bar. I ask around the foreign women from the United States, Canada, and Europe that I recognize – some of them have moved here, others are regular visitors like myself, others are on holidays – to see if anyone knows her. One woman tells me, "Oh, yeah, I've seen her. She's just a random tourist, I think." The following week, the sunburned woman is not around town.

On another occasion I notice a blonde woman in one of the open-air bars on the front street, directly across from the beach. It is late, at least for me, about one o'clock in the morning. It is raining. The street is as crowded as the bar inside, where the dance floor is packed with people. Before the rain stops long enough for the people who perform the fire twirling to come out, the woman makes a public display.

She seems to have arrived with her tourist boyfriend, a white-skinned man wearing cropped cotton pants and a tie-dyed T-shirt; however, she is now flirting with a dreadlocked Afro-Caribbean rasta.[1] Her boyfriend tries to intercept but is brushed off. Eventually she tries to leave the bar with her boyfriend, who has momentarily recaptured her attention. Finally, she wanders off towards the beach with the Afro-Caribbean young man, their arms interlocked. She pulls away from him and looks back – a gesture that suggests some ambivalence in her decision.

A group of us watching the action wonder aloud where she might be from. A *Tico* (Costa Rican) friend thinks that she is German.[2] A few of us think she is American. We all hope she knows what she is doing. A few days later I hear that the man she left the dance hall with has been identified: he was an outsider referred to as "the man who lives in the tree" because he seems to have made a home in a tree along the main road in town. They are seen walking around town together for the next day or two and then, apparently, she departed.

A third scenario was described to me by an American woman who recounted in her interview with me a particularly upsetting experience she once had with a former Afro-Costa Rican boyfriend: She was standing on a dirt road in a village. After a long day at the beach she was waiting for him to meet up with her, as they had pre-arranged earlier that day. The sand between her toes was itchy. With the sun setting in the early evening the thin cotton sarong she had tied around her waist over her bathing suit suddenly felt much too thin. She was cold. She ached for a hot shower. When her boyfriend, towering above her in height, showed up several long moments later, he stood before her with his hands stuffed in his jeans pockets, barefoot, bare-chested, and sullen faced. He told her that he did not want to go out to eat with her. He wanted to go home, alone, instead.

With her finger pointing in his face, she screamed up at him in the darkening sky, "I thought we were going out? I thought we had a date. What do you mean you're going home? We were going out on a date! A blinking date! Do you even know what that is?!"

With the rising voices of the white foreign woman and black patois-speaking local man, a few curious people poked their heads out of windows nearby. Tourists scurried past with their faces averted from the arguing couple. When he started to walk away from her, his apparent sulking set her off and in a swift movement she took one of her rubber thong sandals and began to hit him with it, whacking one arm, then the other. Mercifully, a friend of her boyfriend's happened to walk by and witnessing the escalating battle between a six-foot-tall man and his five-foot-tall girlfriend, he had defused the situation, pulling the American woman away from his friend.

Later that evening the couple met up at a local disco, where they resolved their earlier battle. But, as she told her side of their story, the relationship had been peppered with similar violent outbursts, each assaulting the other on different occasions. Eventually she left him and returned to the United States with bittersweet memories of her passionate transnational romance.

These observations of mine as a cultural anthropologist provide a glimpse of the diverse experiences of North American and European women when they were tourists in Costa Rica and had intimate and sexual relationships with local men. Such representations are gleaned from eleven months of fieldwork when I lived in the community and spent time with women who were short-stay tourists, longer-stay tourists, temporary residents, regular visitors (tourist migrants), and expatriate residents. I conducted interviews and participant observation within their social worlds in order to understand women's intimate and sexual relationships with local men and how women negotiate their sexual subjectivities in and through international travel. While several anthropologists and sociologists who study tourism and sex in Latin America and the Caribbean have written books about Euro-American tourist men seeking sex with Latin American and Caribbean men and women (e.g. Brennan 2004a, b; Cabezas 2009; Padilla 2007; Rivers-Moore 2009), tourist women's practices of sexual tourism are less well known (although see Pruitt and LaFont 1995). While a growing body of literature has emerged on the topic in the past two decades, the bulk of published material is in journal articles rather than full-length books (although see Jacobs 2010), which means that the complications and nuances of very complex relationships have not yet fully surfaced. Yet, on the other hand, websites, films, trade books, and Broadway plays have taken up this topic (e.g. Aston 2008; Cantet 2005; Virmani 2010).

Given that much speculation has been made within the public imagination and popular media about women as "sex tourists," a term that I critique in the book,

I raise many basic questions: What are the material practices through which women in a foreign country meet and "hook up" with local men who are strangers to them? What are the meanings that women give to these encounters? Do sexual feelings, identities, and practices change when visiting another country? How does "being a tourist" (Harrison 2003) bring about new possibilities for sexual expression as well as reproduce and sustain familiar patterns of gendered and racialized sexual and intimate behavior? How do "local men" come to be so highly appealing, and which ones in particular? How and why are these transnational inter-ethnic erotic encounters heady and exciting but also confusing and, as one research subject put it, "messed up"?

This book moves back and forth between my observations of what women do as tourists, what they say themselves (their words recorded from interviews, conversations, and email messages), and my interpretations of what they do and say, as well as what other people do and say in relation to tourist women. I try to capture some of the lived experiences of women from Canada, the United States, France, Germany, Austria, Australia, New Zealand, England, and Italy in their everyday actions and interactions as temporary dwellers in one locale in a foreign country where they were sexually active. Who are these women? What do their experiences abroad, as tourists, travelers, and temporary residents, tell us about sexuality, and more specifically, heterosexualities, shaped through geographies of mobility? What insights do their stories of cross-border sex and desires bring to new understandings about tourism?

"Wild about local men"

> Puerto Viejo is such a complex place, okay? We have a lot of factors there ....
> (Interview with a doctor at a local clinic, December 2007)

The scenarios described above took place in Puerto Viejo de Talamanca, a small town in the southeastern corner of Costa Rica in the province of Limón, just a few kilometers north of Panama, nestled between the Atlantic Ocean and the Talamanca mountains (Figure I.1).[3] A local physician described the area as "a complex place," when he was explaining to me the situation regarding sexual practices within the community. His statement evokes a "scene" for which the tourist town has become known, a pattern of foreign tourist women who engage in sexual liaisons and romances with local men.

A popular travel guidebook describes a town called Cahuita, a few kilometers north of Puerto Viejo, as notable for its friendly "resident dreadlocked hustlers" who like to "chat up," that is hustle, foreign women (McNeil 2001: 173). However, when I visited Cahuita in 2004, a European resident gave me advice that set me on my research course: "Puerto Viejo [and not Cahuita] is the place to go if you want to learn about foreign women's sexual appetite for local men," said Georgette, a Swiss woman in her thirties married to a *Tico* she met several years earlier when she arrived on a holiday.[4] On her suggestion, I traveled further down the coastal highway, a two-lane paved road peppered with gaping potholes, until

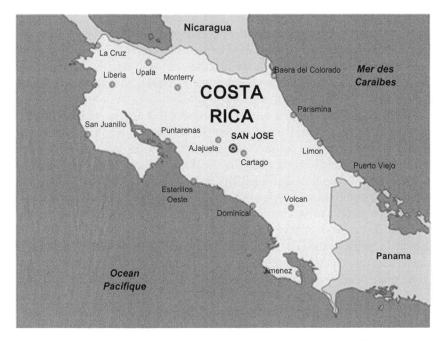

Figure I.1 Map of Costa Rica showing Puerto Viejo de Talamanca, located in the southern Atlantic near the Panama border.

I reached Puerto Viejo. There, without any prior social contacts and as "a lone ethnographer" except for my travel companions (my sister, on the first trip, and my young daughter on subsequent trips), I asked questions to anyone I felt comfortable enough to approach, which eventually led me to a wealth of information.

One day the woman who ran the guesthouse where we were staying introduced me to a friend of hers. Ted was a *gringo* in his late forties who had moved to Puerto Viejo from the United States in the 1990s.[5] After hearing my explanation of why I was in Costa Rica and specifically Puerto Viejo as a cultural anthropologist studying gender, sexuality, and tourism, he told me that I had come to "the right place." His comment was based on his observations over the years of seeing many tourist women pursue sexual relations with local men. He suggested that the reason as to why "American and European women, especially from Germany, 'go wild' for local men" is "because of all the hormone-laced meat they eat [in their home countries]."

It was, for me, a fascinating metaphor to hear deployed: Women consuming hormones, presumably testosterone, that compels their sexual conduct with men from another country and culture, who, in turn, are also endowed with uncontrollable sexual urges and an equal insatiability for foreign women. A metaphor lucidly connecting women's erotic desires with food, and with the ingestion of substances responsible for sexual maturation, it is as though women acquire "tastes" and insatiable appetites and become "like men" who are seen to be driven inherently with a "drive" and "impulse" for sex. In this framework European and North American women are sexual subjects of modern food production and consumption and are at the mercy of their hormonally altered biological drives. A socio-cultural perspective takes a rather different view; that they are subjects situated in complex cross-cultural and interracial terrains with agentive interests in the pursuit of erotic sociality and sexual pleasure.

It is the latter theory that as a cultural anthropologist I wish to offer as a counter explanation. In this book, I discount the possibility that European and North American tourist women in this Caribbean tourist town in Costa Rica were attracted to and formed intimate ties with local men because of the meat they ate back home or the impulses that raged within them and changed their biology and bodies, explanations that were given a great deal of currency and validity amongst townspeople and expatriates based on overly simplistic and deterministic physiological understandings of sexuality. Instead, I look at women's erotic desires for Costa Rica men as embodied practices that take place in very complex contexts of cultural notions about tourism, about sexuality and love, about Caribbean and Latino masculinities, about Western femininities, and about the heterosexuality that they brought with them on their travels and that intersected with local and translocal notions and practices of sexuality and intimacies. I offer a counter explanation that does not refute the claim that "women go wild for local men" because, although I frame it differently, the observation is roughly true. In the words of Annabella, an American woman I introduce later in the book, many, many tourist women acted as though they were "boy crazy." Rather than reproduce stereotypes about "boy crazy" and "wild" and "loose *gringas*," this book addresses Euro-American women's attraction to Costa Rican men by situating their cross-border, cross-cultural attractions and transnational travel sex encounters in social and cultural processes and local and global political economies of desire, instead of in biologically driven or pathological bodies. This does not mean that, to restate Judith Butler's (1993) phrase, "bodies don't matter." On the contrary, I show in this book how "apparently empirical bodies" and "apparently interior experience" are entirely intertwined, such that "bodies come into being" through "collective formations [that] are social, political, subjective, objective, discursive, narrative and material all at once" (Farquhar and Lock 2007: 9).

This book features Puerto Viejo and surrounding towns as a place within Costa Rica where North American and European tourist women are attracted to and have sexual, romantic, and a range of intimate relations with local men, from casual "hook up" sex to longer term co-habitation unions. This array of intimacies are "cross-border" in that they are formed through and structured by physical movements across national borders and also by social relations of crossing ethnic, class, and racial borders that dictate what anthropologists rather coldly refer to as "mate selection," or rules of endogamy and exogamy between and within different social groups. They are "cross-cultural" or "transcultural" in that the actors (tourists and locals) are from different cultures (white Euro-American and Latino/

Caribbean) and, at times, move between two cultures. At times I refer to these patterns of sociality (that is, how people relate socially to one another) as "transnational" because of how the cross-border, cross-cultural intimacies entail not only "flows" of tourists and tourist migrants from one country into another but also "connections made between two places" (Levin 2002), in this case Costa Rica and the home countries of the tourists. As feminist scholars point out, "transnational" is thus a key analytical term in thinking critically about sexuality and the making of sexual subjects through travel, and in examining "the power relations of travel" that include "contacts and transactions of all kinds" and the "material histories embedded in the encounters" (Grewal and Kaplan 2001: 671). I use these various terms – cross-border, cross-cultural, transcultural, and transnational – at different times to emphasize one aspect or another of this range of sexual unions.

Within the quotidian spaces and places in Puerto Viejo, transnational sex plays out in the everyday lives of locals and tourists who comprise two social and culturally differentiated groups. Although by no means homogeneous, these two groups bring their "homegrown" or cultural notions of romance, love, and sexuality into the "negotiations" of heterosexual subjectivity and intimacy that transpires within the materiality of encounters and which, crucially, are often at cross-purposes with one another. As a young man, a resident of mixed parentage, once explained to me, somewhat exasperated by my seemingly relentless attempts to complicate what he saw as so straightforward, "The men want money, the women want sex, love, and '*una experiencia*'; it's as simple as that." This book examines more closely this idea of incommensurability and cross-cultural impossibility that seems to permeate transnational sex between foreign women and local men in Costa Rica but, importantly, it also looks critically at the production of desire that takes place within this specific context of touristic consumption, recreation, and bodily transformations. I do this by looking ethnographically at what people do and say.

This region is not the only place in Costa Rica where tourist women from the global North temporarily reside on short holidays or extended visits and have sex with, and form emotional attachments, with local men. Several other areas, including Jacó and Montezuma on the Pacific coast and Monteverde in the Santa Elena cloud forest, have been documented in academic literature (Freidus and Romero-Daza 2009; Ragsdale *et al.* 2006; Romero-Daza and Friedus 2008) and also mentioned by tourist women as towns where hook ups and unions with local men are common. These communities on the Pacific are linked to the Caribbean region by the Costa Rican men who travel between these places for various reasons – to surf, find work, to party, and hang out with foreign women. Even though there are various other places in Costa Rica where foreign women engage in sex with local men, in the minds of many locals, and foreigners too, Puerto Viejo stood out over and above these other places, which hints at the local specificities of women's cross-border desires and encounters.

As my first interlocutor, Georgette, kindly pointed out to me when I was a newcomer to the community, the area is "notorious" for the sexual relations

Figure I.2 A local man and tourist woman on Playa Negra, a beach just outside the village.
       Photo by author.

between foreign women and local men. These sexual relations, which are also social, cultural, and economic, as well as historical and political – and their materiality in the form of bodies dancing in the reggae bars, riding on motor-scooters through the town and on the coastal road between villages, sitting in the small *sodas* (small informal restaurants) situated in the back alleys, and hanging out on the beach watching surfers, in the form of new kin (daughter-in-laws, sister-in-laws), and as new things acquired by male townspeople (a boom box, a new shirt) – constitute the central feature of Puerto Viejo in this ethnographic representation, as the iconic photograph of the local man and a tourist girl hanging out on a beach in solitude together invokes (Figure I.2). Although other patterns of tourist–local and tourist–tourist interactions took place, foreign women's erotic attractions to, and encounters with, local men remained prominent in the social imagination (see Maksymowicz 2010).

   With this specific region of Costa Rica in focus as a localized place that is connected to wider structural processes at the regional, national, transnational and global level, the main questions I raise in this book are: How do women while on holiday and traveling away from home understand their attractions to, and desires for, Costa Rican men? How is sexual subjectivity affected by international travel as a particular form of mobility, set of ideas and discourses, as well as feelings and material–social relations? As tourists and tourist migrants situated within a late capitalist global economy and the contemporary social phenomenon of international travel, how do their multiple desires (especially their desires for "difference" – for a different culture, for different food, a different way of life, a different masculinity, and a different experience) and their own cultural backgrounds shape women's understandings of their sexuality and their sexual subjectivities? In answering these questions and focusing on a specific locale, I also aim to contribute to the growing ethnographic scholarship on ways in which crossborder romance, sex, and intimacies involving female tourists that are occurring in many tourist destinations of the world are shaped by local, national, transnational and global processes and in turn are affecting women's sexual subjectivities (e.g. Dragojlovic 2008; Meisch 1995; Piscitelli 2001; Takeyama 2005; Tucker 2003; Yamaga 2006).

By addressing these questions, this book engages in a wider conversation in anthropology and other disciplines – including women's and gender studies, geography, sociology, tourist studies, and cultural studies – about how sexuality and gender are constructed, produced, performed, and embodied by particular social actors in specific contexts of tourism. In thinking about sexual subjectivity, I am also concerned with how social processes, in this case tourism and related desires, are lived through the body and thus are enacted through emotions, affect, senses, and bodies marked by gender, race, class, and nationality. Another way of putting my basic theoretical aim is that I want to show how sexuality – as a broad realm of erotic desires and practices, and not only identities but also feelings and subjective experiences associated with the sexual (Cameron and Kulick 2003) – is produced, or given shape and meaning, in a particular locale in the contemporary world of movement and tourism mobility. Because my research focuses on women's sexual relations with men, the book will also show, more specifically, how heterosexualities – as "socially dominant performances" (Alsop *et al.* 2002: 101) that remain unmarked by virtue of entitlement and naturalization – are enacted within a context of pleasure travel. Within touristic spaces and through touristic movement, hospitality, consumption, cosmopolitanism, and quests for alterity (or Otherness) are important shaping factors on the formation of heterosexualities, even when women do not necessarily identify as "straight."

I concentrate on one tourist destination with its multiple meanings and try to impart to readers a sense of the social and cultural geographies of transnational sex that took place there during the years of my fieldwork, between 2004 and 2009. It is the perspectives of foreign women who as tourists and as temporary residents were involved in a range of sexual and intimate relationships with local men that readers will hear about most of all. The book is about relationships, experiences, and encounters more than it is an ethnographic account about a place or a cultural group, although to some extent it is that too. It addresses the broad issue of women's sexual agency and the formation of sexual subjectivities in the context of contemporary tourism travel, and the readily accessible opportunities and privileges for passport-holders of countries in the global North to live and work in another country and meet other people. As an American backpacker framed this point in an interview in 2005, "I know that if I'm going to stay here

I'm going to be sexually active." I examine the meaningfulness that women ascribe to their desires, feelings, and interactions with men. More specifically, the book is about the particularities of European and North American women's embodied heterosexualities, formulated and negotiated through cross-border, cross-cultural, opposite-sex relations that took place within touristic spaces and socialities in a transnational tourist town on the Caribbean coast of Costa Rica in the early twenty-first century.

My own reasons

Flashback to one of my fieldwork trips in August 2009   I wait for a friend to finish her shift in a local shop. Killing time, I notice the dozens of photographs of local people and visitors plastered on one wall. From the images captured over the past decade or so, and amongst the smiling faces, I notice those of local Afro-Caribbean men, taken as they perform as reggae artists, drummers, and musicians, and their foreign mostly light-skinned girlfriends. I recognize some of the faces. Traveling back and forth from my home in Canada for numerous visits over the past five years I have had the incredible good fortune of meeting many local townspeople, expatriates, and tourists. Some of the women whose faces are on the wall of the shop I had the chance to interview and know them personally. Others, I knew a little about them through social contacts, introduced casually by friends or while taking yoga classes, going to restaurants and out at night. Still other faces I did not recognize at all. I look at the photographs of people caught in a snapshot and frozen in time while I wait for my friend whom I met initially as a research participant. What strikes me is my own fascination with these women and how this fascination of mine has shifted over time. The reasons that initially prompted me to carry out research into the experiences and social worlds and subjectivities of foreign women who are involved with local men have changed.

Euro-American female tourists who are attracted to and involved with local men while on their travels, no matter where the destination, were once exotic to me.[6] "Strange" in their cross-border inter-ethnic romances and sexual relationships but yet also familiar to me as a white heterosexual Euro-Canadian woman and travel enthusiast from a "sending" nation in the global North, dimensions that I shared with my interlocutors. My own history of traveling to Europe and other countries abroad as a young woman in the late 1970s and with meeting men from outside my home country and from different cultures as an important and exciting aspect of my traveling experience and memories is part of the reason why the women's sexual desires and practices in Costa Rica were familiar to me. Growing up in Canada as a teen in the late 1970s, the moment in history when women first began to travel en masse, I was part of the new flows of pioneering backpackers moving across Europe and into the so-called (back then) "peripheries" of northern Africa and the Middle East. Like many other women in that era, at the tail end of the baby boomer generation, I was exposed to the emergent travel-and-youth practices developing during those times and recall my experiences of being exposed to different cultures as a heady mixture of adventure, naivety, risk-taking, and cultural curiosity, all the while trying to make sense of my own sexuality as a young woman. When I was in Spain, to me and my female backpacking travel companion, the Spanish men seemed so much more exotic and thus more intriguing than the Canadian men we knew as relatively sheltered Canadian teen girls, and so on, as we traveled throughout southern Europe, northern Africa, and Israel.

When I began to conduct research on the topic of women's sexuality and tourism travel in the early 2000s, I was in my forties. European and North American women who, in my mind then, had crossed ethnic and racial boundaries to engage in sexual relations with Costa Rican men – men who were Latino, lighter skinned, brown, black, Afro-Caribbean, mixed, and, for the most part, poorer and darker skinned than the women – were intriguing subjects to me as an anthropologist (in contrast to, for instance, tourist women who had sex with tourist men). I had lived in the United States Virgin Islands and British Virgin Islands during my twenties, and several of my Canadian and American female friends were involved at the time with black "West Indian" men, the term commonly used in the 1980s. As Euro-American white women who had children with black Afro-Caribbean men and had forged lives and kinship ties with their relatives, I saw them as not only sexually adventurous but I also envied their intimacy with Caribbean culture – a culture that remained quite distinct from and well outside of my own social world as a white Canadian woman married to a white Canadian man – accessed through what I perceived then as their "daringness."

Now, after living periodically over the span of five years in a Caribbean community on the Atlantic shores of a Central American country with many foreign women who were intimately involved with Costa Rican (and also Nicaraguan and Panamanian) men, and after spending time with them and their children and sometimes their male partners at the beaches, restaurants, yoga classes, and private gatherings, I no longer regard them with the exoticism I did at the beginning of my field research. I see their erotic desires, romantic interests, and physical attractions to local men arising in and structured by many complicated factors and a wider social, cultural, and economic context. This view stands in contrast to an earlier view of mine where I saw "sexual behaviors" as those actions that derived from inherent personality traits such as "daringness" or inner drives, or solely determined by women's relative wealth and privilege of mobility vis-à-vis the local men they had sex with.

The materiality of their intimate entanglements – from the rice and beans and pizza they eat with their local boyfriends, to the dwelling spaces they share for sleeping and cooking, to the walks they take in the dense verdant coastal rainforests, to the chill "vibe" of the reggae bars where dancing brings bodies together, to the Spanglish sentences they yell out in jealous rages – are the fodder for my anthropological account of love, friendship, sex, and sexuality in a country not-so-far from home (a mere five hours from Toronto and less than four hours from Los Angeles), yet at the same time another world away. With that aim in mind, my ethnographic account proceeds with the following broad questions in mind: How and why do North American and European women choose to have sexual relations with men situated in different cultural, social, racial, and economic positionings than their own? Which women? What aspects of tourism influence their decisions? What are the central mediating discourses that shape their sexuality through travel?

These are complex relationships to comprehend, rather than an overly simplistic matter of individual bravery or resistance to normative sexuality, ideas that underpinned my earlier much more naïve notions of intrepid women travelers. As I look at the photographs once again, the women's faces smiling back at me, images that are meant to capture the quintessential tourist experience of spontaneous authenticity and cross-cultural connection and intimacy with a local culture, jolt me into my anthropologist's mode of analysis. How did the women get there? What are the meanings they gave to their experiences?

Arriving in Puerto Viejo (Old Harbor)

The paved highway south from Puerto Limón stops abruptly at the three-way intersection of Hone Creek, the road to BriBri, and the gravel road to the southernmost communities. Driving into Puerto Viejo on the dusty, bumpy road that starts at the intersection and passes by the iguana farm and a steady smattering of small homesteads whose yards are framed by Indian paintbrush hedges, the town begins to spill out once you reach the short and narrow bridge.[7] At that small concrete bridge, where at any given time, people are walking, riding bikes or scooters, and buses and trucks pass by along with town dogs and black turkey vultures, the road splits off into four directions. One road, known as "crack alley," (also, *el ghetto* and *la zona roja*) veers sharply to the right and heads inland a few blocks, past the barrios of corrugated tin dwellings and resident substance users referred to, not always benevolently, as "*craceros*" ("crack-heads"). Two or three women are often standing near this corner, asking tourists for money or food, and, if the rumors are true as I suspect they are, selling sex to men in town who do not mind paying a *rojo* (a local currency note worth approximately US$4) or trading crack cocaine for a furtive "quickie."

Veering to the left, another road follows the Atlantic coastline snaking its way parallel to the beach where the sand abruptly changes in color from black to beige. At the bridge, the town's main road juts straight ahead, and here cars slow down over the massive speed bumps, especially the extra big one right in front of Esmeralda's Soda; here in 2004, the town's only bank and drug store were located, along with dozens of restaurants and guesthouses crowded together over a few blocks. Only a few side streets intersect with the main road forming a small grid that constitutes the town's center. On these pot-holed roads, nestled between residents' homes and the town's several churches are numerous types of small-scale lodgings (guesthouses, *cabinas*, hostels) and tourist enterprises,

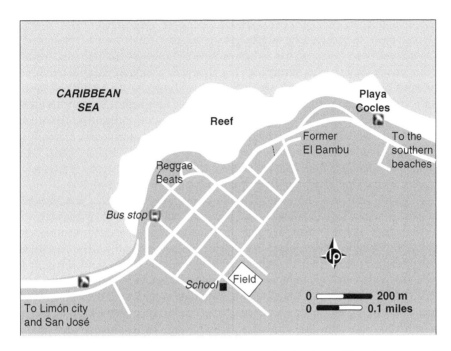

CARIBBEAN
SEA

Reef

Playa
Cocles

Former
El Bambu

To the
southern
beaches

Reggae
Beats

Bus stop

School
Field

To Limón city
and San José

0 ⊂=====▬ 200 m
0 ▬====⊃ 0.1 miles

Figure I.3 Map of Puerto Viejo de Talamanca, showing its size and location as a small
coastal tourist town close to several prominent beaches in the South Caribbean.

adorned in a mishmash of Caribbean, Central American, and European styles of architecture and offerings of goods and food. Tourists can find *sodas* serving rice and beans, the preferred Caribbean meal, and *gallo pinto* (the national dish) for breakfast; Italian bakeries where chocolate puff pastries can be found in the glass cooler covered in condensation and eggplant panini is served on the front patio for lunch; a vegan restaurant that also sells vitamins, ointments and other health foods run by a local Seventh-Day Adventist family; and an art gallery shop owned by a French expatriate, infused with bright tiles of every color, fluttering banners, and artwork spilling outside and brightening up the otherwise street dark in the early tropical nightfall.

Walking or riding a bike through town takes only a few minutes, although once I came to know many of the townspeople it could take an entire morning, stopping to talk along the way. Riding my bike from Zeldas, a beautiful guesthouse located at the back of town near the soccer field, to the Internet café located in the center of town a mere three blocks away could take an hour! While the geographic center might well be the strip of shops (beachwear and souvenir shops, several tour agencies, a small hardware store) near the corner where *La Casa Cultura* (Cultural or Community Center), a bright one-story building used as a cultural community center that also houses the high school during school days, is located, there are several social centers of the town.

For many of my interlocutors, the heart and pulse of Puerto Viejo were the various nightclubs or reggae bars sprinkled along the very edge of town, where the road meets the beach. One of the most important of these "sites of encounter" was Reggae Beats, a reggae bar and dance hall just a few meters from the ocean, where on the busier nights during high tourist season people would spill out from the open-air dance floor inside the shuttered building onto the beachfront lined with candles melted onto rocks and driftwood. On slower nights, local men would sit on the benches outside talking amongst themselves and chatting up the occasional tourist who might wander over to check out the pulsating music. Local DJs spun their favorite music in the DJ box situated above the bar. Roots reggae, reggaton, dance hall, hip-hop, and, on occasion, deep house kept locals, expats, and tourists dancing until late into the morning, no matter what time of year.

If Reggae Beats was a nostalgic place for many of the European, Canadian and American women I got to know (as many of them had met their boyfriends there), it also held bittersweet memories and, for some women, quite dark memories in fact. A shooting had taken place just outside the bar; women I knew had been close friends of the victim. A young American woman, a long-stay tourist, had been the person holding him when he died. Another time, a carjacking had occurred right outside of Reggae Beats, resulting in the tragic murders of two young American women who had been close friends of women I met and came to be friends with through my research (see Frohlick 2010). Other women spoke of near-rapes outside of this club, incidences where they had gone out to the beach, just a few steps away from the dance floor accompanied by a local man who had tried to press them into sex right then and there, mistaking their interest in a few kisses or flirtatious exchanges as an expectation of sexual intercourse. A Canadian woman was once able to extricate herself from such a situation by telling her aggressor that she had *SIDA* (AIDS), something she later bore the brunt of as he spread the stigmatizing rumor to other townspeople as a kind of punishment for her non-compliance with his demands for sex.

Two other nightclubs marked the southernmost edge of town. Both changed hands during the time I spent in Puerto Viejo and several times before I arrived and after I left. Compared to the low key and authentic "vibe" of Reggae Beats and its rustic aesthetic that appealed to the Marley followers, located at the opposite end of town, the El Centro disco was the modern monstrosity of a San José style club (or at least it tried to be, was what Illondra, a young American woman, once told me as we stood together one evening on the periphery of the property watching in amusement the spectacle of choreographed dancing of the girls on stage with strobe lights flashing). At El Centro, young *Ticos* from the Central Valley would dance the weekends away, and DJs from the city, another world away, would bring their high-tech equipment to light up the starry sky in artificial light, presenting a striking contrast with the candles and swirling fire sticks of the fire dancers outside the beach at Reggae Beats. El Centro was akin to "Babylon," I was told, a Rastafarian reference to the "White colonial and neo-colonial world" (Chevannes 2010: 216) and, more loosely, to the damaging Westernized, commodified, and sexualized culture that encroached through globalization. Most of

Figure I.4 El Bambu, a legendary reggae club in Puerto Viejo. Still standing in December 2004, "Bambu" was a popular spot for tourist women and local men to meet before it was destroyed in a fire. Photo by author.

the women I knew did not go there unless they were desperate for a change of scene, or if, like Illondra and I, they wanted to watch the spectacle of middle-class San José culture.

In 2004, a few yards away from the expanse of beach that marked off the El Centro property stood an icon of Puerto Viejo's party culture. Although I never had the opportunity to experience firsthand the "Bambu," for many people I knew it had been "the place" that was the most special of all – the ultimate reggae bar and cool place with the best vibe (Figure I.4). When I returned in August of 2005 the cement building was reduced to a pile of rubble, reportedly closed down because of a drug-trafficking charge against the Italian couple who rented it from a local Afro-Caribbean matriarch to operate the nightclub. Later again, in the following years, this rubble had been cleared, so that people could hang out and eat their food in the shade by the beach on the cement platform that was once the building's foundation. By the time I returned again in 2008, a bright green trailer was set up on the cement slab of the old foundation, where someone had put up curtains and perhaps was living there. On a later visit still it had become a vendor's stall, and lights were strung up between the coconut palm trees that had once held the large driftwood sign for Bambu, where people now bought trinkets rather than danced barefoot under a starry sky to the roots-style reggae music of one of the resident DJs, DJ Raul, a Nicaraguan Rastafarian.

Across from the old Bambu site, a restaurant marked the site of one of the best surfing waves in the country, the Salsa Brava. During the surfing season the sand parking lot was filled with SUVs and jeeps from all over Costa Rica, a combination of international tourists and domestic visitors coming in throngs to try out the Salsa Brava wave. Further south on the road, clusters of small businesses catering to tourists, everything from surf rental shops, laundry services, small *tiendas* selling beach towels and suntan lotion, *sodas*, and backpacking hostels, were interspersed with vacant lots and stands of jungle, until the pavement ended and the potholed gravel road began. Beyond Puerto Viejo a ten-kilometer length of road connected numerous beach hamlets – Cocles, Playa Chiquita, Punta Uva – to Manzanillo, a sleepy beach hamlet almost on the Panama border and situated in the middle of the Gandoca Manzanillo Wildlife Refuge, a state-protected refuge for flora and fauna in the mangrove swamp and lowland rainforest. Soccer fields, *pulperias* (general stores), and real estate offices (springing up seemingly overnight between 2005 and 2007, and then closing down in 2008) were scattered alongside this road.

I use "Puerto Viejo" to refer to both the specific town of Puerto Viejo and also more broadly to the area that encompasses a number of towns and hamlets in the area, including Cocles, Playa Chiquita and Punta Uva, and to a lesser extent, Hone Creek and Cahuita. Sometimes I use the accurate name of the town or village when recounting specific incidences but more often I am purposely vague in order both to protect the anonymity of individuals and also to represent the vagueness reflected in conversations with tourists. Local residents used town names precisely while tourists tended to gloss over differences between places with all-encompassing (and inaccurate) references to "Puerto Viejo."

I provide here a sketch of what one of my interlocutor's, the town doctor, so aptly characterized as "a complex place" that has been transforming in its transnationality since its early days as a stopping off point for the cocoa brokers and government officials when the area's first hotel, Maritza, housed such visitors in its one room for rent. Since then, like other towns in the southern Caribbean and the entire Limón province, it has shifted from the transnational worlds of bananas to global tourism (Harpelle 2001).

A crucial point I want to get across to readers is that Puerto Viejo is a place that revolves around tourism in ways that profoundly shape not only the built environment but also the social space. Vandegrift observed during her fieldwork there in 1999 how "the town had no bank, high school, or health clinic, but housed three souvenir shops, three discotheques, as many Italian restaurants, and a surf shop" (2007: 126). Although by 2005 there was one bank and even an ATM machine, there was no high school or health clinic. When I first arrived it seemed as though the growth of tourism and land development was on an unstoppable path. One of the first real estate offices was constructed in Cocles, just a few kilometers south of town. By 2009, several real estate agencies existed, from Puerto Viejo all the way to Manzanillo, and "*se vende*" (for sale) signs were everywhere. During a brief visit in the summer of 2008, friends told me about a brand new mall, described as a "Pacific-like" monstrosity, similar to the large-scale development on the Pacific side of Costa Rica, being built, ironically, right across the street from one of the first locally owned and run non-profit ecotourism organizations in the area. In 2009, I saw the immense cavernous concrete building with my own eyes and although its architectural style detracted from the Caribbean aesthetic of the nearby structures, residents and tourists alike appreciated its spaciousness. The upstairs restaurant was lively and packed, and the "Reggaeland" store on the main floor was bustling with tourists and locals forking out money for surf shorts, bathing suits, and reggae and "Bob Marley" paraphernalia.

The town was changing! But as an Afro-Caribbean young man explained to me in response to my trivial observation, "Maybe we have more buildings now, but the place, it stay the same." By this he referred to the history of neglect by the state and the subsequent lack of physical infrastructure but also to the patterns of migration and mobility that had long marked the town's sociality.

A busy intersection

> The stew is now rich and thick with an exotic, provocative flavor. These are the children of the rainbow, Caribbean youth, young Talamancans, multi-lingual Costa Ricans – the future!
> (A leaflet distributed by American hotel owner and resident,
> Eddie Ryan, June 2004)

While the geographical features and the built environment of the town were constantly fluctuating over time, the social contours were equally in flux. The area is populated by what an American expatriate has called "an ethno-cultural rondon" or a "melting pot" of black and mixed Afro-Caribbean residents, descendants of earlier Jamaican, Barbadian, St. Kitts, and other Afro-Caribbean settlers of this area including those from Nicaragua and Panama; as well as *Ticos*, indigenous BriBri and Cabecar peoples, and recent internal migrants from other regions of Costa Rica; black, white, and ethnically mixed labor migrants from Panama, Columbia, and Nicaragua; and expatriates from many countries from all over the world.[8] Labor migrants, tourist migrants, vacation-home owners from the Central Valley, retirees from the United States and Canada, and foreign business owners resided alongside families who had lived in the area for generations.[9] A flow of Afro-Caribbean kin members continued to move up and down along the Atlantic coast from Nicaragua, to the north, and Panama, to the south, a pattern of migration and transnational residency that started when the first turtle fishermen settled their families in Cahuita and Tortuguera in the 1800s, the first being William Smith, from Bocas in Panama, in 1828 (Lefever 1992; Palmer 2005).

A census in 1998 stated that residents from forty different nationalities co-inhabited Puerto Viejo and the surrounding area (Vandegrift 2007).[10] A rough estimate for the small region where I conducted fieldwork, covering many small hamlets spanning roughly a ten kilometer distance, is a population of between

3,000 and 5,000 people; a figure that can rise drastically during the week of Semana Santa (Easter Holy Week), one of the busiest vacation weeks of the year, and then drop dramatically in the month of May when businesses close down and many foreign women return to their home countries to visit family or take on work to save money.

While in the twenty-first century the town is made up of a diverse mix of people, its earlier history had led to the creation of a racial enclave (Harpelle 2000). The area was, and continues to be in many ways, marginalized from the rest of Costa Rica. Since the beginning of nation making, dominant members of Costa Rican society from Spanish backgrounds saw the nation as "white" and "racially pure;" therefore, those inhabitants with "ethnic" backgrounds were discriminated against (Harpelle 2000: 58). By the mid twentieth century a long history of systemic racism had effectively "spatially incarcerated" black Afro-Caribbean-Costa Rican residents into this area through various regulations, as well as imposed the Spanish language onto a predominantly English-Caribbean English- and patois-speaking population (Harpelle 1993; Sandoval-García 2004; Sharman 2001).

As I describe in more detail in Chapter 2, when tourists arrived in the 1980s during the country's boom of tourism development they traveled from Europe and North America looking for a nascent "ecotourism" experience (Raventos 2006). In the twenty-first century, women tourists head to Puerto Viejo with a range of motivations. Many head there from other parts of Costa Rica on a whim, as a last-minute decision based on a scant but glowing recommendation, and often as an unplanned excursion to see what is constructed in national tourism media as "remote" and culturally distinct from the rest of the country. Many women are participants in volunteer and other humanitarian types of tourism, or are interested in adventure sport and health-and-wellbeing kinds of tourism – and many of the women I interviewed were part of this growing trend in tourist mobilities. Many tourists in Puerto Viejo are drawn by the infusion of New Age spirituality into the growing tourism options, such as yoga retreats and healing retreats. The flow of tourist women since the 1980s, traveling alone, in pairs or small groups, single, married or otherwise, has altered and indelibly marked the social landscape. A local *Tico* uttered a commonly stated sentiment: "There are so many of them [tourist women] coming and going... . One leaves and another busload arrives!"

As an international and domestic tourist destination, and a home to European, Canadian, American, and South American expatriates (many from Argentina), Afro-Caribbean, black, white, mixed ethnicity, and indigenous residents as well as documented and undocumented immigrants from Panama, Nicaragua, Columbia and countries in the global North (McIlwaine 1997; Vandegrift 2007, 2008), Puerto Viejo is situated at a very "busy intersection" (Rosaldo 1989) of different discourses about sex and sexuality. A Catholic nation, Costa Rica has legislation against abortion and assisted reproduction technologies, and advocates against birth control, sex education, and sex outside of marriage. On the Atlantic coast, the population of Limón province is predominantly Protestant. In Puerto Viejo, numerous churches including Baptist, Seventh Day Adventist, Catholic, and independent evangelical denominations exert their own sanctions against non-procreative and putatively "free" sex, recreational sex, and the notion of sexual leisure. Expatriates and other foreign residents have brought New Age spirituality and yoga from Northern urban centers and from Southern towns in Argentina and Uruguay. Rastafarian notions of sexuality, where women's putative "natural inferiority and power to contaminate" (Chevannes 2010: 222) justifies the subordination of women's sexual pleasure to men's and women's subjectification to a naturalized male promiscuity (Lake 1998), and where homophobia is central (LaFont 2009), enter the mix too. Rastafari messages of women needing their "king-man" and attaining enlightenment through "Jah" (Chevannes 2010: 222), disseminated through the lyrics and apoplectic messages of redemption and Babylon in reggae and dance hall music, were heard in the clubs and hawked by street vendors selling CDs and rasta trinkets.

It is this complex hybridity of overlapping and competing beliefs about sex as reproduction, condoned as pleasure only within heterosexual state-sanctioned marriages, as male privilege associated with *machismo*, as temptation and sin, as health and spiritual connection within the philosophy of tantric yoga, and as a normative aspect of international travel, especially for Euro-American young adults, and about gender subordination where women are regarded as "impure," as *gringa*s and sluts, as liberated and fun-loving, and as Rastafarian Empresses upholding male supremacy, for instance, that Northern women stumbled into as newly arriving tourists. Some women were intentionally seeking out sexual adventure as part of their travel experience. But most of the women I interviewed and spent time with during my fieldwork research felt that the sexual encounters they had been involved in as visitors or temporary residents in Puerto Viejo were for the most part almost entirely unforeseen. As I have only sketched out here, a complicated history has unfolded in this region of Costa Rica of tourist–local encounters and of mutual desires based on racialized and exoticized stereotypes, some of which I have previously written about in several published journal articles (Frohlick 2007, 2008a, b, 2009). A graduate student of mine, Kris Maksymowicz, wrote his master's thesis on the topic of European and North American men's heterosexual relations with local women. This book attempts to unravel some of these complications at length and to provide detailed contextualization of the experiences and practices of North American and European women's transnational encounters in Costa Rica.

These encounters that we Northerners write about, in turn, are situated in a much wider array of transcultural relations that are played out in a place situated at many different crossroads and borders, not only those of tourists and locals. An Afro-Caribbean friend, who is a public nurse, put this in perspective for me when she explained, "Puerto Viejo is not a frontier but an intersection of people coming from everywhere." Naming a bordering country and border towns as origins of migrant laborers in Puerto Viejo, she went on to say, "Cahuita, Sixaola, Panama, [this mobility] creates opportunities to have 'easy sex' here."

Curiosity about tourist women was rampant in Costa Rica. Georgette, the Swiss woman who initially steered me to Puerto Viejo, was the first but not the

Figure I.5 Flags marking associations with Rastafari, Bob Marley, Africa, Jamaica, Ethiopia, the United States, and Costa Rica hang from a second-story bar along the main street, signaling a "busy intersection" of cultures in the area. A biblical proverb appears on a poster in a restaurant below. "Love them that love me and those that seek me early shall find me." Photo by author.

only person to tell me that sexual relations between tourist women ("strangers," as she referred to them, in a translation of the Spanish term for foreigners, *extranjera*) and local men are rampant yet they remain "*escondido*" (hidden) to townspeople and daily life in the community. I conducted my first interview for this study in December 2004, sitting with my interviewee in an open-air café one rainy morning while my sister, Jane, read her book nearby. Near the end of our hour together, Georgette explained to me: "You [do] see it but, in Spanish, it's '*escondido*,' hidden. Nobody will ever, ever really talk about it. [Everyone knows it goes on and] nobody really likes it, but nobody talks about it." This observation of hers stuck with me, and has piqued my anthropological curiosity for years now. I would later hear different opinions, such as Miss Matthews' notion that within the Afro-Caribbean community people are not secretive because, in her words, "in our culture, it's not so bad having a companion." In writing about these "hidden" and "not so secret" social relations, I participate as much in the ongoing public secrecy of transnational sex in Puerto Viejo as I do in "exposing" what others already talk openly about (Frohlick 2008a). In other words, it is through stories, and praxis, that places come into being (Rodman 1992: 642). This is one more story but only one.

A common observation that the town is different between night and day articulates two of its many touristic faces – by day, an eco- and adventure tourism destination favored by backpackers, families, nature and adventure sport enthusiasts, and a spiritual destination for yoga and health and wellbeing seekers; and, at night, a reggae music and "fiesta tourism" scene reveled in equally by an international cosmopolitan crowd and local people, mostly men (although more local girls and women were starting to show up in the evenings over the course of my fieldwork).[11] As I have written elsewhere, this Janus-faced formation persuaded me to think about sexual tourism in the area not as "public performance of sex," a term used by Manderson (1992) to describe sex tourism in Thailand, but rather as a kind of public sexual secrecy (Frohlick 2008a: 24). Taussig has defined "public secrets" as "knowledge that is generally known but is left unspoken" (1999: 50). That is a salient way to describe the ways in which sex was kept under wraps yet talked about all the time in specific modes of telling, namely rumors, gossip, and speculation. These particular modes of telling, in turn, served as discursive mechanisms by which social knowledge about sex and sexual relations were empowered through strategic revelation. A young American woman named Bethany who had been visiting Puerto Viejo for several months and had dated several local men when I spoke to her had explained this to me: "Women just don't talk to one another in this town. It's all kind of a secret really. Women seem to compete with one another when they first arrive to attract a black Costa Rican man and nobody says anything because word spreads like fire." The threat of being the subject of gossip as much as losing out on the attention of an attractive man shaped the social practices of transnational sex for heterosexual tourist women.

"Sex in Puerto Viejo is abundant," some locals insisted, as did some foreigners. But which sexual relations and which people were the fodder of gossip and scandal? This was not a town where sex was plainly evident, and therefore it contrasts with the descriptions of Jamaica, Barbados, and Dominican Republic where public displays of affection in broad daylight between foreign women and their local lovers are evidently common (see O'Connell Davidson and Sánchez Taylor 2005; Wright 1992). Although sometimes plainly visible (such as the tourist couple making out on the town's beach within plain view, or frenzied couples fondling inside the nightclubs) and other times obvious but not visible (such as the telltale signs of long line-ups outside the bar's only washroom), the town's sexual cartography was marked, more or less, by discretion. Another way of framing it that draws on my interlocutor's description: By concealment. *Escondido*.

In a Costa Rican town experiencing many changes due to the recent forces of global tourism, including those related to the sexual practices of its townspeople and the thousands of visitors per year, transnational sex was the fodder for gossip and for secret keeping. I came to know the place through the stories, experiences, behaviors, performances, and biases of European and North American women who led me through their everyday worlds as they moved about Puerto Viejo doing things that tourists and temporary residents do.

An ethnography of Euro-American women tourists

Those alien lovers have their own stories to tell....

(Tsing 1996: 299)

Alex, a Canadian woman I met early on in my fieldwork and whom I introduce in more detail later in the book, told me that she thought it was fascinating that an anthropologist was actually going to study the sexual relations between tourist women and local men in the town. It was a topic on the minds of so many people yet a source of confusion and puzzlement. It was immediately clear to me that my research might be of interest to the women I was working with as well as to some townspeople in the local community (including the physician who described Puerto Viejo as a "complex place" and the public health nurse who was treating tourists for sexually transmitted infections in her newly opened clinic in 2009).[12] But I would also need to address the question of how cultural anthropologists would be interested in the sexual practices of women who traveled to a Central American country as contemporary tourists.

A main reason has to do with how "Western women" as a study population represent a strident break in the object of inquiry from a disciplinary fascination with the sex lives of "primitives." In a recent history of anthropology and sexuality, Lyons and Lyons talk about the "ghosts of oversexed [and undersexed] savages" that "haunt" contemporary studies of sexuality in anthropology (2004: 322). The forefathers and mothers of anthropology including Malinowski, Margaret Mead, and Ruth Benedict examined sexuality as "local customs" in the antipodes of Europe and North America and sites of colonial encounter – the Trobriand Islands, American Samoa, and the Native American reservations of North America. The anthropological study of sexuality represented in textbooks continues to emphasize "culture" and thereby to address the sexualities of "different" cultures (e.g. LaFont 2003) or non-normative "different" sexualities (e.g. Robertson 2005). However, more recently, as Boellstorff (2007) has pointed out, anthropologists have begun to investigate the changing formations of sexual subjectivities through and in global and local contexts, rather than as fixed in time and place. While these new shifts in how anthropologists and other social science researchers have re-conceptualized sexuality in the past decades are undoubtedly important, the anthropological record remains skewed. As Kulick notes, "the sex of 'the Other' has provided endless fodder for reflection, speculation and flourish" (1995: 3). Therefore, an examination of Western heterosexuality constitutes an important shift away from a sustained disciplinary gaze on non-Western and non-normative sexualities, and also paves the way for nuanced understandings of "normative sexualities" and the ways in which heterosexualities are multiple and not always "straight."

While feminists agree that women as a gender category in opposition to men have also remained a kind of "Other" in scholarship on sexuality, in anthropology "it is always the other woman, the native woman somewhere else ... the !Kung woman, the Balinese woman, the National Geographic woman" (Behar 1995: 1) who anthropologists study. Behar went on to say, in a provocative passage in

Women Writing Culture, that it is only the native women somewhere else who seemingly have breasts – "breasts that can be seen, exposed, pictured, brought home, and put into books" (1995: 1) – implying that the breasts of Western women (who write about other women) have remained hidden, "behind her pen and pad of paper" (1995: 1). Behar's words were deployed at the time as a feminist challenge to the masculinism of the anthropological canon, where men's authorship had been championed at the expense of women's authorship. Yet her words serve my purposes here, that of challenging the reluctance of anthropologists in the cultural examination of sexuality to look at the erotic subjectivities, especially normative erotic subjectivies, and the fleshy, corporeal, bosomed, and white-skinned bodies of women, especially heterosexual women, from Western cultures.

In the anthropology of tourism it is also non-Western subjects who tend to be the ones studied, often as the victims of the deleterious forces of Western tourism or as local tourism producers. When tourists are looked at "male bodies remain the normative performing active mobile tourist subjects" (Frohlick 2010: 52; see also Kaplan 1996; Veijola and Jokinen 1994). Although there is an established body of literature on colonial women and travel (e.g. Blunt 1994: Ghose 1998; Grewal 1996; Mills 1991), women tourists as relatively elite mobile subjects partaking in contemporary international travel and tourism have yet to become the focus of much research on travel and tourism, particularly ethnographic studies. This is in spite of pleas by Clifford (1997) more than ten years ago to investigate the gendered practices of travel and by feminist scholars to look at gender as one of the many power differentials, including ethnocentrism and colonialism, that "are always implicated in the activity of travel" (Grewal and Kaplan 2001: 673), although fortunately a body of literature is emerging (e.g. Jacobs 2009, 2010; Lozanski 2007; Pritchard *et al.* 2007; Small 2007; Wilson and Little 2008; Yamaga 2006).

Within anthropological accounts looking at travel as encounter, non-Western women as *objects* of desire have been looked at tangentially (e.g. Clifford 1997; Enloe 2000; Gagnon 2004; Pratt 1992). Tsing speaks of the way "the contemporary fantasy of transcultural romance" features "the bourgeois male traveler," and the ever-familiar story line, appearing in science fiction novels and television shows as well as historical accounts, where "the white male explorer is rewarded with an alien lover" (1996: 298). These "alien lovers" are most often represented as passive and conquered victims in contrast to the white men who conquer, that is, "women as weak betrayers of third-world communities, seduced by the colonizer" (Tsing 1996: 299). To rectify these sorts of victimizing accounts of women Tsing set out to show how "alien lovers [the third-world women 'seduced' by the male travelers] have their own stories to tell, stories that show women's initiative as well as their deference" (1996: 299), a corrective that fits the current media representations of Western women tourists as lascivious and excessively transgressive, an issue that I return to later in the book.

Within a long history of heterosexual cross-cultural encounters, men and women have engaged in an array of "transcultural romances." In the eighteenth-century voyages of Captain James Cook, European men first encountered Polynesian women. Gagnon (2004) has looked at the sexual aspects of these historical encounters to show that due to the lack of language sharing, sexual relations between the European men and Polynesian women in those first cultural contacts must have relied upon non-verbal communication between strangers. His work is influential in current studies of cross-cultural forms of sexual relations through travel because he resisted the idea that "the men's interest in copulation with women" and the Polynesian women's apparent lack of sexual "inhibition" were inherent, biological attributes of gendered bodies. Instead, the question he asked is this: How is sexual conduct actually "accomplished between members of culturally different peoples" (Gagnon 2004: 248)?

While anthropologists have grappled with the question of how gender (bound with race and nation) has shaped sexual relations between exoticized travelers and eroticized locals within colonial and postcolonial encounters, women in the role of traveler and tourist have largely been ignored (Clifford 1997). Scholarship on transcultural encounters raises a larger question that directly relates to North American and European tourist women, of how feminine desire shapes contemporary travel practices. Subsequently, heterosexual subjects also shape the social contours of local places that are the profuse "borderzones" created through contemporary tourism as destinations spread throughout the Third World. My book shifts from an examination of local women as desired subjects in contexts of encounter (such as the Polynesian women in Cook's "penetration" of the Pacific) to the study of "foreign" women as desiring subjects in the context of modern tourism. Borrowing and inverting Tsing's term, I use "alien lovers," in this instance, to refer to the men of the global South "discovered" by tourist women arriving from the global North. The notions of "foreign" and "local" and how they are relational have long been of interest to anthropologists. Kelsky's (2001) work on contemporary middle-class working and internationalist Japanese women, the notorious "yellow cabs," and their attraction to American and European men shows how the women's desires are situated in wider contemporary and historical patterns of attraction in recent Japanese society for many things "foreign." My book also looks at desires and aesthetics for particular foreign bodies as cultural and historical, and also sees the opposition between foreign and local as relational and that which can produce erotic tension. My viewing point, from the perspectives of Western women tourists as "foreign," places the Costa Rican men as "local," and as desired for their local-ness.

Anthropologists, geographers, and other scholars are beginning to document the various patterns of foreign women's heterosexual attractions and sexual tourism practices with local men in different destinations throughout the world (e.g. Dragojlovic 2008; Jacobs 2010; Piscitelli 2001; Tucker 2003). Within a global scale of tourist movement or "tourist flows," most long-haul travelers, that is, those who cross international borders, originate from countries in the global North, although this is changing and, morevover, historical patterns are actually more complicated than this (Chambers 2000).Within these flows of international travelers outbound from Northern countries, as many women as men are traveling in both of the main categories of pleasure travel and business travel (Harris and Wilson 2007: 235). To provide a mere glimpse of the complex picture of international travel with regards to point of origin, in 2008, out of a total 922 million international arrivals across the globe, more than 50 percent of outbound international tourists originated from Europe, while North America was the next leading source, followed by Asia and the Pacific, mostly China and Japan.[13] As the broad statistics regarding the source countries of outbound tourists suggest, these flows of tourist groups tracked according to citizenship originate from both Western and non-Western countries; and Japan has been a significant "sending" country of female tourists since the 1970s internationalization movement (Kelsky 2001; Yamaga 2006). Nevertheless, in the early twenty-first century the colonial legacy of the Grand Tour and other earlier forms of colonial travel is reflected in the continued predominance of women from Europe and North America who participate in, what Smith refers to as, "the cultural logic of the individualizing journey" (Smith 2001: xi), an apt characterization of contemporary tourism, although it is also so much more than that. My book builds upon this literature, and provides nuanced ethnographic detail to the emerging scholarship on women, sexuality, and tourism, a topic of great interest in the public imagination where stereotypes and generalizations abound.

1   Desiring Costa Rica

"Costa Rica"

> "Costa Rica – No Artificial Ingredients."
> (International Advertising Campaign by the
> *Instituto Costarricense de Turismo*)

In 2008, Costa Rica, a country encompassing an area of roughly 51,000 square kilometers, received more than 2 million international tourists, approximately half the country's population at the time of 4.1 million.[1] Among these visitors, 55 percent were from the United States, 6 percent from Canada, and 16 percent from European countries. While the majority of international visitors arrive in Costa Rica in couples or family units, almost one-third of international arrivals were traveling unaccompanied by a partner, family, or friend.[2] These statistics mean little in the way of the subjective experiences of touristic travel or of transnational encounters except to provide the broadest scope in which to situate Euro-American female tourists in Costa Rica. My interlocutors, who were from Canada, the United States, Austria, Germany, the Netherlands, Spain, Italy, France, England, Ireland, New Zealand, Australia, and Switzerland, and who were mostly independent travelers, although some traveled with family members or friends, were part of statistics that categorize and track the movement of people across national borders but reveal little else and provoke many more questions: Who were the tourist women in Puerto Viejo between 2005 and 2009, and why did they travel to Costa Rica in the first place?

"Costa Rica," like all tourist destinations, is depicted in thousands of representations circulating globally, on the Internet and other travel media. By the late twentieth century, the small country situated between Panama and Nicaragua on the Central American isthmus had secured "its image as a peaceful country" (Honey 2004: 407), born out of international media attention on the country's Nobel Peace Prize-winning president, its stance against militarism, and its progressive national park system and conservation measures. Costa Rica is lauded for its "exceptionalism" as a Central American country whose relative wealth, political stability, and ecological abundance in comparison to other Central American countries has earned it such nicknames as "Little Switzerland" and "Shangri-La" (Palmer and Molina 2004: 1). Yet it has multiple faces. Depending on the audience, it is a "safe haven" for American retirees, a "utopia" for environmentalists, or an "international hub" for sex tourists and pedophiles.

A burgeoning global sex tourism industry contradicts its reputation as peaceful and "exceptional." While accurate figures as far as economic scope or human resources are impossible to obtain, as Rivers-Moore has indicated, "the sex industry occupies a significant place within the tourism trade in Costa Rica" (2009:60).[3] In San José, the capital city located in the Central Valley of the small mountainous country, prostitution is widespread. While commercial sex is carried out on the streets, local bars, and massage parlors throughout the city, it is the tourist hotels and nightclubs in the central tourism district, notably the "gringo" area with its concentration of men's clubs and American-style sports bars (Rivers-Moore 2009), that are the prime and "enviable" locales for sex trade workers (Downe 1997). In addition to the capital city the coastal beach resort towns are also popular sites for sex tourism.

While prostitution is legal in Costa Rica, sex with minors seventeen years and younger is not. Alongside its global standing as a destination for legal commercial sex, Costa Rica suffers a tarnished reputation for child sex tourism. In a 1995 research paper prepared for ECPAT,[4] O'Connell Davidson and Sánchez Taylor state that:

> [Costa Rica] hosts large numbers of dedicated, seasoned North American and European sex tourists … it seems probable that many of the male tourists who are ostensibly drawn to Costa Rica for other reasons (surfing, water sports, ecotourism, etc.) … also sexually exploit local women and children during the course of their stay.
> (O'Connell Davidson and Sánchez Taylor 1995: 1)

With estimates ranging from 120 "*casas*" with underage minors working illegally as prostitutes (Downe 1997: 1575) to "more than 300 brothels in San José alone" (O'Connell Davidson and Sánchez Taylor 1995), it is not surprising that the Costa Rican government has been mired in scandal over child sex trafficking and human rights abuses. One online travel magazine has recently expunged the country from a list of "the world's most ethical destinations" for this reason, chiding, "Costa, 'the capital of eco-tourism' Rica ain't on the list [of ethical destinations] mostly because of its booming underage sex trade."[5]

While a plethora of online websites berate Costa Rica for an alleged "booming underage sex trade" and "thriving" sex tourism industry, the government strives to retain a much more sanitized image. As one of the world's first "green" destinations, due in no small part to the state's large-scale efforts over several decades, Costa Rica continues to be highly regarded by tourists for its ecological diversity and conservation practices (Honey 2004). Nature-based tourism has been the focus of tourism development and state promotion of a global image since the 1980s. Beginning in the 1990s the state tourism ministry began to brand the country with the trope of "pure nature," as I will explain.

Differing media images can intersect in "the tourist imagination" (Crouch *et al.* 2005: 1). The concept "tourist imagination" reflects the independence between tourism and media; that is, how it is through media that particular images are "converted" into tourist activity or the creative possibility of mobility and crossing over into a sphere of life different from work and quotidian life (Crouch *et al.* 2005: 1). Another way of putting this idea is that places become "places for play" in part because of how people imagine themselves to embody those spaces and landscapes (Sheller and Urry 2004). Tourists draw upon seemingly disparate images to imagine a multitude of roles. Therefore, Costa Rica as a site for sexual consumption coincides with the promise it projects as a surfing and water sports haven, as alluded to by O'Connell Davidson and Sánchez Taylor (1995) in their report on child sex tourism. Another example is how the country's allure as a destination for cosmetic surgery tourism dovetails, ironically, with its image as a "nature" mecca (Ackerman 2010). Different tourist imaginations are thus mobilized – for erotic pleasure, for sporting pleasure, for health and healing, for the beautification of the body, to commune with nature, to access affordable technology and unadulterated landscapes, for instance – which carries implications for the social and spatial organization of tourist activity and the physical mobility of tourism.

In a striking way, media contributes to a bifurcated gendered geography of desire in Costa Rica; that is, a mapping of the country split between the Caribbean and the Pacific in terms of where male tourists and female tourists travel to experience intimate encounters with locals. Despite evidence that indicates the presence of Euro-American female tourists across multiple tourist regions in Costa Rica, including Jacó and Monteverde (see Freidus and Romero-Daza 2009; Ragsdale *et al.* 2006; Shaffer 1996), a powerful notion of gendered sexual travel practices underpins a prevailing tourist imagination. The Pacific coast and its large holiday resorts is where foreign men go for a "girlfriend experience" or to buy sex locally from male and female sex workers. (Manuel Antonio National Park and the town of Quepos, a "gay enclave," are popular with American gay men.[6]) The Caribbean coast and its small villages and small-scale tourist development is where budget and alternative type female tourists head and where local men avail themselves in numerous ways. I am not suggesting that these patterns are fixed. Undoubtedly the allure for tourist activities that conjoin desires for nature and "eco" experiences with desires for erotic experiences are played out in locales that span the country. The point that I wish to underscore is this: The consumption of attractions and landscapes by international tourists is mediated by suggestive imagery that carves up the nation into gendered sites of play and touristic performances, including activities and performances related to sex, love, erotics, and intimacy.

A conversation I had when I was on a side trip to the Pacific coast helped me to understand this. Montezuma, a seaside tourist town in the Puntarenas province, was once primarily a fishing village but has become popular with ecotourists and backpackers and has gained an international reputation for yoga and healing arts. While spending time in an Internet café, I struck up a conversation with an American woman staffing the front desk. When I told her that I was a cultural anthropologist conducting research in Puerto Viejo de Talamanca on tourist women's relations with local men she looked at me knowingly and said, "Yeah, I heard that there was a lot of *that kind of thing* going on *over there*."

Then she proceeded to ask me, "What gives with *that*?"

I found it curious that during my visit in Montezuma I had witnessed firsthand several inter-ethnic couples walking together and interacting, so presumably transnational sex was part of this local scene too. The young woman's comment about "that kind of thing" taking place "over there" (rather than in many places in Costa Rica) served to align the Caribbean region of Costa Rica with a particular naturalized pattern of cross-border sex between foreign women and local men.

This powerful image is reproduced over and over again in tourism media, and is sanctioned by the state. Two examples illustrate this point. In a guidebook called "*Culture Smart! Costa Rica*" the section on Puerto Viejo and Cahuita features an iconic image of a dreadlocked bare-chested rasta interacting with a Western female tourist, an image furnished by the Costa Rica Tourist Board (Koutnik 2005: 40). A similar image appears in a poster published by the national tourism ministry used to promote the southern Caribbean (see Figure 5.1 in Chapter 5). Appearing as a part of the quintessentially Caribbean landscape, emplaced between the crystalline azure water, sparkling white beach, and exotic fruits and other Caribbean foods, are a dreadlocked Afro-Caribbean man and a white woman dancing in synch together (while a white man, presumably her spouse, looks on). Notably, the implied erotic sociability between rastas and white women is not represented in tourist media for other regions of the country, where, instead, white couples interact solely on their own in the nature landscapes or with their children in family groupings (Frohlick and Johnston 2011).[7]

For the majority of women I interviewed choosing Costa Rica and eventually the area of Puerto Viejo as their travel destinations, as well as partaking in flirtatious and sexual relations with local men, were actions that were meaningful to Euro-American women as unplanned events. Most of the women I interviewed, whom I describe in more detail below, and spoke with in casual conversations, like the conversation I had with the woman in the Internet café, had some prior knowledge about Costa Rica, especially ideas about the country as peaceful, safe, and ecologically "green." However, very few of them had heard about the town of Puerto Viejo prior to their arrival in Costa Rica. The metanarrative of spontaneity was central to women's tourist mobilities and cross-border sex, an idea I develop further in the following chapter.

In this chapter, I highlight some of the seductive images of "Costa Rica" as a destination that influenced tourist women's decisions to travel there and that shape twenty-first century cosmopolitan desires for safe adventure and nature-infused experiences. What ideas about the country influenced North American and European women to travel to Costa Rica? Not surprisingly given the million-dollar branding of the country as a top-ranked global ecotourism destination, the trope of "nature" was a strong "pull" factor. The "safety factor" was also significant.

Pura vida

"Costa Rica" was a compelling idealized landscape for Northern women tourists in particular ways. My interlocutors gushed about how beautiful Costa Rica is, how green and lush it is, how beautiful the beaches and jungles are, and about how easy it is to travel within the country. They described the waterfalls, the colorful, exotically scented flowers, and the feeling of tranquility they experienced in looking out at the azure blue ocean. They talked about how the capital city, San José, is not the "real" Costa Rica – as it is regarded as notoriously dangerous and unfriendly. As one woman put it, "San José is a place to leave as quickly as possible once you've arrived from your international flight."

The "Costa Rica" conjured in women tourists' narratives was a place consisting of national parks and small, cosmopolitan villages and towns. It stood out as an ecologically diverse and ethically responsible, peaceful country free of any notable human rights abuses, where people are friendly and "happy and healthy" (Downe 1997).[8] Life is harmonious with nature in Costa Rica, many women told me (Ackerman 2010). The phrase *pura vida*, a colloquialism used in a range of ways, including for greetings, departures, approval, agreement (like "okay" or "great"), and to express appreciation of a good life, was incorporated by tourist women in their Spanglish, in their Facebook posting, and on T-shirts emblazoned with the words. Translated literally, the phrase means "pure living." "*Pura vida*" encapsulates the significance of the exceptionalism wedded to the country's self-image and tourism branding, as the following description appearing on a website about the culture of Costa Rica indicates: "So, if you want to know what living a peaceful, simple, uncluttered life with a deep appreciation for nature, family and friends [is like], just come to Costa Rica and experience it yourself! ¡PURA VIDA!"[9]

Costa Rica is constructed, then, as a utopia. Not only imagined as warm and sunny, like any other sun–sea–sand destination in the global South, what stood out for my interlocutors is how Costa Rica is unique as an ecologically pure and salubrious place. Because it is constructed as unpolluted, it is desired as a place to cleanse and purify the body and soul. Ackerman describes how medical tourists, too, regard Costa Rica as a place of recuperation, and how they "reproduce spiritualist aesthetics of Costa Rican nature" (2010: 415). I found that in Puerto Viejo the kinds of "spiritual aesthetics of nature" and apparent healing qualities of the nation, as described by Ackerman (2010) in her research on the cosmetic surgery industry in Costa Rica, were manifested in the number of services that catered to tourists looking for such experiences. Yoga, massage therapy, meditation, and other New Age health-oriented offerings were plentiful in Puerto Viejo, especially in relation to its small size and population (Figure 1.1). This aesthetic and its material manifestations in the spaces where yoga and meditation classes took place and where massages were given are important context to the women's narratives.

From the Latin word *destinare*, "destination" means to make firm, establish, choose. Tourist destinations are cultural landscapes that are "at once ambiguous, attractive and important" and reflect "the human values and ideologies of the resident and the viewer, serving as a palimpsest of place attachments between individuals and social groups to specific locations and places" (Ringer 1998: 7). Tourists are thus co-producers of destinations and through their embodied actions and language contribute to the establishment and concretizing of places as choice. Tourists' narratives suggest how words and vocabulary render unfamiliar places

Figure 1.1 Yoga, massage, meditation, and reflexology advertisements are prominent amidst notices of house rentals and language classes on a billboard located in an area south of the village popular with tourists and foreign residents. Photo by author.

in more familiar terms (Coleman and Crang 2002). "Costa Rica," a relatively unknown country to many tourist women prior to their travels, was envisaged repeatedly as a place of "pure nature." The reflections of a female anthropology student from an American university, appearing in a report from a field school in the late 1990s, illustrate this:

> When I first heard of the Ethnographic Field School that was being offered at North Carolina State University, the only words that really caught my attention were "Costa Rica." I had visions of a wild, undeveloped nation with lush rain forests and beautiful unsullied beaches. I wanted to see nature unmarred by pollution and unaffected by man [sic].
>
> (Shaffer 1996: 99)

Northern women I spoke with also engaged in the construction of Costa Rica as a paradisiacal destination. Women who were interested in therapeutic and healing practices, environmentalism, "green" consumption, and nature-based experiences talked about Costa Rica as a place they were *destined* to go rather than a place they chose by rational means; it was a place that moved them and that held the promise to be beautiful, unspoiled, health-giving, and friendly.

The "No Artificial Ingredients" campaign

While these images may seem to come out of thin air, in actuality the tourism ministry (*Instituto Costarricense de Turismo*) has directed costly and sustained efforts to create its brand as a nature-based tourism destination. In other words, "visions of a wild, undeveloped nation with lush rainforests and beautiful unsullied beaches" and of "nature unmarred by pollution" (Shaffer 1996: 99), and other such naturalizing global representations, are mediated through extensive campaigns that serve to focus international attention – and primarily the attention of potential US tourists – on particular aspects of the country.

The history of its destination branding goes back several decades to the 1980s, when Costa Rica's international reputation was at risk of being tarnished (Honey 2004) and when a global economic crisis was unfolding.[10] The government hoped to shift its politically unfavorable image to one of being a progressively and proactively conservation-minded country. By highlighting its burgeoning inventory of national parks and protected areas, the government attempted to transform its image from "a southern front for the contras" into a "mecca" for "green" tourism (Honey 2004: 408). During the recession, tourists, especially American tourists, wanted affordable and peaceful destinations. The idea of "eco" tourism was emerging, and Costa Rica was able to jump "the ecotourism queue surpassing older nature travel destinations such as the Galapagos Islands, Kenya, and Nepal," becoming recognized as a world stage both for its peacemaking and conservation leadership (Honey 2004: 407).

Euro-American women's experiences of transnational sex and romance unfolded in the aftermath of these historical and geopolitical economic developments. Although Costa Rica was imagined as a naturalized eco-utopia, the nation's tourism development had actually been through several different periods of development by the 2000s. Raventos has identified three distinct periods since the 1980s.

During the "Ecological Tourism Pioneering Period" (1980–1988), "dedicated ecologists and academics were drawn to the country by its natural attractions and by its image of peace" (Raventos 2006: 376). The next phase, in the early 1990s, was the "Growth Period," marked by the arrival of "ecologically minded tourists … interested in experiencing nature or in combining sun and beach with some kind of nature-related experience" (Raventos 2006: 377). The third phase (mid-1990s) is identified as the "Evolution Period from an Ecological Tourism Destination to a Nature-Based Tourism Destination." During those years "nature" became the central signifier and unifying feature in an increasingly multifaceted, niche-marketed industry. As Raventos explains, "Tourism segments, such as sun and beach, adventure, convention, those seeking health, and intercultural knowledge – all of them leaning to natural experiences – start to become more clearly defined" (2006: 377). This was the time when efforts to transform Costa Rica into "a place where the tourist could have a nature related experience and be very

Figure 1.2 One of ten posters in the 2004 "No Artificial Ingredients" campaign sponsored by the *Instituto Costarricense de Turismo* (Costa Rican Tourism Institute). Each poster depicts a different geographical region of the country and links "nature" with embodied tourism consumption, here featuring a white, Euro-American, mono-racial, heterosexual tourist couple.

comfortable" (Raventos 2006: 377) were intensified. It was during that period that the government hired a large international advertising firm to create the hugely successful campaign entitled "Costa Rica – No Artificial Ingredients." The "No Artificial Ingredients" campaign, featuring lush, vivid green exotic landscapes and light-skinned tourists performing a variety of outdoor recreational and adventure sport activities, appeared in glossy advertisements in upscale US-based magazines such as *Travel and Leisure*, *Surfer*, and *Backpacker* (Figure 1.2). Such images appealed to diverse tourist imaginations linked by tropes of purity and nature (Frohlick and Johnston 2011; Raventos 2006; Rivers-Moore 2007). The objective of the campaign, which was massive in economic scale relative to the GNP of the small nation, was to promote and circulate the idea of a "nature-based experience" in Costa Rica to millions of people worldwide.

However, the primary target demographics were upscale, middle-class, university and college-educated, urban dwellers and consumers residing in major US cities (Raventos 2006: 377). As Rivers-Moore aptly remarks, "the current global reality of the US hegemony plays a major role in structuring the ways that a nation and a people can be depicted in order to appeal to US tourists and their dollars" (2007: 352). Moreover, the fact that an international European-based marketing company was hired to design the slogan for the nation's newest image as a branded "nature" destination with US citizens in mind as the predominant consumers of Costa Rica's eco-scapes is important context in the consideration of how women understand their embodied engagement in this tourism destination.

A "woman's (safe) destination"

Alongside the ubiquitous imagery of Costa Rica as a place for embodied immersion within natural, green, and untainted spaces, an equally alluring image coexists. Not only is Costa Rica "pure" but also "safe." Gender plays a central role in these constructions. Web-based media as well as newspapers and travel magazines attest to the safety that women can be guaranteed when they travel within Costa Rica.

An article posted on the online *USA Today* names Costa Rica one of the most "women-friendly" destinations worldwide for women traveling on their own, third on a list of five countries and cities (following Amsterdam and Ireland).[11] Another article in *The Tico Times*, an English-language newspaper out of San José for expatriates, foreign business owners and tourists, ranks Costa Rica as the world's "third safest destination for women travelers" (after Holland and Ireland).[12] In a third article the editor of an online women's travel magazine suggests that Costa Rica is safer than her hometown in the United States. She writes: "In La Fortuna, as my friend and I descended a steep hill on a hot day, a man in a pick-up truck pulled over and offered us a ride. In the US, I never would have accepted the ride, but *I felt so safe in Costa Rica* that I hopped in. The man dropped us off a few blocks from our hotel with a wave."[13]

In these media examples "safety" as a key criterion in the naming of a destination especially suitable for women tourists is one that Costa Rica seems to meet. This is because the people are regarded as happy and healthy, as I have explained. But it is also related to the focus on "untamed" and "pristine" nature in visual representations such that, as Echtner and Prasad (2003: 675) have shown in their analysis of Costa Rican tourist marketing, "civilization" is largely absent so that tourists can participate in expeditions to "discover and observe the frontiers." In an analysis of the "No Artificial Ingredients" campaign, Rivers-Moore argues that gender and race is utilized in its imagery that effectively re-inscribes the putative "whiteness" of its citizenry and displaces bodies of color, such as indigenous and

Afro-Caribbean people, so as to project a sense of safety – as well as purity (2007: 345). White spaces are linked to safety (Rivers-Moore 2007). A supposed racial homogeneity (whiteness) is central to the narrative of the nation. This myth is invoked as the explanation for social peace in a country where both violence and racism continue to be lived realities for many of the nation's citizenry and residents alienated by the system (de Regil 2009; Palmer and Molina 2004; Sandoval-García 2004).

Despite deep cracks between the myths and lived realities, which are not unique to Costa Rica but are systemic in Third World tourism marketing where "any difference contrary to the myth is silenced" (Echtner and Prasad 2003: 679), many women were taken by notions of Costa Rica as a "safe place." Crucially, however, it was not all of Costa Rica nor was it the places deemed the "safest" by the government where women felt safe. Particularly in contrast to the "Americanized" Pacific coast and urbanized San José, the Atlantic held a positive attraction for women looking for safe travel experiences and encounters with purity and nature.

"Safety" is thus linked complexly to the Atlantic. While warnings spread by urban white Costa Rican society intended to discourage travel to the Caribbean "as an area of high crime" (Momsen 2005: 211), these warnings had the opposite effect with the tourist women I interviewed. This was in part because, as Momsen has pointed out, "locals and critics interpret the government's warning as a reflection of institutionalized racism as Costa Rica's Caribbean coast was historically populated by black Jamaican and other islands and has a distinctly Afro-Caribbean culture" (2005: 211). However, the southern Caribbean was not constructed as a completely "black space," insofar as the international community of foreign expatriates and long-stay tourists is also strongly present in tourists' representations on the Internet as well as in my interlocutors' narratives of Puerto Viejo. Here we see the "whitening," as Rivers-Moore (2007) points out, associated with safety. They saw the Puerto Viejo area as Afro-Caribbean but also "multicultural" and like "every color of the rainbow," as I explain further in Chapter 4.

Through such complexly racially coded imagery, foreign tourist women associated Costa Rica, and in particular, the southern Caribbean beach towns, with a sense of freedom of mobility. They felt free from the gender-based troubles of sexualized surveillance associated with women traveling to a foreign country (Jordan and Aitchison 2008), such as the physical or sexual harassment from local men that they experienced in San José and elsewhere. This was the place to which they arrived "by chance" and as a kind of "fluke" and in which decisions to partake in local sexual cultures and practices were regarded as spontaneous and unpremeditated, an idea that I demonstrate further in the next chapter. While a diversity of tourists travel to Puerto Viejo, one of the common "typologies" of tourist flows into the area that I observed closely fits the demographics targeted by the *Instituto Costarricense de Turismo*: so-called "alternative" tourists in middle to upper income brackets, well educated and with a proclivity for a range of ecotourism and also volunteer type tourisms – such as therapeutic and transformation type tourism, health, wellbeing, and spirituality tourism (spas, retreats, yoga, and so forth), bodily oriented adventure sport tourism (such as surfing and whitewater rafting), and education-based tourism (such as Spanish language home-stays) – are drawn to the southern Caribbean and especially Puerto Viejo.

Constructed as a popular tourist imaginary for "women's travel," Costa Rica attracts hundreds of thousands of female tourists every year.[14] In looking at the sexual practices of female tourists more broadly, fewer numbers of women in comparison to male tourists participate in sex while on holiday, according to large-scale studies in Australia (McNulty *et al.* 2010), Canada (Egan 2001), and Peru (Cabada *et al.* 2003). The numbers of tourists, male or female, who engage in sexual relations with locals are lower than those who engage in sexual relations with other tourists (Cabada *et al.* 2003). With these very broad contours of travel sex in mind and given its allure with North American and European women as a top-ranked "women's destination," Costa Rica is an important locale for querying the particularities of women's sexual agency and subjectivities as social actors in the wider global phenomenon of transnational sex. Out of the large numbers of female tourists each year in Costa Rica, who are the women who engage in transnational inter-ethnic sex and heterosexual material–erotic exchanges with local men? What are the contextual and subjective factors that influence their actions? Why do these encounters matter?

Feminist researchers studying sexuality and tourism have acknowledged the importance of social context and physical locale in shaping sexual intimacy (Flowers *et al.* 2000; Thomas 2000, 2005). With this in mind, Thomas urges, "whilst quantitative studies have been useful in exploring the extent and correlates of sexual behaviour abroad, a more qualitative understanding is necessary in order to further understand the context in which these sexual relationships occur" (2005: 573). She is interested in the implications for women's sexual decision-making on holiday for sexual risk and the transmission of sexually transmitted infections and HIV/AIDs, as HIV-risk has been the focus of many studies of women's international travel (e.g. Bauer 2009; Bloor *et al.* 2000; Ragsdale *et al.* 2006; Romero-Daza and Freidus 2008; Thomas 2000; Thomas *et al.* 1997). Because my interest is on heterosexuality and sexual subjectivity, as I explain further below, in my fieldwork I was trying to understand the ways that being in another country as a tourist in a gendered, sexualized, racialized body influences sexual experiences and the meanings that are given to those experiences. I wanted to know what the common narratives were as far as trajectories, or paths, tourist women took in their sexual, erotic, and intimate heterosexual encounters from beginning (arrival in Puerto Viejo) to their departure. In order to get at these material realities, the patterns and meanings of women's experiences, as well as the social and spatial contexts that shaped cross-border erotics, I used qualitative methodology, which I outline next before explaining the main theoretical concern of the book how does tourism shape sexuality and sexuality shape tourism?

Living in the village and researching tourists

> They flit around town with their blonde hair, on their bikes, like they are special.
> (Afro-Caribbean male townsperson, August 2005)

Research, like travel, can be unpredictable. I had originally traveled to Costa Rica to investigate women's adventure tourism. During a winter break from the university, I set out to investigate the Atlantic coast as a field site, and took my sister along as a travel companion. During a two-day visit to Puerto Viejo I became acutely aware of sexualized interactions between local men and foreign women. Countless times the two of us were approached by male taxi drivers, surf instructors, Internet café personnel, and hotel staff. An Afro-Caribbean taxi driver from Puerto Limón told us outright that he would "set us up," presuming that because we were traveling without men we must be looking for local boyfriends. When we questioned him, in defense of his mistaken assumptions he replied, "After all, 80 percent of women traveling alone are coming for sex tourism!" This impressive number struck me as odd. Did women actually travel to Costa Rica to pay for sex with local men, we wondered? As I would learn, the situation is far more complex than what was suggested by our taxi driver.

The sanitized images in tourism media that depicted the area as an "adventure playground" steeped in "tropical nature," indigenous culture, and other wholesome elements contrasted with the eroticized interactions that played out when two white Canadian women in our forties arrived to partake in kayaking, surfing, and hiking. The taxi driver offered to find us the "world's best lovers," while our surf instructors suggested they set us up with "sexy Caribbean boyfriends" – these narratives compelled me to shift my ethnographic attention from women's adventure tourism to women's transnational sex (although these are not disparate activities). The contingent, open-ended nature of ethnographic research methodology, where researchers are not detached from the phenomenon they study (Amit 2000; Madison 2005; Marcus 1998), inspired the modification of my research plan. Back in Canada I submitted new protocol to the university research ethics board and made plans to return the following summer to begin the multi-year project.

Carrying out fieldwork with tourists, who are by definition mobile and transient subjects, carries its own set of problems for anthropologists, who by disciplinary convention need to gain rapport and build trust before gathering data. One of the biggest problems generally in studying with tourists is how to get people to stay in one place long enough to talk to and to spend time with in order to observe their everyday lives (Frohlick and Harrison 2008). On my first return fieldwork trip I found it very easy to strike up conversations with residents and expatriates. Entering a tour office, for instance, to inquire about their tours I let the agent know that I was a cultural anthropologist studying tourism (or sometimes I would mention my specific interest in tourist women's sexual relations with local men) and they would generally have lots to say. But because I wanted to understand the phenomenon from the perspective of Euro-American women tourists, I had to develop a strategy to access their social worlds.

In the chapters to follow I expand further on my methods. In this chapter, I explain how I situated myself in the community and amongst women who became my research participants. I made nine trips between two weeks to three months in length, for a total of approximately eleven months, between 2005 and 2009.[15] I returned again in 2010 for two weeks, to start a related project, and again in 2011. Because I aimed to use participant observation and unstructured interviews as my main methodology, it was imperative that I situate myself amongst tourists and participate in shared activities. I became an ethnographer-tourist (Bruner 1995), positioning myself constantly back and forth between each overlapping role. The classic issue of needing to gain the trust of a suitable "sponsor" (DeWalt and DeWalt 2002: 39), someone connected to the people I wished to meet and who was well-respected and willing to introduce me, was resolved when I attended a yoga class, a strategy that combined a personal interest with research goals.

I met Carolyn in a café, and she invited me to her yoga class. A Canadian woman living in Puerto Viejo for several months, she was interested in my project and eager to help. At the end of the class, she introduced me to the rest of the students (all women). Several women approached me about participating in my research. From that exchange, which led to five initial interviews, those women in turn introduced me to other women who, in turn, introduced me to other women. Once the word was out in the village about my research project, women from different social networks approached me on my frequent trips to Puerto Viejo over the next five years at various times of the year including high and low tourist seasons, or, in Costa Rica, what are referred to as "wet" and "dry" seasons (referring to the precipitation).

Through my multiple interests and responsibilities, as an anthropologist from Canada, a mother with a school-aged daughter, a yoga student, a Spanish student, a tourist (who loved hiking trips in the Talamanca mountains and kayak trips on the Sixaola River), a friend with a rented jeep to take local kids on excursions to the beach or elderly parents to the clinic, a grocery shopper, and Internet café user, I met people who contributed to my research in immeasurable ways. Many of the people with whom I had conversations over the years about the topic of foreign women and local men appear in the "shadows" of this book (that is, they inform my analysis and are part of the general story) but are not directly heard. On the other hand, the "voices" of women I interviewed are foregrounded through my use of their stories and experiences as the centerpiece of each of the following chapters. Due to issues of interpretation and selection necessary in any representation, these are necessarily partial accounts. Moreover, I do not purport to speak "for" actual women but rather "with" and "about" tourist women.

As a feminist ethnography of women as international travelers and mobile subjects, as I explain in the Introduction, the book takes "an inclusion approach to the voices that must be heard" (Cole and Phillips 1995: 10). As such, I focus on the experiences of foreign women. It is important that readers recognize how I came to understand their experiences, since my interpretations are based on the relationships I formed in the field with research participants and on the methods of data collection I used. Fieldworkers are often referred to as the main "research tool" in ethnographic research, or, as Amit (2000: 14) has aptly suggested, we act as the "fulcrum" in the network of individuals that come to form the subjects of our fieldwork who are not necessarily a collectivity or self-conscious social group.

Figure 1.3 The author and her daughter in town during a fieldwork visit in 2006 on our bike, a common form of local transportation. Photo by Maria Perez.

Ethnographic methodology hinges on "being there" as being essential to the knowledge produced, and as such there is epistemological weight accorded to the "sheer physical, emotional, and psychological experience of being in the field" (Watson 1999: 2) wherein experience is transformed into social knowledge (Hastrup and Hervik 1994). For me, "the field" became the shared social spaces occupied by Euro-American tourist women – wherever they were and what they did there. I was both a tourist-ethnographer, that is, learning about tourism as a tourist as well as an anthropologist, and a fulcrum in constantly emerging social networks both among women who previously did not know one another and among those who did. My main research techniques were participant observation and interviewing. I also collected some tourism media *in situ*. This means that the data from which my interpretations and representations are crafted were derived from what women told me in interviews and in informal conversations, what I noticed as a participant observer while spending time with them or within the community, and what others said.

Because individual women were departing "the field" on a regular basis, my account of "tourist women" is an account of a contingent cohort rather than a collectivity. The sociological characteristics of the individuals are neverthe-less imperative clues to how readers will situate and interpret the voices and experiences presented in the book. I interviewed sixty women and had conversations with countless others.[16] Some of those conversations were conversations I was given permission to include in my book, while some remain "off the record" and therefore indirectly inform my analysis. The women I interviewed ranged in age from nineteen to sixty-five years old. The majority of participants were between twenty-five and forty-five years old. Nationalities varied. I interviewed women from Canada, Ireland, the United States, England, Australia, New Zealand, Austria, Germany, France, Italy, Switzerland, and Norway.[17]

Some women were short-stay tourists (a weekend to two weeks or so), while others had been in Puerto Viejo for several weeks or more when I met them. Some women considered themselves semi-permanent residents. Among the women in this latter group many of them spent months at a time in their home countries every year, or their plans to stay in Costa Rica were tenuous; therefore they can be considered "perpetual tourists," "residential tourists," or, another useful term, "tourist migrants" (Bowen and Schouten 2008). All these women remained connected to Puerto Viejo through relations with local men (Frohlick 2009).[18]

To be a "tourist" has many meanings (Harrison 2003), and is a polythetic "category of person" that varies across cultures (Hepburn 2002). The World Tourism Organization defines a "tourist" as any person "traveling to and staying in places outside of their usual environment for not more than one consecutive year for leisure, business, and other purposes."[19] For anthropologists, the phenomenological aspect of being a tourist is underscored such that tourists are those who "engage in temporary travel for the purpose of experiencing a change" (Gmelch 2004: 5; also Smith 1989). I use "tourist" as a flexible and broad socio-legal and phenomenological category that, while not a perfect solution to the problem of categorizing a range of tourism-related mobility, fits most of the women in my study even though they varied in length of stay in Costa Rica, from a few days to several years: They arrived in the country on three-month tourist visas and were seen by-and-large as tourists regardless of their major activity (such as temporary worker or volunteer) or whether they had serially renewed their visas in order to stay in the country at length, which was a common practice.

Hepburn usefully draws attention to the ways in which "tourist" in its local usage in non-Western countries can mark race, ethnicity and class rather than "someone who travels somewhere to visit" (2002: 623), and thus is a term not always used in the same way by local people as by those who travel. In a similar way, tourists in Costa Rica become "types" of people associated with, for instance, apparent inherent wealth and related behaviors such as the "giving" of sex. In some respects women who stayed in Costa Rica more than three or four weeks were sometimes "locals," in that local discounts were extended to them in foreign-owned restaurants and they participated, along with foreign residents, in local community events. At the same time, they saw themselves and were regarded by Costa Rican nationals and long-time residents in Puerto Viejo as "tourists," or "*turistas*," a relational term and category of personhood (Hepburn 2002). While domestic tourism is growing in Costa Rica, as a "receiving country" in global tourism, "tourist" is a term reserved for international visitors.

Their legal status as temporarily in the country on tourist visas conferred them with certain privileges but also with a social distance associated with not belonging. Tourist identity was a personal issue for some of my interlocutors, regardless of whether they were short-term or gap-year travelers or hoped to migrate permanently. Many women spoke about their inability to "get close to local people" because the town's native inhabitants (especially families that had resided there for generations) kept a certain distance in their relations with foreigners, which hints at the underpinnings of desires for cross-cultural connection and intimacy in women's sexual relations, which I explore in the book. In short, I use "tourist women" to categorize an amorphous group whose individual members were referred to by many emic and etic labels, such as "foreigner," "foreign resident," "*gringa*," "*extranjera*," "tourist girl," and "expatriate," by others in the community but for whom being an international tourist in Costa Rica was salient and meaningful to their experiences of transnational sex.

Regarding socio-economic characteristics of this group, their financial situations varied. Many women voluntarily shared details about their personal finances, especially those who were trying to find ways to remain in Puerto Viejo by finding work or some means of support. Money was a popular topic, as is often the case with tourists and especially those tourists who prefer the "traveler" identity (Desforges 2001; Errington and Gewertz 2004), but specifically in terms of the price of food, restaurant meals, lodging, and airfares – key expenses for most tourists. As people who traveled from the global North, tourist women were situated within a socio-economic position, whatever it was in their home country, where being able to afford plane tickets to Central America and to support themselves for the length of their intended stay including the costs of food and lodging and tourist activities was regarded as middle-class or even elite. In the eyes of local residents struggling with increasing costs of living during the time of my fieldwork (before and during the global recession in 2008), tourist women were "rich," especially those who ate in the more posh restaurants rather than the local rice-and-bean establishments associated with backpackers, and those who stayed in the bigger hotels rather than modest *cabinas* (small-scale independent-type lodgings very common in Puerto Viejo). It was common practice to mark the "class" of a tourist by the type of accommodation they stayed in. For instance, tourists at a budget backpackers' "camping resort" near the edge of town or at a surfer's budget hotel in the center of town were placed in categories by local men who paid attention to and constructed their own indicators of Northern wealth, which I expand on in the following chapters.

While socio-economic class broadly was a shared characteristic of my interlocutors, what I saw as common attitudes about international travel as a beneficial and rewarding endeavor fundamental to their self-development and personal growth were also central similarities. They can be seen as "embodied cosmopolitans," insofar as they espoused "cosmopolitan worldviews" and they were also well-traveled individuals by social practice and lived experience (Molz 2006). Most of my interlocutors had traveled outside of their home countries prior to their travels to Costa Rica. Most were independent tourists who eschewed all-inclusive resorts and the American-style tourist development popular on the Pacific side of the country, or they had traveled to Costa Rica as volunteer tourists or for humanitarian tourism or study-abroad programs. Most of the women spoke two languages; many spoke three or four. The Western countries of their origin, "sending countries" in the pathways of international tourism, were places where dreams of traveling were part of the childhoods and young adulthoods of middle-class citizenry. Many women referred nostalgically to childhoods or their youth where "always wanting" to live somewhere else outside of their home country played a huge role in their decisions to travel. These kinds of sentiments reflect a discourse of "pro-travel" and internationalism (Harrison 2003) through which women became world travelers. More specifically, proclivities for nature and small-scale development drew many women from the United States, Canada, and Europe to Puerto Viejo, an idea that I expand on in the book and show how these desires, and the economic underpinnings of these desires, shaped their sexual experiences and subjectivities.

I was hanging out with Milo, a Costa Rican man in his thirties, biding my time in the heat of the afternoon under the cool porch of the *tienda* (small shop) where he worked, when two tourist women cycled past on the dusty gravel road. He looked at them nodding his head in their direction and said to me, "You see those tourist girls? They ride their bikes around here like they own this town."

On another occasion, Kylia, a woman who worked in one of the tour offices selling ATV tours, nature hikes, and boating trips to Bocas del Toro in Panama, said to me, "These girls, you know, they all look alike – blonde hair, thin bodies, going to places I never would go." By this Kylia meant that tourist women, who blurred together in her view, visit tourist attractions that were, to her as a Costa Rican, uninteresting, such as a hike in the rainforest, or that were too rustic, like the local backpacking hotels and budget guesthouses.

Although a diversity of tourists came through the town on a daily basis, a certain image of female tourists propagated. The term "*gringa*" held a particular connotation, more specific to American women. "Tourist girls," or "tourist women," these categories referred to foreign women who were Othered by what they wore – short shorts or skirts and bikini or tank tops – and the light or "clear" color of their skin, their blonde or light brown hair, and by the way they rode bicycles through the town and up and down the coastal road that linked the beaches and villages with an apparent freedom to go wherever they wanted and to spend their money on whatever they wanted. These are the women who embodied a myth of the "blonde tourist girl," the notion that all foreign women were "blonde" referring both to hair color and other bodily attributes (such as "skinny asses") and to sensibilities associated with an American lifestyle, notably a Californian lifestyle and identity.

Not all of the individual research participants fit this description (although many did). Nevertheless they were affected by stereotypes of foreign women and were often regarded with suspicion and, sometimes, antagonism by *Ticas* and Afro-Caribbean female residents. It is at once this group of actual people and the constructed social categories that the reader needs to be aware of, and whose lives I write about here, because in some ways the two are inseparable. My own representation contributes another layer of fact-and-fiction to the complicated social history and to the well-trafficked stories about foreign women in Puerto Viejo and their ("unconscionable") sexual desires for local men.

Local men in Puerto Viejo

> The world comes to me.
>
> (Interview with Juan, a local resident, February 2006)

I met with Juan in a restaurant. He was curious about my research, after hearing about it from his European wife. It was a rainy Saturday morning in February. I found him at the farmer's market, and waited while he finished his business with the vendors. After the stalls were closed, we headed to a popular café near the beach across from the police station. Luckily, we found a table inside, as the rain dripped down on the patio tables. He was curious about why an anthropologist would want to find out information about relationships instead of native plants, animals, or indigenous people. When I explained my rationale to him, that tourism all over the world was putting new groups of people into contact with one another and therefore changing the nature of intimate relations, he agreed with me. He shared his own fascinating explanation with me for why local men are interested sexually in foreign women.

"Men here," he told me, sipping his coffee, "they eat not when they're hungry, [but] when the food is there."

I looked back at him curiously.

He smiled, patiently, and continued his explanation: "Well, Susan, you must see it too, all the foreign women who come through the town showing off their bodies. It is as though everyday is a Miss Universe contest being held for all the local men to watch. Everybody can see this, all the women walking down the road waving their hands."

For the next two hours we sat at the white plastic table while other patrons came and went, and Juan generously offered his views on relationships between foreign women and local men. He regards foreign women as very brave because they are willing and able to travel, for instance, to Honduras and Guatemala on their own. Foreign women are direct and open in their interpersonal communication, he said. He can speak with them in ways he cannot with local women, whether the local women are black, white, or indigenous. Local men like to show the foreign women what they know, Juan explained, and to share with the foreign women whatever they have. While most men in Puerto Viejo do not own cars or have much money, they are knowledgeable about the trees and the beauty of the sea. They share this with tourist women, he offered, because the men like to make them happy and to see them smile. While Juan understood local men's motivations to meet foreign women, he was much less sure about the motivations of tourists. He did not understand why tourists are so fascinated with books, and why they find it enjoyable to lie in the hot sun on the beach to read when it would be much more comfortable to do this activity somewhere else. But, Juan hastened to add, he was fascinated that they know how to read and use computers. He explained to me that while he had many opportunities to go to Europe, he had decided not to go since he was afraid that people might not be very nice there and that, in his words, he might be "put in a box."

"Juan," I interjected, confused, "What do you mean, 'be put in a box'?"

He recounted a story he had heard from a friend who once traveled to Germany with a tourist woman he had fallen in love with. For several months he had stayed with her in her small apartment in a large city. While she went to work during the day he remained in the apartment, all day, day in and day out. When he had ventured out to the streets and shops unaccompanied by his German girlfriend, he found that German people were racist, and they would treat him with disrespect. So, he had avoided going out during the day without her. He did not leave "the box" very much during his stay in Germany, which was an unpleasant experience for him that contrasted sharply to the freedom and mobility of his lifestyle back home in the village where he grew up, roamed the coastal forest (referred to as "the jungle") and streets, and knew everyone.

Juan used this story as a kind of allegory to explain why he does not have an interest to travel.

"Why should I?" he asked, "I know everyone in Puerto Viejo. And, besides, the world comes to me."

I sat on the bed with Lucia and watched her three-year-old daughter, Maria, and my seven-year-old daughter, Breck, play together with Maria's "Barnie" collection of toys. The queen-size mattress served as the couch, and a fan placed high on the wall near the open window blew cool air on us as we chilled out in the middle of the hot day. I was taking a Spanish class with Lucia, a Columbian woman who had moved to Costa Rica several years ago with her husband. I had met Lucia at the Internet café where my daughter and I often went at the end of the day, and we quickly formed a friendship. She asked for my advice on English spelling and grammar for their advertisements and notices in the shops, and I had asked her to help me with my Spanish. We met at her house. Their two dogs met us approached us, barking but their tails wagging, when we approached the gate. After offering us a cold drink and distracting the girls with toys or books or sometimes a movie on my laptop computer, my lesson would begin. Lucia was fascinated with my research topic and we often ended up chatting about relationships between foreign women and local men for the duration of the lesson.

That afternoon we began to discuss the differences between two main groups of men in the town – local men and foreign men. Lucia was trying to understand why foreign women find local men more attractive than "their own" men.

"But why wouldn't they find them attractive?" I asked her, after suggesting what seemed like implausible reasons to her: To foreign women, the local Latino and Caribbean men were more handsome, more fun to spend time with, and less demanding than North American and European men.

Getting up from the bed to grab something for the girls, Luccia turned to me and with her quick wit and a sparkle in her eyes replied, "*Porque ellos son perros.*"[20]

"*Todos son perros?*"

"*Si, todos hombres son perros,*" she replied, still smiling.

Settling herself back onto the mattress she explained that in her understanding of Latin American men so far in her twenty something years, sure, there might be some differences between individual men. Some men were funny, while others were smart, for example. But, overall, when it comes right down to it, they are all pretty much the same, she said. "They are all dogs." She laughed again, teasing me, the one who was supposed to be the expert on these relationships: Why are such smart, beautiful, and rich women so interested in men who have sex with anyone and everybody? Like dogs, Costa Rican men, like all *machismo* Latino men, need to have sex every day.

Lucia's comments reproduce a number of common stereotypes about Latin American and Caribbean men (as well as about foreign women): They have uncontrollable sexual urges. They need to have sex every day. They are completely indiscriminate in their random and feckless choice of sexual partners. The "dog" metaphor also picks up on the associations of laziness and freedom in the streets with local men and masculinities (dogs are not leashed in Puerto Viejo but have the run of the town). Juan's explanations, too, that men "eat when they're not hungry" but because "the food is here," echo similar themes about Costa Rican men (and men in Puerto Viejo, in particular, who meet many women from different parts of the world as part of their everyday lives) and their seemingly biological proclivities to have sex as a response to their surroundings, not to fulfill nutritional needs. These metaphors and claims to "what local men are like" serve to paint all men from Puerto Viejo with the same brush – whether indigenous, "white"/*mestizos* Costa Rican, "black"/*negro* Costa Rican, or mixed – and in doing so, become part of the way in which hearsay, gossip, and over-generalized claims tend to "reinvent hackneyed truisms" about Latino and Caribbean masculinity (Gutmann 2003: 11).

What people say about the "local men" in Puerto Viejo is not what the men are. Not only do the stereotypes obscure the heterogeneity of masculine identities in the town but also, more generally, masculinity can appear to be an "essence," because gender is often regarded as biologically determined (Cornwall and Lindisfarne 1994). In this way, the abundant claims about what they are, what they do, and how they "do it," (like a dog) coalesce to produce durable narratives. Costa Rican, Nicaraguan, Panamanian, Jamaican, Afro-Caribbean, Central American, Latin American masculinities and men become an undifferentiated pack of wild and hungry unneutered dogs ....

In the pages that follow, I try to keep the representations of men in tension with the men themselves while pursuing my wider aim, which is to look closely at the complexities of local masculinities in order to understand foreign women's attraction to men's bodies, personalities, performances, and "vibes." For my account of foreign women's sexual encounters of local men in Costa Rica, I am interested in what foreign women say about local men and their interactions with local men (as well as what local men themselves say about themselves and what they do as men), rather than producing an account of Costa Rican's men's experiences or an analysis of masculinities.[21] I refer to "local men" in anthropological terms rather than by any geographically correct categorization. Men who are regarded as "local" or who regard themselves as "local," regardless of where they are from or where they were born or what passport they hold, are included in this broad, relative term. The population of the area is diverse, in contrast to more culturally homogeneous communities in Costa Rica. "Local men" therefore includes a range of native or resident men and immigrant locals and also a range and mix of men who identify themselves and are identified as "black," as "Caribbean," as "white," as "Costa Rican," as "Indian," as "indigenous," as "Nicaraguan," and so forth. While most of the men I met had lived in the area since they were born, many had migrated there later in their youth, either domestically or from outside the country, mainly from Panama and Nicaragua. Many of the men traveled, to the Pacific for surfing, for instance, or to visit girlfriends in Europe or the United States. Others, like Juan, might have had the opportunity to travel but preferred to stay in Puerto Viejo and seldom traveled "outside," not even to San José, the capital city about four hours away.

"Local" invokes a relationship to the place, specifically to Puerto Viejo and the Talamanca. My use of the term does not necessarily mean that local men are not mobile subjects or that they are Costa Rican citizens necessarily either. Some men did not have Costa Rican "papers" (legal status) but they had lived in Costa Rica for many years, as long as the community could remember. "Local" refers to residency in the area (so men from San José might not be considered local, or even men from Límon city, for that matter, only thirty-five kilometers away) and to a particular integration into the community that was not possible for foreign men (Maksymowicz 2010) or even for men who were nationals but had not established the required but arbitrary duration of residency or "rootedness" in the community.

I came to know local men through my daily interactions as a visitor and tourist, a customer at the restaurants and shops in town, a yoga student, a Canadian taking Spanish classes, and as an anthropologist. I formally interviewed ten men, whose voices are interspersed throughout the book, and spoke with several others, whose opinions, experiences, and stories inform my own evolving understanding of what being a man means for different local men in Puerto Viejo. Mostly, however, my knowledge about "local men" derives from talking to foreign women. Occasionally, like my exchange with Lucia recounted above, I had the opportunity to speak with female townspeople. Opinions about local men came from foreign men too – business owners, mostly, who had lived in Puerto Viejo for several months or years, and had formed fairly negative opinions, telling me that foreign women "throw themselves" on men who treated them "like shit," for instance. Relations between foreign men and local men were complex, and I only touch on them in this book as they pertain to tourist women's experiences. While sometimes antagonism across groups of men was evident, there also appeared to be a kind of camaraderie between the surfers, the musicians, and other cross-cultural groups of men (Maksymowicz 2010).

I did not spend a lot of time hanging out with men, foreign or local, except with the boyfriends of foreign women I knew, who sometimes regarded me suspiciously as "the woman writing the book." I was lucky enough to become friends with a couple of local men who generously allowed me to spend time in their social worlds and even to travel with them within Costa Rica. Frequent casual interactions with local men took place throughout my movements in the town during the day, such as in shops and *sodas* (small restaurants that serve home-cooked meals), while waiting in line at the ATM machine outside the town's one bank, buying groceries at my favorite *pulperia* in Cocles, and often when I was with other foreign women. My knowledge of the social worlds of local men is defined, facilitated, mediated, and delimited by and through these specific, contingent interactions in contexts largely where any other foreign women might also meet local men. To some extent I tried to create a research context for hanging out with local men as an anthropologist but, as the focus is on women's experiences, most of my time was spent with foreign women.[22]

Notes on language

Another important fieldwork consideration, always, is that of language. Due to its history of Afro-Caribbean settlement, notably English-speaking Jamaicans, the transnationalism of the plantation economy and the presence of the American United Fruit Company, followed by the influx of global tourism in the late twentieth century, English, along with creole, is widely spoken in the southern Atlantic region. According to Afro-Caribbean residents, it was when Spanish was imposed as the national language into the state school system that Spanish began to replace English as the predominant language in the homes of Afro-Caribbean families in the 1950s (also see Palmer 2005). Nevertheless, Madrigal notes the "great linguistic flexibility" of the local population, and she found that Afro-Caribbean townspeople in Limón "deeply appreciated a Hispano-Costa Rican approaching them in English and not in Spanish, validating their culture and language" (2006: 177). By the time I arrived to conduct my fieldwork, various forms of English (American English, English-based creole, Standard English) were a predominant form of communication in the public and tourist spaces of Puerto Viejo. In the tourist businesses and in the street, along with creole and various Spanish dialects (from Spain, Costa Rica, and the rest of Central and South America), as well as Italian, German, and other European languages, English was the most widely spoken language by expatriates, foreign residents, and many but definitely not all of the Afro-Caribbean and other Costa Rican residents. While a discussion of the politics of language is beyond the scope of this book, it is important that readers are aware of local and national language issues. More broadly in Costa Rica the increasing presence of American English has been resisted as much as adapted in popular culture and the transnational business sphere (Mellom 2006). Within the southern and northern Caribbean regions, however, English has been the *lingua franca* for decades (Lefever 1992; Palmer 2005).

As an Anglo-Canadian researcher, although I was learning Spanish while living and doing fieldwork in Puerto Viejo, my research is English-centered. The interviews were conducted in English, both with native English speakers and with people whose second or third language was English. The study focuses on women whose lives I was able to immerse myself in. Due to the nature of tourist mobility this was often on a temporary and peripheral basis. Language was a central pragmatic parameter in this regard.

Theoretical beginnings

> Desire: "The fact or condition of desiring; that feeling or emotion which is directed to the attainment or possession of some object from which pleasure or satisfaction is expected; longing, craving; a particular instance of this feeling, a wish; physical or sensual appetite, lust; longing for something lost or missed."
>
> (Oxford English Dictionary 2010)

"Why do foreign women go wild for local men?" This is a question that many people – tourists, expatriates, foreign business owners, and local townspeople – raised. Contained within the question are several assumptions about sexuality. Female sexuality is seen as "wild" when directed at particular groups of men, and therefore untamed, uncivilized, and transgressive. Sexual relations between foreign women and local men are seen as out-of-the-ordinary and problematic. Local men are seen as questionable sexual partners for foreign women. To challenge these assumptions, I shift the question to ask: How are North American and European women's heterosexual desires expressed in another country and outside of their own cultural group, and what do the social and cultural processes of tourism and international travel have to do with sexual practices? This re-formulated question allows us to think about the material and social dimensions of sexuality, which thereby moves away from biological deterministic explanations of female sexuality rooted in sexist and racist notions of the body, femininity, and interracial sex.

I argue that tourist women's erotic and romantic interest in local men in Costa Rica is expressed and produced within the context of tourism as a set of social relations and desires for many things. Subsequently, I see women's participation in cross-border sex and intimacies as part of ongoing formations of sexual subjectivities, that is, how they are sexual subjects, and in the materiality through which sexuality is given shape. Rather than an inherent physiological impulse where First World women are "freed up" to act out their otherwise repressed impulses with Third World men, which some accounts of female sex tourists seem to imply (e.g. de Albuquerque 1998), heterosexuality and desire are formed and shaped by many complex factors, which include social processes and relations of tourism and travel, as well as political economic, historical, and physical aspects. Given the increasing prevalence in the contemporary world of international travel to Third World locales as a means by which identities are not only forged but are "stretched out" "beyond the local to draw in places from around the globe" for many women and youth in North American and European "sending nations" (Desforges 1998), global tourism and international travel is a highly meaningful context for the production of women's sexual subjectivities (Alexeyeff 2008; Jordan and Aitchison 2008).

The question of where sexual or erotic desire originates, in the body or in social processes, as a physiological impulse, or as a learned response or script embedded in patriarchal heteronormative institutions, for instance, has been an important question in feminist scholarship on female sexuality (e.g. Beasley 2011; Butler 1993; Curtis 2004, 2009; Grosz 1994; Hockey *et al.* 2007; Jackson 1999; Ross and Rapp 1997; Rubin 1984; Tolman 2002; Vance 1984). Purely biological models of desire have been rejected on the basis that social and historical processes construct and produce sexuality as a heterogeneous and continually changing aspect of personhood, subjectivity, social practice, and culture; that is, what it means to be sexual is constructed differently across time and space and therefore much more than physiology is involved (Curtis 2004: 94). Heterosexual desire for females involves attraction to men and yet it also involves a broader "straight culture" in which implicit and explicit rules about sexual relations and practices shape individuals' actions (Bhattacharyya 2002).

From this foundation in social constructionist and poststructuralist theories of sexuality, which I expand on in the next chapter, I explore how heterosexual desire plays a significant role in and is shaped by women's travel practices and experiences. My interlocutor's explanation, mentioned in the Introduction, that foreign women eat too much testosterone-laced meat and therefore enact sexual lasciviousness, normally associated with men and male hormones, towards Costa Rican men, suggests that "sex" is a "natural" "appetite" that is caused by the hormones they ingest. A problem with this claim is how it rests on Freudian notions of "a repressed, sublimated, and projected sexual impulse" that posit desire as "a basic biological drive, restricted and repressed by a civilization that forces our sublimation of it" (Stoler 1997: 30).

Rather, feminist poststructuralist frameworks see "desire" as a social practice and, at the same time, as separate from social practice. In other words, what people actually do in the way of sex acts and acting sexually does not match neatly onto sexual feelings, fantasies, attractions, identities, or to the ways that particular behaviors, such as vaginal–penile intercourse, are deemed "heterosexual," for instance (LaMarre 2011). Ward suggests "homosexuality and heterosexuality do not refer to essential aspects of the self or some quantifiable set of sexual practices, but to the culturally and historically specific language used to explain and regulate sexuality" (2010: 28). Heterosexuality does not narrowly denote particular opposite-sex sexual relations but rather "a system of erotic relations and a cultural experience that appeals to people who choose to be straight" (Ward 2010: 31). While the women I interviewed did not talk explicitly about heterosexuality or straightness as an identity, in part because heterosexuality is the unmarked dominant sexual subjectivity (Hockey *et al.* 2007; Kitzinger 2005), their interest in being sexually desired by men and in looking at men as erotic subjects and sexual bodies was bound up with heterosexual femininity as an embodied way of moving through the world. In short, heterosexual culture, rather than hormones or repressed impulses, shaped their behaviors.

In tourism scholarship, sexuality is looked at almost entirely in the context of sex tourism (Frohlick 2010). "Sex tourism" has been defined as travel where the main purpose or motivation is to "consummate sexual relations" (Ryan and Hall 2001: x). One of the key motivating factors of sex tourism, as outlined by Ryan and Hall, is "the important cost differential that exists in the provision of both tourist and sexual services in the developing world compared to such provision in the industrialized world" (2001: x). Within this predominantly political economic framework, where analyses have been narrowly focused on transactional sex, sexuality has been under-theorized. Stoler has referred to the "hydraulic" theory of sexuality that has often been used in accounts of travel and transnational sex in the context of imperialism and colonialism, which limits our understanding of complex phenomenon and subjectivities. By the "hydraulic theory of sexuality," Stoler refers to conceptualizations of sexuality that have "depended not just on a dam within the male body, but also on the attribution of release and freedom to others – to working class or racial 'others' of the bourgeois European self" (in Jolly and Manderson 1997: 7).

Rather than a "release" that is derived from relations of economic privilege and power for tourists vis-à-vis their already victimized Third World hosts, I take the view that the sexualities of tourists are better understood as those which are

Figure 1.4 A hand-painted sign marks the entrance to a residential property close to town. Photo by author.

produced, resisted, negotiated, and given meaning through wider forces (the economy, markets, and capital) where people have some measure of personal agency and control over their actions, rather than simply "unleashed." Moreover, geography, place, culture, sociality, and embodiment are all factors in how and why sex occurs within tourism and pleasure travel spaces. Key to my framework is the idea that sexual relations occur in tourist places and within the domain of international travel because tourism and travel as an idea and a set of material relations foster and produce desires for a *range of things* (from bodies and beaches to helping build schools and saving endangered turtles). By thinking more expansively about the linkages of sexuality, embodiment, intimacy, and erotics with tourism processes, I aim to expand the ethnographic record and also theoretical knowledge about cross-border desire beyond just "sexual exchange," although material–erotic exchanges remain central, which I explain later in the book.

Subjectivity is thus at the heart of this theoretical framework. By "subjectivity" I refer to the ways and means by which individuals become a subject, and how the sense of being a person is formed through subjective experience structured and produced by social processes (Biehl *et al.* 2007). Language and discourse, that is, the things people say as well as "that which can be spoken at any given moment" (Curtis 2009: 8), in tandem with materiality (bodies, money, things, and relations) form the foundation of sexual subjectivity as an ongoing constitutive process. The term "subjectivity" in regards to sexuality invokes the way sexual desires and sexual practices are bound up with emotions, feelings, and sensations that are rooted in the body and embodiment as well as cognition, language, and identity-formation. Sexuality is much more than identity and a person's orientation or sexual preference, however; it is also a central organizing principle of many (but not all) people's lives.

In the chapters that follow I address some of the key debates in contemporary social theory about women's sexuality, and more specifically, heterosexuality. I touch on theories about social constructionism and biological determinism, about the role of the body in gendered experiences of tourism, about the associations of intimacy with normative heterosexuality and feminine desire, about the role of race in the production of inter-ethnic desire, and about the relationship between economics and erotics in women's sexual pleasure (supposed to be completely free of economic underpinnings), in order to bring these theories to bear on the overarching question of how sexualities are shaped through travel and how travel is shaped through sexuality. Tourism, therefore, can be a lens through which the production of sexualities comes into view rather than only a site in which sexual acts are "released" and expressed in liminal states. Tourism in the "tropical paradise" of Costa Rica is one such lens (see Figure 1.4).

2   Sexuality

Zoë

"How did you meet him?" I asked, sitting across from the blonde American woman swinging in a hammock chair on the shaded porch of my rented *cabina* overlooking a garden of hibiscus and carambola trees.

It was a hot mid-July day in 2005; any breeze from the ocean a kilometer away was barely making its way up Monkey Hill, a small knoll that rises from the back of the sea-level town past the soccer field and primary school. Even in the shade it already felt stifling in the intense summer heat! My daughter played in the garden in the center of the circle of cabins, looking for baby geckoes. For the time being she was content while I conducted an interview. Last night a Canadian woman living in Puerto Viejo had introduced me to several tourist women, and Zoë was amongst the first to volunteer for an interview. We had agreed that the morning would be the best time to meet up, before the hot sun became unbearable.

Zoë seemed relaxed and happy to share some of the details of her new and unexpected holiday romance with me. She smiled before replying to one of my first questions.

"How did I meet him?' she repeated back to me, before telling her story. Another local man, not her current boyfriend, had tried to hit on her before she met Marco.

"Well, we [she and her sister] had this one friend, this guy, who is a surf instructor somewhere. He does tours. He was taking us to do stuff. I wasn't interested in him at all but he was, you know, taking us to do all this stuff. I had to tell him straight up, 'I'm not interested.' But he was still, like, and I was, like, 'Can we be friends?' He was nice. He was doing all this stuff for us. [But] he really took it too far. One night, I said, 'Listen, I don't like you.'"

As she continued on, I began to understand how the interactions she had experienced with a pushy "player" contrasted to the laid-back approach taken by another local man she had met while out dancing with her sister one night. In her words:

When I ran into this guy [Marco], he never did anything to me. He was just different. You go out, you start to recognize people. We danced a couple of times but he wasn't really aggressive. We just danced. It was more, like, chill. Then we danced a couple of times one night. I went home, that was that. Then I saw him a couple of days later and I went, "Oh, there's my friend," to my sister. We ended up hanging out, talking most of the night. He speaks patois. It was interesting. It was fun, just trying to talk. Then we just started hanging out. That's basically what happened. My sister left. I wanted to go to the Panama. I was like, "Do you want to go with me?" I don't know. I just asked him. We ended up having a really good time.

An American woman in her mid-twenties, Zoë had traveled to Central America as a post-college gift for herself. Joining up with her sister for a two-week vacation to Costa Rica, when friends from home invited them for a few days on the Caribbean beaches they made their way to Puerto Viejo. The four-hour journey by bus traverses up and over the central mountainous region, which eventually gives way to expanses of banana plantations as the land flattens before reaching the water's edge at the port city of Limón. From Limón, a bustling town of low-rise cement buildings, *supermarcados* (supermarkets), super-sized gas stations, and endless rows of shipping companies with their huge lots of containers made ready for the freighters anchored in the harbor, the road turns sharply to the south and forms a strip of pot-holed pavement, parallel to the ocean and beach, and bordered with palm trees.

Within days of their arrival in Puerto Viejo, the sisters had been approached by several young male townspeople interested in taking them to the beach or to the jungle for a nature hike. Zoë's sister had hooked up immediately with a local man she met at the reggae bar. Zoë did not meet Marco until near the end of their two-week vacation. After her initial encounter with him at a bar, she saw him several times again in town hanging with his friends outside of the tourist restaurants and shops on the street corner. She knew very little Spanish but she could understand enough of the patois he used to communicate with her to carry on a conversation with him.

At the end of the two weeks, her sister returned to the United States. Zoë decided to stay longer. On a whim, after knowing Marco only a few days, she asked him to join her on an excursion to the Bocas islands in the Panama. She was surprised but happy when he accepted her invitation. They spent three days together on a mini-holiday outside of Costa Rica. Zoë paid for everything – the hotel room, food, and bus and water taxi transportation. Her budget was tight so they spent time hanging out at a local park and in other public spaces in Bocas. She watched him interact with the local kids, talking to some skateboarders and taking pictures of them on her digital camera. Zoë found his mannerisms and habits interesting – how he smoothed and folded his T-shirts so carefully before putting them in his backpack, the attention he gave to his hair (worn in short dreads), and his preference for bare feet. She was also intrigued with how other people reacted to her as a white American tourist woman, a *gringa*, with a local Afro-Caribbean black man. Although she felt awkward at times, she was also very curious about what was a new situation for her, having a local boyfriend in a Central American country.

Back home in California she had dated men from various cultural backgrounds. Marco was her first black boyfriend. The reactions she received from the hotel staff, as well as from Marco's friends, once they returned to Puerto Viejo made her feel in some ways special but in other ways ambivalent. One day after their trip to Bocas, when Zoë had run into Marco and his friends on the street, he had asked her to turn around in front of him and his friends to show off her trim and athletic figure. Laughing anxiously when she recounted this story to me, she referred to it as "doing the little trophy thing."

A European business owner had offered Zoë a job to work in his bar. Accepting his offer, she decided to stay at least until her three-month tourist visa was up. Zoë continued to see Marco, leaving their relationship casual until she had decided whether or not she would stay longer. By the time I met Zoë, her original two-week vacation had turned into an open-ended stay. She rented a small room at a guesthouse situated near the soccer field on the very last street in town, at the foot of Monkey Hill. It was clean, cheap, and relatively quiet. Her plans to return to the United States were up in the air.

Her connection with Marco, which began as a holiday fling, had now become a relationship that was, in her words, "complicated." His seemingly laid-back personality had become overshadowed by his persistent requests that she become pregnant in order to have his babies and, also, his requests for money, albeit small amounts.

It was during a point in the interview when I asked her about condom use, that Zoë articulated her encounter with Marco as "unexpected." I had asked her if the men in the town used condoms. She replied that, according to her own experience and also from hearsay, no, they were not regularly used.[1] She recounted a recent experience with Marco when a condom had broke at an inopportune time. Because I had heard several women tell me that the condoms available for sale in Costa Rica and other Central American countries were of poor quality and broke often, I wanted to know if she had brought American-made condoms with her. As Zoë told me in her reply:

> Yes. I mean, like, I had no idea what this place would be like, but I was going on vacation. I'd just gotten out of college. I have a lot of liberal girlfriends. I'm not going to be stupid. I was going to bring condoms. But I didn't expect

anything like this, that I'd be having sex on a regular basis. That scared the shit of me. Who knows? Especially when I thought he was thirty-seven. A 'thirty-seven'-year-old black man in the Caribbean, who knows what he could have? That really scared me. But it's like, some shit that happened. That's the best I can do but the condom broke. That scares me.

She had anticipated the possibility of casual sex while on holiday, stopping at a store on the way to the airport with her sister to buy condoms to pack in her suitcase. But the notion of hooking up with a Costa Rican man (rather than a male tourist) had not crossed her mind. She had not imagined herself in an interracial transcultural relationship. She was perplexed about the local ways of dating and sexual interaction. At first she had been confused about his age. Mishearing a patois accent, new to her ears, she mistakenly thought he was thirty-seven years old, an age gap that she was uncomfortable about. Relieved when she found out that he was equal to her in age, she was nevertheless unsure of the dynamics between them, especially regarding the economic underpinnings. She wondered if he was taking advantage of her and worried that he might ask her again for money.

Near the end of the interview, Zoë spoke about the secrecy that she felt her transcultural romance was mired in. She was making new friends with other tourists and foreign residents through her work and everyday life in the town, yet she had not shared with them any information about her involvement with a local man, which bothered her.

"I'm not ashamed of him but it is the stigmatism of it that I don't like. That's another aspect that is weird for me," she explained.

When I asked her if Marco might want to spend time with her foreign friends, Zoë expressed doubts, not only about how he would act and feel but her own ambivalent feelings.

"He's from a completely different world," she said, "I just don't talk about him much with other people. I have so many doubts and I just don't want to deal with other people's questions. Not that it matters. I shouldn't care. But I know what people think about it."

On several occasions I would run into Zoë again, on her bicycle in town and outside of the Internet café. She updated me on the unfolding drama that seemed to be associated with local romance. Eventually I heard through expatriate networks that she had returned home disheartened by the intensified conflict over money and other incommensurable aspects of her relationship with Marco that she could no longer bear.

There are many threads in Zoë's story to unravel – how a casual encounter had affected her travel plans, and thus how gender and sexuality shaped her mobility, for instance, and also the ways in which racial and class-based differences and asymmetries played out in her choice of a sexual partner and the feelings of shame and need for secrecy this incited. These elements, as well as the economic contestations she struggled with, will be addressed in subsequent chapters. Here I pick up on the particular meanings an American tourist woman gave to her sexual experiences in Costa Rica with regard to sexual agency and intent.

Due to exposure to public sex education in her schooling in the United States, Zoë was knowledgeable about sexually transmitted infections, HIV, and birth control. "Safer sex" was on her mind before and during her holiday in Central America. She had not been sexually active for about a year prior to her trip because she had wanted to focus on her studies and also because she was disillusioned with men and the dating scene in general back home in what she felt was "American materialism" and consumer culture. Although it seemed entirely possible that she might have foreseen the events in which she was an active participant, Zoë regarded her transcultural sexual and romantic experience with an Afro-Caribbean man in Costa Rica in terms of spontaneity.

Unplanned destinations, fortuitous arrivals

> But yet again … nothing can be decided in advance about what tourists actually do.
> (Crouch *et al.* 2005: 12)

Later that summer, I was sitting in the coolness of the lush garden at Zelda's Cabinas, situated in a lively residential neighborhood in the back streets of the main village. I liked to stay at Zelda's, with its beautiful scented flowers and bushes, because it was close to the activity in town yet close enough to walk to the beach. Also, the owner, Zelda, had taken me under her wing as she did with many other foreign women who arrived wanting to start a business, buy a house or property, and settle. She was hospitable, and generous in providing me with useful contacts for my research. Zelda's Cabinas felt like home-away-from-home for me.

It was there where I met Angelika, a young German woman in her mid-twenties, who told me what became a favorite story of how foreign women arrived in Costa Rica. Speaking in English, her voice carrying a distinctive and charming, almost musical lilt, of a German accent blended with Caribbean patois, Angelika told me, "I came to Puerto Viejo just by luck." I was curious about this because other women had recounted similar experiences to me. Over the next five years, I would hear many stories from tourist women about their arrivals in this small tourist town. Most stories were about arriving in this place by some odd chance rather than by advanced planning and premeditation.

I had met Angelika through my own good luck.

> That afternoon I was waiting for Erica, a friend of Zelda's, to show up for an interview. While I was enjoying a few minutes of quiet after a long day of fieldwork, my prospective interviewee came rushing up to me.
>
> "Susan, Susan," she called out to me, her cheeks red from the quick sprint on her bicycle to the guest house, "I have a favor to ask you."

"Yeah, sure, of course," I replied, half expecting her to postpone or cancel the interview.

"I have a friend who wants to come too. She wants you to interview her too. Can she come over now?"

I smiled, relieved.

"No, I don't mind at all! That's really great if your friend wants to join us."

Erica scooted off again, dashing back to her house in the next block to retrieve her friend, who was watching Erica's infant son and her own. The two women hurriedly made alternate childcare arrangements with a neighbor, and then walked together to meet me in Zelda's garden. Lean and wiry, Angelika's athletic body fidgeted the entire time that Erica gave me her story. She was practically bursting when I turned to her to pose my questions.

"Can you tell me a little bit about how you first got to Puerto Viejo?"

She smiled what I came to know as her warm and engaging smile that lit up her whole face and drew people into her charming personality. It was infectious.

I suspected that she liked this question by the look on her face when she replied, "I came to Puerto Viejo just by luck."

"By luck?" I asked her.

"I didn't even know, well, I knew that Costa Rica was in Central America, sure, but I was looking for a ticket to Africa actually," Angelika began.

A year earlier back in her hometown in Germany, Angelika had gone to a travel agent to buy a ticket to Africa. While waiting for the agent to help her, she noticed the name of one country blinking on his computer screen. Knowing nothing about Central America, she asked the agent to book her a ticket to the country – Panama – the name still flickering on the monitor when he turned to help her. Days later, the twenty-three-year-old college student was bound for Panama. When she arrived in Panama, within hours she changed her mind and headed for Costa Rica.

She arrived in San José many hours later after a long bus journey. Three o'clock in the morning. She thought she might visit the Pacific coast, as she had heard fellow tourists talk about beautiful Manuel Antonio Park. But while Angelika sat waiting in the Caribé Sur bus station (see Figure 2.1), a ticket agent called out the name of another destination, "Puerto Viejo." She decided once again to change her travel plans.

Once she arrived in Puerto Viejo, she found that she had stumbled upon a place she instantly liked. Near the end of her story, Angelika looked back and forth between me and Erica, emphatically making her point, "From the first second here, I didn't see nothing [else]."

Figure 2.1 Backpackers stand in queue at the kiosk selling tickets to Limón and Puerto Viejo de Talamanca at the bus station in San José. Photo by author.

One night shortly after, she felt an inexplicable urge to go out dancing. As Angelika tells the story of how she met her soon-to-be husband, she had tried to convince a girlfriend to come along with her that night, pleading with her, "You should stay outside with me. I feel something is going to happen." When her friend decided to stay in and get some sleep, Angelika went on alone to reggae night at Bambu, following her intuition that something important was going to happen. In her words, "I didn't know what it was exactly, but it was 'the vibes,' you know?" At the club, a young dark-skinned Afro-Caribbean man with long dreadlocks was dancing alone. Totally immersed in the music, he caught her eye.

Her face lit up when she described this moment to me, "My husband was inside there dancing. He didn't really even look up, he just bust a smile at me."

The two of them spoke for a little while before leaving the club for the beach, where they spent the rest of the evening together. He moved into her rented house shortly afterwards. They eventually married and had children together, and moved back and forth between Costa Rica and Germany so that they could earn better wages to afford the lifestyle they aspired to in Costa Rica.

On the day I first met Angelika, she had just returned from Germany and was ecstatic to be back. She could barely contain her happiness as she described exuberantly what she loved about the place. Everything was better in Puerto Viejo, she told me, from the landscape to the energy of the place. As the three of us sat together at Zelda's in the coolness of the fading light of the tropical dusk, the women lingered, not wanting the conversation to end or to rush back to relieve the neighbor of her child-minding duties. In that flash of falling daylight that contrasts with the long hours of twilight back in the northern summers of Germany, Angelika explained to me and her *Tica* friend how Puerto Viejo had always been so beautiful to her and how her love for the place had brought her back:

> I want to feel the sun. I want to feel the beach. I don't want to be surrounded by mountains. I want to be outside and to see the ocean. I like the feeling of wide open and feeling free. To feel the nice vibe. I like this much more than Germany. Sure, the grass is green there and the forest is green. It's true. But there's a very big difference. I like the jungle, the birds. I like this atmosphere. And, of course, he grew up here, his life here, well, he's living in a paradise.

Years later I would meet up with Angelika under very different circumstances. Her marriage was dissolving. There had been bouts of violence she had both suffered and inflicted. Her family was in a crisis, and she was struggling to make her life in Costa Rica work out. But on that day in July what stood out for me was the delight she took in telling me how she arrived in Costa Rica as a young, adventurous, solo woman backpacker from Germany who had simply followed her "gut feelings" rather than any kind of planned itinerary. In her rush to talk to me, when she otherwise would have been at home making dinner for her family, she wanted to tell me how much she had been drawn to this place she had known only as a name stamped on a bus ticket by a set of coincidences rather than by "rational choice."

Angelika's story has several fascinating elements: The glimmering computer screen the young solo backpacker took as a sign in her choice of destination for a long-haul trip; her reliance on hearsay and intuition to decide where to go once she arrived in a country she knew relatively nothing about; and, the way in which she "went with the flow" when a ticket to a place completely unknown to her manifested itself. While I was charmed by her story-telling abilities and her lilting patois-inflected accent, Angelika was just one of many people who felt that they had arrived fortuitously in this sleepy-but-cosmopolitan Caribbean beach hamlet. Like Angelika, many of them made sense of their eventual arrival in terms of chance, luck, or "a complete fluke," rather than as a consequence of pre-trip planning or otherwise calculated intentions. Puerto Viejo was a special and unique place that they had been drawn to by an inexplicable pull. They had not expected to travel to Costa Rica. Once there, they had not expected to travel to the Caribbean side. Once on the Caribbean coast, they had not expected to fall in love with the place the way that many of them did, nor had they expected that they would have sexual relations with a local man. Moreover, many Euro-American women did not anticipate becoming entangled in a transnational romance that would last a few weeks, a few months, or, for some women, several years.

Spontaneity and authenticity in tourist experience

Angelika's story describes the "how" of women's travel practices, always enacted by gendered, raced, and sexed bodies. Angelika was not only white, German, middle-class, university-educated, single, and female but she was also tall and athletic, spoke several languages, loved to dance to reggae music, held a soft spot for stray dogs, and had strikingly bold green eyes – embodied dimensions of her corporeal being. Women's "arrival stories" reveal a key linkage between how "Costa Rica" is imagined as an authentic place for spontaneous, serendipitous (and transformative) experiences and how women experience the place through embodiment, a theme I expand on in Chapter 3. In this chapter I focus on how tourism is enacted as a culturally embedded set of particular desires, aspirations, and motivations. I want to show how tourism is a lived experience shaped by a notion of travel as worthwhile, that is, a "sanctioned use of time and resources converted into geographical or spatial social mobility" (Smith in Nash 1981: 475).

Spontaneity is a salient "metanarrative," or dominant discourse, about touristic travel for the European and North American women who traveled to Costa Rica with an expectation of unforeseeable events and the credo, "whatever happens, happens." Bruner describes metanarratives as powerful tourist stories. Not just any tourist stories, they are "the largest conceptual framework through which tourism operates" (Bruner 2005: 21). One example of a tourism-metanarrative is that of "the wild and the civilized," where wild nature exists in a state of purity and fixedness to be appreciated by those tourists living civilized lives (Bruner 2005). Tourist women use "wild nature" in relation to their urban, Northern, cosmopolitan, and "green consumer" lifestyles to frame their experiences in Costa Rica, which I explore in the following chapters. Dominant framing narratives organize tourists' individual stories (Bruner 2005; Löfgren 1999).

Tourists tell stories about their travel experience before, during, or after a trip, thereby constantly making and re-making their experiences. In telling me about how they arrived in Costa Rica, the women articulated how at that present moment in time they interpreted the meaning of their travels as well as what had actually happened (that is, events are re-told relying on memory, nostalgia, and other motivated ways of recounting lived experience). Their arrival stories were mediated through a powerful idea that the value of international travel as a transformative experience can be found in its spontaneity. This metanarrative gave meaning to the entire trip, including their entrance into the small village in Limón province where "Caribbean culture" seemingly awaited their "discovery," which I discuss in Chapter 5.

Following Bruner and tourism scholars (e.g. Löfgren 1999), I see "experience" as something desired by tourists and a commodity in itself (such as, "I want to *have* an experience"), which is "made" through stories. "For the story is how people interpret their journey and their lives," suggests Bruner (2005: 20).

Feminists, too, see experience not as "uncontestable evidence" but rather as that which needs to be explained (Scott 1991). Löfgren explains:

> "To have an experience" calls for a situation with a beginning and an end. In the everyday flow of activity the experience stands out, it is marked and distinctive. It is something we enter and exit, and the production of experiences – especially out of the ordinary ones that can be furthered by rites de passage – is a situating that involves both time and space. Experiences always take place, but in ways that combine the realities of both the grounds we are treading and the mental images present. We neither have nor can be given experiences. We *make* them in a highly personal way of taking in impressions, but in this process we use a great deal of established and shared cultural knowledge and frames.
>
> (Löfgren 1999: 95; original emphasis)

As all-encompassing conceptual frameworks, metanarratives thus transform events, interactions, people, and place into meaningful experiences, which are always "both individual and collective" since "discourse is by definition shared" (Scott 1991: 793).

Transnational sex is one mode of engagement with local people that tourists participate in, although certainly one that not all tourists are interested in or choose. Uncertainty and contingency more generally is paramount to "the tourist imagination" (Crouch *et al.* 2005). Tourists choose to take up certain activities depending on a range of factors, including their own bodies, imaginative and cognitive capacities, and proclivities. As Crouch *et al.* (2005: 1) indicate, "[T]he activity of tourism itself makes sense only as an imaginative process which involves a certain comprehension of the world and enthuses a distinctive emotional engagement with it."

Tourism marketers, on the other hand, see "tourist behavior" as that which can be predicted and, therefore, controlled. Tourism management literature addresses "destination choice" and "cost factors" (Papatheodorou 2001: 165). In contrast, anthropologists and geographers conceptualize tourists' actions as imaginative processes that play out "within a wide range of constraints according to a diverse range of possible negotiated itineraries" (Crouch *et al.* 2005: 12). Papatheodorou offers: "tourism cannot be compared to supermarket shopping" in that it "is a time-consuming activity applied to different spatial entities" (2001: 165). These theories offer a perspective where creativity and agency as well as history, culture, and power come into play – tourists do not have endless possibilities but they constantly make decisions about what to do that cannot be decided in advance.

Yet as much as tourists' actions are contingent, "unplanned" tourism, a popular travel ethic in contemporary travel practices, is also an exertion of control. Whether tourist women were on their gap year between university back in Australia, on a backpacking trip through Central America as a sabbatical from a job in the United States, or taking an "unplanned" escape from an organized tour as a volunteer tourist from England, like many contemporary youth travelers, they held up and constructed Third World countries "as a series of differences to be known and experienced" (Desforges 1998:176). Costa Rica was imagined as a country to be experienced without a set itinerary (like a flickering dot on a computer screen). The "unplanned" – as a relationship with time and with the world – was, in other words, a highly valued travel ethic and organizing metanarrative.

Tourism media and factual information undoubtedly influence people's decisive actions – which travel agency to use, which destination to choose, which bus to catch at three in the morning when you are bleary eyed. So, too, does intuition, "gut feeling," embodied knowledge, "vibrations," and other visceral forms and forces of affect that allow us "the capacities to act ... other than conscious knowing," all which influence and direct peoples' ways of moving through the world (Seigworth and Gregg 2010: 1). Authenticity is a highly contested term in tourist scholarship but most important, argues Olsen (2002), is how it is claimed as a value, a code of behavior, and guiding principle. The central question is not whether or not authentic culture or authentic experience exists, as this is an essentialist view that sets up a binary between the authentic and inauthentic, but instead to understand how "authenticity" is "a cultural value constantly created and reinvented in social processes" (Olsen 2002: 163).

Tourist women saw Costa Rica as a place to be discovered through the authentic experience of spontaneity. They wanted unique and deeply meaningful experiences, as many Euro-American travel enthusiasts do (Harrison 2003). They wanted to meet people who were more in tune with nature and "simple living" than the people entrapped by materialistic lifestyles in urban centers in Europe, the United States, Canada, and Australia. Authenticity *was* a quest and a meaningful assertion for Angelika and many other women, and is thus an "emic experience of authenticity" (Olsen 2002: 160) that I explore in this book. I show how "authenticity" was "aroused in certain social contexts" (Olsen 2002: 160). The comprehension of time as a scarce commodity and as an essential feature of their quest for something out of the ordinary was central. Spur-of-the-moment was a claim to authenticity and a metanarrative that profoundly mediated their travel stories and gave meaning to their sexual experiences.

Josie

I met Josie through a network of foreign yoga practitioners visiting the area. While on research leave in the winter of 2006 I rented a beautiful old house just meters from the ocean in a community popular with expatriates, tourist returnees, and middle-class *Ticos* from the Central Valley who stayed for weeks or months at a time. While living there with my seven-year-old daughter, Breck, we interacted socially with our neighbors, a mix of Europeans, Costa Ricans, Americans, and Canadians. One day I took a yoga class with Josie, a vibrant, energetic, dark-haired, and olive-skinned woman in her thirties, who had traveled from the United States to visit friends. Josie offered daily classes from a thatch-roofed *cabina* nestled in a thick strand of guanacasta trees along the Rio Negro. After class, we spent a few minutes chatting. Sharing our respective reasons for being in Puerto Viejo, when I told Josie about my research, she had asked if she could participate in an interview.

A few days later we rode our bicycles together to a seaside hamlet down the road. Wanting to get away from the curious scrutiny of friends and neighbors, Josie had a beachfront café in mind where she would feel more relaxed.

While waiting for the waitress to bring us our fruity *batidos* (milkshakes), Josie made a joke about needing a much stronger drink before feeling comfortable enough to start the interview. I laughed with her, agreeing that an alcoholic beverage might ease the tension involved in talking to a complete stranger about private aspects of her life. But by the time the pineapple and papaya frothy drinks arrived, Josie seemed ready to answer my questions. Still, she remained a bit on edge throughout the interview. Talking with her was like being on a roller coast ride. One moment I thought I had her figured out and then next moment she would surprise me with another twist and turn in her story.

Josie was a complex research participant (like most of the women I interviewed, whose experiences were more complicated than I had assumed). While Zoë's life seems marked by privilege, Josie might be considered a "survivor." Raised in a working-class family by a single mother who had moved her family from place to place in search of work, Josie's youth had been influenced by migration and the ups and downs of economic strife. She struggled in her twenties to become a successful clothing designer and yoga instructor, overcoming substance abuse and related health problems along the way. With her stylish short hair, hemp T-shirt and skirt, and bold tattoos emblazoned on both arms, I saw a smart, savvy, sophisticated woman who exuded confidence and a certain don't-mess-with-me attitude. Her social world seemed to hinge on hybridity; her friends were world travelers, immigrants of mixed ethnic identity, and people who espoused liberal attitudes towards gender, sex, and sexuality.

Years of yoga and attention to the physicality as well as spirituality of the body in her yoga practice and New Age beliefs showed in the way Josie carried herself and how she interacted in a sensual and even eroticized manner with people. One of the things that surprised me, then, was when Josie told me that sex did not matter much to her.

She described to me how she met her current boyfriend on her last trip to Costa Rica. Without prodding from me, she described the first time they had sex together, which had happened, she said, completely "by chance" when they were at the beach. She had not anticipated a sexual relationship with him because, in her mind, they were only friends and also because she had not been interested in sex, although she felt he was attractive. However, the way that she describes the encounter (see below) clearly left an indelible impression on her because, as she said, it "woke up" her body in exciting, new ways. When she returned to Puerto Viejo to meet up with him a second time (which is during the time when I met her) they resumed their sexual relations. When she spoke with me, she was reflexive about the development of their relationship.

Twirling the straw in the remains of her fruit shake, she pondered aloud her relationship with Michael, "I consider him 'my man,' yes, but with no expectation whatsoever. That's the beauty of this transaction, from this relationship. As a whole, for me, being here, it's about letting go, letting go of something that ... doesn't come easily."

I nodded, encouraging her to continue.

Josie went on: "Expecting and just allowing myself to have a good time. Because I'm not the most sexual being, by any means. I've always thought that I have ... a low sex drive."

"Yeah?" I asked.

"Yeah. You know, there's a lot of stuff that I just, I just don't give a shit about sex. It [sex] doesn't mean much to me. I can so do without it [sex]. I prefer to have friends."

"I know what you're saying," I replied, believing that I had correctly interpreted her to mean that her sexual involvement with a local man, who was principally interested in the sex, was important to her in the development of a friendship rather than the sole pursuit of sexual pleasure.

But Josie's story took an abrupt shift from where I thought she was going. Looking at me straight in the eye, she stopped fidgeting with her drink and said, "That crap [referring to casual sex that occurs in the town between tourists and locals], just isn't me. But meanwhile, *I'm like an animal here*. I *love it*. I'm human. I'm a woman...."

"Hmm?" I asked, revealing my surprise.

"I have desires. I'm kind of just getting in-touch with that, I guess.

I was at a loss for words. She had gone from "I don't give a shit about sex" to "I'm an animal" in a few sentences! I wondered: Did she or did she not find sex enjoyable enough to "care a shit" about it? Was she suggesting that sexual drive is so completely changeable and unpredictable that she can go from "not giving a shit" to feeling "like an animal," and by virtue of what? Was it an experienced Latin American hot lover and a holiday setting that revved up a "low sex drive" to such capricious desire?

"You know?' Josie asked me.

"Yeah, I guess," I stalled.

"And it's all fun and exciting. Whatever my story or my issue is, it's always a fun time. Usually I just kind of shut down, you know? That's been an issue for me and my partner, but, you know, one of the beautiful things about here, too, I have just embraced, and I am forced to, is the concept of 'one day at a time,' more than ever here, you know?"

Josie went on to explain how she felt that taking advantage of all of the opportunities for enjoyment in any given day were important in this small

Costa Rican Caribbean town for both tourists and locals alike in ways that were different from back home. She described a sense of immediacy, reflected in the *"pura vida"* expression, that she felt was part of the local culture as "a way of life" that "doesn't occur any place else." Josie was referring not just to Costa Rica, however, but also to what she saw as the unique qualities of the intersecting Caribbean and transnational elements that undergirded the sociality in the town.

"Because," she said, "one minute later it could just be gone. People come and go. This is probably why a lot of the men, or women, are the way they are. It's gotta be lonely. They make a sport out of it, you know? It's all they know if they're born here. This preying on people. They're human. They experience the loneliness of that flux, I'm sure. So why not?"

"Yeah," I offer, not exactly sure by now what she was talking about.

"Sport fuck. Why not?"

Did she understand her own motivations to have sex with Michael as "sport fucking"?[2] Or was she telling me that she could understand why Michael wanted to "sport fuck" because of the flux of people in his life growing up in a tourist town?

Josie's travel narrative was complex. She had visited Costa Rica for the first time several years ago when she was in her late twenties and had now returned. She had arrived feeling stressed out from her hectic lifestyle in the United States and recovering from poor health. She had not been sexually active for more than a year but had also, as she told me, intended to keep it that way. Her motivation for the trip had been mental and spiritual renewal, and not for partying or casual sex ("Urgh," she had said when referring to what she saw as "the hordes of tourists" who partake in "hook up sex" after the discos and bars close.). She felt attracted to and close to Michael, a notorious local "player," who had surprised her with his sexual advances. But yet in another breath she was saying that she did not especially care about sex. She regarded "sport fucking" a normal practice for local people and for other foreign tourists, not her. Her sexual involvement with a *machismo* sweet-talking Latino hustler had caught her off guard. She did not see herself as someone to have casual sex with a "player." She regarded herself as a woman with a low sexual drive. Interest in the opposite sex had not been high on her priority list as a single woman trying to get her life on track.

Therefore, given these circumstances her sexual relationship with Michael occurred as a surprise to her. Yet at the same time she does not see herself as completely passive either. Her reaction to his "moves" is highly contextual though: She had been uninterested in sex back home but in Puerto Viejo (a "different" kind of place) her body "was starting to wake up."

Josie's description of their first sexual encounter reads like a Harlequin romance novel:

I didn't know it was going to happen. He picked me up in front of my hotel. We went for a bike ride down to Punta Uva. He's just, he's from the bush, you know? He's a total Mowgli, right from the Jungle Book. He knows the beach just like the back of his hand. He can tell you cool spots to hang out. We're just hanging around and he's incredibly respectful. Never once laid a hand on me. Well, we were lying in the sand. We just talked. Eventually I put my head on his belly. We just talked and hung out there until the sun went down. And rubbed sand on each other and eventually started kissing. It was really sweet.

And then we jumped in the water and played with all the phosphorescent fish. It was like a dream. Something you go home and tell your girlfriends about. It was short, sweet, and completely innocent. No grabbing, no groping. It was pure sweetness. Coming home in the pitch dark. Through the jungle in our bare feet. I was like, "Oh, my god." It was such a little adventure.

As she described the event, the idea of spontaneity was fundamental to the meaningfulness of her sexual experience, which was also a travel experience. By this I am picking up on how Josie referred to their encounter as "a little adventure" and how she gives the local man a nickname from an adolescent character in a childhood story whose attributes (boy-like guilelessness and living close to nature) are wedded to an anachronistic racialized exoticized sexual identity. That the sex took place within the "pure" and "natural" spaces of the Costa Rican Caribbean was memorable to her. Like a souvenir, the story that she would share with friends was about an emotional and physical connection that caught her unawares – and that had exposed her to new and heady erotic experiences as a person with a normally "low sex drive" and as a thirty-seven-year-old woman with, as she explained to me, limited sexual experience.

Josie said that she "could count on one hand" the number of men she had ever slept with. At the same time her social world was a sex-positive one, and in Puerto Viejo she spent her days and evenings with foreign residents and tourist acquaintances involved in sexual relations with local men and women. These circumstances suggest that she could easily have foreseen the transnational sex that unfolded, in another sense, rather predictably.

Sexual "impulse" – powerful narratives

December 2006 *Fieldnotes* Carmelita [a young Costa Rican woman married to an American man, a local surfer] wants to know why so many (foreign) women come here and act like they are sex crazy, and have sex with men who otherwise they wouldn't touch. She tells me her theory of genetic memory; that long ago men hit their women, and because the people here are not so educated they haven't been socialized to repress those impulses, and so their genetic memory kicks in and they treat women badly.[3]

What to make of the apparent contradictions in women's stories? Were women such as Josie and Zoë merely naïve in not recognizing the circumstances that made it likely that local men would be sexually interested in foreign women? Were they being disingenuous and hiding their "true" intentions and lustful feelings for Costa Rican men, anxious perhaps about their reputations? My own question is worth reflecting on, for in wanting the women to "admit" that their sexual liaisons were perfectly foreseeable, I am suggesting that sexual desire follows a rational, predictable pattern, that heterosexuality will result inevitably in particular sexual behavior. Moreover, reflected in my question is the Western idea about sexuality as an aspect of selfhood that we can "know" through self-reflection and that desire, as a fixed aspect of our sexual "orientation," ought to be controlled via our self-awareness. Yet my interpretation of tourist women's sexual practices differs from Carmelita's above.

Carmelita's claim that foreign women become "sex crazy" when they travel to the southern Caribbean links the "uncivilized" behavior of Afro-Caribbean men as an exertion of power over acquiescing foreign women. Her comment echoes a widespread belief in the town, and further away, that foreign women's sexual attraction to Costa Rican men, irrational and out of control, is due to Latino and Caribbean men's genetically hard-wired sexual urges. A view of sexual impulse as rooted in genetics is a powerful notion about desire as one "thing" or another; that is, as a traceable and "clearly demarcated thing" (Lancaster 2003: 258).

But what "sets off" desire, defined in the dictionary as a "strong sexual feeling or appetite," and is desire – as "appetite" – always rooted in rational self-knowledge or, conversely, that which comes about by external forces ("men hitting their women")? Can we think beyond desire as an internal force that tourist women either acquiesce to or control, to consider desire as a relationship not "a thing within us" (Lancaster 2003)? Sexuality as a way of being sexual does not map neatly onto fixed or pre-set objects (e.g. a straight white middle-class man). As I mention in Chapter 1, the view of desire as an internal innate aspect of an autonomous self or a "hard-wired" physiological response mechanism set off by hormones where sexual identity and sexual practice are seamlessly connected obscures the culturally diverse range of feelings and affective experiences that constitute desire and that are produced intersubjectively and contingently in social relations and through movement, the senses, and embodiment (Lambevski 2005). Hormones and bodies play a role but the critical shift here in thinking is away from "purely physiological explanations (lust) toward the importance of how we make meaning out of our bodily, emotional, and relational experiences (desire)" (Tolman 2002: 14). Lancaster offers:

> Desire is an opening, not a closure, a relationship, not a thing. It is not within us, but without. It encloses us. We cannot quite see our desires, because we are immersed within them: They are the very medium of our actions and thoughts, the perspectives from which and through which we see and feel.

> (Lancaster 2003: 266)

The element of movement to a poststructuralist framework of desire is critical too. As Lambevski suggests, "a human body is *erotically potentialized* by the entire world that *infolds* and *unfolds* around it" (2005: 582; original emphasis).

Like travel, desire is neither necessarily predetermined nor erratic. My rationalization that Josie and Zoë could have predicted their cross-border liaisons with Marco and Danny misses the crucial point that who and what people are attracted to, and trajectories of attraction and "appetite," are contingent on time and space. Spontaneous desire for tourist women, sex that "just happened," is a spatially and temporally mediated embodied experience – at the same time that it is delineated. I am not suggesting that in actuality "anything goes" (i.e. that human actions are completely random) but rather that "anything goes" is a framework by which socially and historically shaped sexual relations between particular categories of people are possible.

For these reasons, rather than sustain the misplaced idea that deeply buried innermost desires exist within us all, following poststructuralist, feminist, and queer theories, I argue that it is through a combination of mental images and material realities that sexual desire is crafted into a particular experience. Desire is made meaningful in the process of narration; yet, "sexual stories" are "issues to be investigated in their own right" (Plummer 1995). Not reducible to but profoundly shaped by cultural codes and discourses, desire is creatively produced and negotiated within power relations and wider social processes. How sexual "appetites" arise – for dark-skinned, barefoot surfing dudes, or smooth talking patois-inflected "jungle boys" – and how women's tell the stories of these encounters are overlaid, not separate, phenomena.

Women's experiences of desire are enacted and produced through the proscribed behaviors and implicit codes bound up in gender, race, and class by which sexual attraction and erotic interaction – the "thing" that is desire – is supposed to occur. The regulation of women's sexuality as a historical and ongoing aspect of femininity and womanhood thus influences, through Foucauldian disciplinary power, how women themselves understand, talk about, and experience desire (Curtis 2004; Rubin 1984; Vance 1984).

Euro-American tourist women interpreted their cross-border sexual experiences in diverse ways. This is not surprising because, as feminist scholarship reminds us, there is no "one" way of "being" "heterosexual" or "straight," in that "heterosexuality is not a monolithic entity" (Jackson 2009: 149). Rather, myriad practices, experiences, and feelings constitute heterosexuality as a "historically variable" social category and as a means not only of ordering sexual lives but also everyday social relations beyond the erotic (Bhattacharyya 2002; Jackson 2009), some of which is drawn out in the book. What is surprising, though, is how the majority of my interviewees talked about their sexual encounters in the same way as Josie, Angelika, and Zoë – by using a framework of spontaneity that inferred control attributed to external circumstances: The local men were "chill," had a good "vibe," and therefore that it was easy to "let go" while on vacation.

"Not expecting it," "not knowing it was going to happen," "letting it happen" were common ways in which tourist women understood sexual desire, agency, and heterosexual experiences that extended beyond sex acts (to the intimacies of the men's daily lives, such as how the local men folded their clothes, and where the men took them, such as to special swimming spots, for instance). Why did they interpret transnational sex as "spontaneous" rather than as any number of ways that sex is envisaged as an aspiration of travel, such as the possibility expressed by Zoë of casual sex with a fellow American tourist (also see Bauer 2009; Egan 2001)? I explore throughout the book the social, cultural, and economic underpinnings of heterosexuality subjectivity as a constellation of identities, feelings, and embodiment constantly underway and shaped by processes of tourism. Here I stress how women's desire is so thoroughly permeated by "drive" discourses, which are gendered. Being driven by desire, by sexual impulse .... What to make of this powerful narrative? Lancaster's words, again, are useful: "Desire, then, like nature, has no 'nature' apart from the one we give it" (2003: 267). How did spontaneous sexual desire, unplanned and out-of-the-realm-of-possibility, become so rife with meaning for my interlocutors?

Josie determined, "I'm not the most sexual being." Her self-reflection suggests a view of sexuality as an essential aspect of a person's core self and, moreover, of desire and identity fused, resulting in a quantifiable measure of "more" or "less" sexual feelings and capacities that "ought to" match up with "orientation" (a heterosexual woman). She became "in touch" with what she regarded as previously dormant aspects of her "sexual being" when she met Michael, the suave Costa Rican lover. Her story echoes a common experience across many women I spoke with, as the rest of the book will delve into – how the spatiality, the sensory dimensions of the place, the abundance of "wild nature," the women's embodiment and transformations, and the presence of the town's players, in other words, multiple influences, opened up "the eroticized possibilities" for cross-border heterosexual encounters (Lambveski 2005: 582).

At least since the "sex war" debates of the 1980s feminist scholars have wrestled with the dilemma of female sexuality being always bound up in gender power relations, namely patriarchy (Rubin 1984; Vance 1984). According to Tolman:

> Although there continues to be tremendous debate over how to conceptualize and deal with the various forms that sexual desire takes for women, what remains clear is that women's sexuality holds a fundamental contradiction under current gender arrangements: It involves both pleasure and danger. As wide-ranging and variable as the dangers and harm that are associated with sexuality for girls and women are, so too are the potential pleasures and gain.
>
> (Tolman 2002: 80)

This always threatening "danger" of female heterosexual sexuality, be it violence, disease, or unwanted pregnancies, defines and regulates "proper" heteronormative femininity such that the idea of "good"-ness is inculcated into girls and women's understandings of their sexual deportment and subjectivities.

In a study in the United States with adolescent girls who talked about their sexual experiences in terms of "it just happened," Tolman contends, "'good' girls do not have sexual feelings of their own. 'It just happened' is a story about female desire" (2002: 2). In a study in Canada and New Zealand with young women, Beres and Farvid, too, noted, "some women depicted casual sex as sex that 'just happened'" because casual sex in particular is "a contested site of gendered relations" for women (2010: 384). They argue, "the prevalence of 'sexual double standard' means that young women who openly engage in casual sex are often labeled as promiscuous and/or are blamed for any associated negative consequences" (Beres and Farvid 2010: 380). By depicting casual sex as sex that 'just happened' young women express a lack of control that can be an act of "self-preservation," strategically deployed to manage identities as "good girls" and to distance themselves from putative "sluts" (Beres and Farvid 2010: 385).

Feminist scholarship raises the issue of how girls and young women are compelled to follow particular "scripts" in talking about casual heterosexual sex or else "take heat" for participating in "sexual encounters that occur outside of condoned space of one particular form of relationship," that is, monogamous romantic heterosexual partnerships (Tolman 2002: 201). Even within the "new normative" sexual practices of "hook up culture" amongst college students in North America, that is, "recreational sex with no strings attached," gendered notions of femininity and compulsory heterosexuality set the parameters for young women such that, for instance, expectations of romance and concerns about protecting their reputations affect their experiences differently than their male counterparts (Kalish and Kimmel 2011). Certainly it is plausible that cross-border encounters in Costa Rica present ambivalent desires for some women to defend, such that they want to bolster their reputations as "decent women" in a context of antagonism against "slutty" and "loose" foreign women who are seen to be perverse in their sexual attractions to non-Western hypersexual dark-skinned men.

However, I wish to extend the argument, following Lancaster (2003), to reiterate how "the nature of desire" is that which we make it. Desire is not one thing but many; it is not a "true" inner essence or buried authentic experience and it is diffuse, not focused on a singular object (the men, or more specifically the "big black male dick" claimed to be rastas' *pièce de résistance* for white women) but rather on the entire surroundings in which co-inhabiting and transmitting bodies are immersed (Lambveski 2005). In my analysis of tourist women's sexuality, I view "it just happened" as partly a "cover story" that allows women to keep under wraps the societal pressure "not to feel, know, or act on their sexual desire" (Tolman 2002:13). But I also see it as a claim about and therefore the production of a particular sexual experience.

The experiences of Zoë and Josie hint at the ways in which women's sexual pleasure is realized through encounters imbued with a sense of "the unexpected" and initiated by the men; in other words, the women find pleasure in being "won over" by men's advances and in knowing relatively little about their respective sexual partners, yet enough for the women to feel safe. Zoë did not have sex right away with Marco, but she did travel to the Panama with him alone "on a whim" after knowing him only for a few days. Josie had a "low sex drive" back home in the United States but acted "like an animal" in Costa Rica, which suggests the fluidity of sexuality as a domain of identity and embodiment that is both intensely personal and unique and completely enmeshed in the social and material. Her narrative thus also draws attention to the slippages in discourses and narratives about sex. As she understands her embodied desire, it was a matter of her bio-logical "innate drive" being affected profoundly by the social and spatial context and by the re-organization of time.

Ethnographic evidence demonstrates how powerful narratives of impulse and spontaneity are used to articulate women's sexuality. These articulations of women's sexual experiences with local men in Costa Rica also reveal the com-plexities and tensions underpinning women's heterosexual desire. Sex that "just happened" and "unplanned" sex are stories about the social organization of women's sexual agency. That the women felt that they were easily swayed by men's "sweet talk" and affable sociability, and by men's situations (regarded as "lonely," for instance) meshes with the metanarrative of tourism spontaneity. Because heterosexuality is so thoroughly naturalized, because scripts of feminin-ity dictate the boundaries of normative sexual agency for women, and because Costa Rica was the ideal setting (naturally and ecologically fecund, and safe for border-crossing), their experiences were couched in the language of external actions, lack of control, and physiological impulse. What, after all, "caused" them to have sex with the local men if not the "waking up" of desires incited by the local context? Tourist women's experiences of cross-border sexualities, and the language they used to talk about and make sense of these experiences, suggest that images of Costa Rica as a country of "no artificial ingredients" are incorpo-rated into tourists' imaginations of a place where erotic desires and sexualities are formulated.

But, at the same time, there were overtones of ambivalence, of losing control in the negotiation of safer sex, and of crossing various lines of respectability that were peppered throughout the women's narratives. Their engagement in interra-cial transnational sex and intimacies places them outside of heteronormativity, an idea I return to.

The ethnographic gaze ... beyond staring to hanging out

> Being ethnographic is really a rather strange way of being in the world that attempts to approximate naturalness. It follows that ethnographic observation is a "strange" way of looking at people ...
>
> (Madden 2010: 98).

When the likeable taxi driver, a young Afro-Caribbean man, shared his observa-tion with me that "80 percent of women traveling alone are coming for sex tour-ism," as I describe in Chapter 1, I transformed his offhand remark into a research question. While I did not wish to undertake quantitative research to measure the actual numbers of women who travel alone let alone those who "come for sex tourism," I did want to know if Mateo's statistical idiom held water. In research methods parlance, did the claim hold any "construct validity" and follow cultural logic – that is, did it reflect a commonly held perception in the community that foreign women were visiting the area for sex? Moreover, if tourist women in abundant numbers seek sex as part of their travel experience what was the empirical, that is, "observable" and "verifiable," nature of "sex tourism" for them?

These questions became methodological puzzles, for it was not a simple matter of approaching complete strangers to ask them about their sexual and, therefore, private experiences. It would be rude to impose upon a person's time, as it would be offensive to make assumptions about people's sexual identities and practices. If women were to agree to speak with me, I worried that their answers to my out-of-the-blue questions might be superficial, at best, and absolute lies, at worst. I also recognized that merely watching the interactions between tourists and locals in the bars and on the beaches as a bystander would put me at serious risk of being perceived by locals, people from whom I wanted to gain respect and trust, as a "creeper," the term my daughter uses to refer to those who inappropriately stare at others. From the onset I endeavored to find ways to be a part of the tourists' worlds in order to access women's subjective experiences while at the same time gaining the trust of the local community, especially since transnational sex was a contested social issue and a topic for which little public discourse existed beyond rumor and gossip.

Madden describes the process of developing a "concentrated form of observation," which must be accomplished "in a manner that doesn't appear rude, overly interrogative or 'unnatural' with regard to the local social and cultural conventions," as "the development of an ethnographic gaze" (2010: 99). Ethnographers "see" differently, based on our respective dispositions, backgrounds, intellectual influences, and personal foibles, and therefore must acquire a "systematic eye," that is, to see things that are ethnographically relevant and important (Madden 2010: 100, 112). As I described in Chapter 1, my methodology focused on finding ways to spend meaningful chunks of time with tourists, in order to gain information that would be helpful in contextualizing what they said and did and also to "attempt to approximate naturalness" (Madden 2010: 98). What they did in their everyday lives became a window, for me, into heterosexual sexuality as "the sex that just is, that needs no explanation" (Bhattacharyya 2002: 18). This strategy aligns with post-structuralist feminist and queer theory projects of "de-naturalizing" heterosexuality; projects that critique the naturalization of heterosexuality and seek to make "strange" the historically and culturally variable practices, social structures and material relations that constitute heterosexuality, and which are normally taken for granted and unquestioned (Bhattacharyya 2002; Ingraham 1996).

Acquiring an ethnographic eye is tricky because it entails attempting to see things of significance to the people with whom we study. For many weeks, I looked for "signs" of women's sex tourism in Puerto Viejo but, as I quickly came to understand, I was missing the point. Where were all these "sex crazed" women chasing men for the "wild sex," I wondered? The "strangeness" of some of the practices of Euro-American heterosexual women became apparent to me when I was able to hang out with them, joining them in everyday activities. "Watching boys" was one such activity.

March 9, 2006   Fieldnotes I spent time with Alex today ... we went for ice cream at a little house across from the surf shop, really delicious, in little bags, for 200 colones.[4] Then we ran into April and invited her to go "watch boys" together. We sat in the fishing boats [the ones lined up on the beach at the front of the town]. A few men came around, to listen to our conversation Alex thought. She pointed out various men going by: This one is Alex's ex-lover. This one was in a fight with April over Rastafari politics (she told him that he was not rasta, he told her that he has "the vibe," apparently he won't talk to her anymore after their argument). This one used to have a European girlfriend but they just broke up. He tried to hit on April, and wants to borrow her CDs. We discussed whether or not he's a good guy. We moved away [from the fishing boats] to watch the soccer game that got underway on the water's edge....

Too much more to remember. Shit, shit, I wish I had better recall skills! This sucks. ... Alex said some interesting things, good words for different things. I've lost it now. And remembering the men's names, shit! Paton was playing [soccer] – his German girlfriend is coming next month to take him back to Germany because she doesn't think he can make it all the way there by himself. She's worried he'll get lost en route.

This excerpt from my fieldnotes shows how my "systematic eye" was developed. Through such moments, when women invited me to join them in activities that were meaningful and familiar to them, I began to look at the men and see things about them that I would otherwise be unlikely to notice and, also, I began to see women watching men. Which boys were cute, which ones were "fake rastas," which ones were off limits, which ones had foreign girlfriends, which ones traveled overseas.... Alex and April were keen, and to me, tirelessly interested in the lives of the "local boys." Spending time in the boats, watching men's *fútbol* (Figure 2.2), and hanging out in other spaces in the town where foreign women checked out the local men were "strange" behaviors that coached me into noticing social practices and performances of heterosexuality that I otherwise took for granted.

As my notes reveal, my methodology was fraught with the perils of human apprehension: I could not remember everything, the men's names and other details escaped me, and my senses were often overloaded. But yet, the ethnographic gaze, which is a thoroughly embodied research method (Coffey 1999), enables understanding, however deficient and fragmented, of social settings that other devices are incapable of recording – the temperature, the smells, the

Figure 2.2 A foreign tourist woman on her bicycle stands out amidst a group of local men watching and playing an afternoon soccer (*fútbol*) game. Photo by author.

emotion, and, what "in ludicrously non-technical terms" is "the vibe" of phenomena (Madden 2010: 101). Because it is through such "ways of seeing" that representations are crafted, how my eye was trained by the women I spent time with shaped my understandings of "women's sex tourism."

While awkward and challenging problems arise from such an intimate, messy methodology (Hume and Mulcock 2004) – including the limitations of memory, perception, and, even, poor eyesight, along with the researcher's age, gender, ethnicity, proclivity for night life, and so forth – this is a long way beyond "the clipboard" approach critiqued by Graburn (2002), which relies on surveys, questionnaires, and brief conversations at sightseeing stops. Ethnographic methodology facilitated a glimpse into sexual subjectivities formed within transnational milieus, from which I, an ethnographer-tourist, was not detached. For me, the abstraction of "sex tourism" mapped out, or transmuted, into complex social relations that disrupt rather than "prove" its empirical existence.

Conclusion

Women's stories about their travel experiences in other countries highlight the complexities and contradictions in what are often taken to be a disembodied rationality of tourist motivations. Tourists are alleged to know what and why they do things (Burns 1999), and to incessantly plan and map out their itineraries. But as Angelika's story shows, "tourist behavior" and attendant "motivations" can also just as strongly be that of sanctioned ignorance and lack of rationality. Gut feelings. Intuition. Fortuitous signs. The explanation, "I didn't expect it to happen," was a common narrative when women explained cross-border sexualities in a country that they regarded as safe, natural, pure, and open. This common framework may well contain several contradictions; for instance, in that women were in many ways expecting or at least hoping that transnational encounters might be part of their travel experience. Zoë brought condoms. As I got to know her better she admitted that she had vaguely heard about Puerto Viejo's reputation as "a hot spot" for "cute rasta boys," which partially influenced her and her sister's decision to travel there instead of elsewhere in Costa Rica. Josie eventually mentioned to me a liaison of hers with a young beach boy the very first time she had traveled to Puerto Viejo, and thus knew full well of the sexual opportunities that she might likely avail herself of on a return trip.

However, the desire for a unique experience and for a sensual experience involving all of the senses and the body, which are key phenomenological, social, and economical structures of tourism in post-industrial society (Crouch 2002; Crouch and Desforges 2003), aligned remarkably well with how women imagined Costa Rica as a "women's destination" that was safe, peaceful, and, possibly, disease-free or, even, pre-disease. Why is it that Zoë and Josie did not imagine themselves in the situations they were in? Why could they not foresee the perfectly foreseeable event of having sex and romantic entanglements with local men in Costa Rica? Why was cross-border sex not expected to happen? How they arrived in this Central American country of "exceptionalism" with expectations of safety carried implications for how they used and emplaced their bodies, in striking contrast to masculinized touristic practices and anticipated risky emplacements in place and engagement with local people such as "danger-zone tourism" and "adrenalin-rush tourism" in places like East Timor and Burma/Myanmar (see Adams 2003). They arrived feeling "open." The possibility of *una experiencia* entailed the promise of pleasure and a measured amount of danger (Rubin 1984) at least as far as acceptable risk taking. This was Costa Rica, after all, not Thailand, nor Panama City, nor Africa.

3 Embodiment

A "special vibe"

This place has special powers … special energy.
(Interview with Iris, an Italian expatriate, August 2005)

Angelika traveled to Costa Rica on a whim. The "nice vibe" captivated her when she first arrived in the town. The translucent shadows of the towering kapoks of the dense jungle canopy, the warm waters of the Caribbean ocean, and the flavorful mangos sold by the elderly vendor on the main street emit an ephemeral magnetism. It is "a place for self-transformation and healing," I heard many times. It is a "karmic and powerful place," people told me. Puerto Viejo produces strong emotional responses, visceral feelings, and physiological sensations, of love, connection, belonging, passion, and sexual energy. "Women are drawn there," more than one person explained, by "the energy" of the place. Serendipity. Destiny. A place they were meant to be. A place dense with the excessive fecundity and greenness of the tropical rainforests and plant life; a place that, as an Austrian woman expressed, "immediately felt like home, as soon as I got off the bus and put my foot down on the ground."

Places of arrival are key sites in tourist–local encounters. They are "meeting grounds" (MacCannell 1992) and "borderzones" (Bruner 1996); they are spaces where tourists, an "ever-changing moving population" (Bruner 1996: 158), and local residents interact, out of various motivations. Touristic borderzones arise not only in "enclaves" created by the tourism industry but wherever tourists and locals converge, and are occupied according to hierarchies of gender, race, sexuality, and class. Bruner indicates that in borderzones the "native" tends to remain disembodied in that Western tourists "possess and control [them]" (1996: 161). Yet, tourist–local encounters are thoroughly embodied. Bodies are central to travel experiences (Johnston 2001; Pritchard *et al.* 2007; Small 2007).

Puerto Viejo was a powerful place infused with possibilities for interacting with local people. Different bodies "arrive" differently in Puerto Viejo. "Foreign" bodies are perceived according to local gender scripts. A woman from Nicaragua was "foreign" but not in the same way as a Canadian woman. A Costa Rican man once told me: Nicaraguan women clean homes, raise children, scrub floors; Canadian women read books, sunbathe, do yoga, and take hikes in the jungle for pleasure.

They are both "foreign women," he explained, because "foreign" is a relative term, as he acutely recognized. Local norms regulate the mobility of tourists and, also, the mobility of local residents allowed to interact with tourists. Local men circle the parameter of the dance halls at night while local women are markedly absent.[1] Who meets the tourists in meeting grounds, and in what spaces? Male vendors, hiking guides, touts at the bus station, and suntanned surfers in the reggae bars make contact with tourist women based on transcultural practices of sociality. Tourist praxis depends on a negotiation of space through embodiment. Power dynamics are central. Given that sexuality and gender (bound up with race, class, and nation) are central aspects of embodiment, by looking at tourist women's experiences of arrival and encounter I aim to show the active fleshy, bodily production of heterosexualities.

I, too, was attracted to the feeling of the area. An excerpt from my fieldnotes in January 2005 evokes the "instant" visceral connection I felt with the physical and social landscape as a newly arriving tourist, with/in a seeing, hearing, smelling, emoting body.

January 2005   Fieldnotes I didn't even intend to travel to Puerto Viejo specifically but rather passed through it in a mini-van en route to a small resort located further south down the road, where I was only holidaying for a few days before starting a new research project. I fell in love with it. The handwritten signs for yoga classes and for bike rentals along the side of the road, the small clusters of wood-framed houses and colorful flowers spilling from windowsills, the groups of children playing soccer on a field so green it was as though each blade was hand colored – such images stayed with me long after I had returned back to Canada in the dead of winter in 2004.

In contrast to the crowded city of San José where women felt threatened, Puerto Viejo promised face-to-face sociality with friendly locals, and a place to feel immersed in green, "pure" nature. My interlocutors were predominantly women interested in health and wellbeing, yoga, New Age spirituality, nature, environmentalism, green consumerism, and ecotourism. Their bodies were central to their identities and to how they interacted with the world around them, including their desires for sensual experiences – such as yoga in the jungle, and dancing in a sweaty open-air nightclub booming with reggae sounds – and sexualized interactions with local men. For many tourist women, local men with dark skin, toned physiques, and infectious smiles and ways of speaking exuded a "special vibe." But the presence of other European and North American women also contributed to the good "vibe" and "special energy" of the place.

I begin with the experiences of an American tourist woman whose body and self-perceptions of her body tell an important story about travel, embodiment, and sexuality. More specifically, they reveal how Puerto Viejo was constructed as a place for "bodily practices" and the expression of heterosexual desires.

Ember: "The twilight zone"

> This place has transformed me. I am definitely alive again.
>
> (Interview with Ember, May 7 2007)

Ember, a blonde, blue-eyed, divorced woman in her late thirties, stepped off the bus tired and disoriented from the long day spent traveling from the Central Valley. Not knowing Spanish ("I knew six words," she said), she relented to a local tout, who retrieved her backpack from the gritty underbelly of the public *Mepe* bus for her. Her guard was up after traveling in San José where men's relentless catcalls bothered her, but she allowed herself to be led to the back of the village through the pot-holed dirt roads to a hotel. Dressed in her travel uniform – "men's pants," as she referred to khaki pants, an oversized T-shirt, and "big sandals" – Ember felt safe. "I dressed like a lesbian when I arrived. I found it easier to travel that way. Men would leave me alone if they thought I was a lesbian," Ember told me. A "lesbian body," in her mind associated with a masculine appearance, served an important purpose when she first arrived, although this would soon change.

Travel has historically necessitated bodily modifications for women, either to confirm or disguise their gender identity (Russell 1994). Surfaces of women's bodies – especially skin and hair, clothing and ornaments – were read in foreign locales as socially appropriate bodies. Russell's (1994) history on pioneering women travelers traces the ways women were compelled to pay attention to their appearances when in foreign countries in order to conform to gender norms that permitted mobility, which meant they had to dress either like men or as "highly feminine" women. That Ember felt that she had dressed "like a lesbian" to "disguise" a heterosexuality identity suggests how the reading of bodies and "the semiotic use" of the body "as representations of the identity of the social person" (Turner 1995: 146) are culturally embedded processes, but not straightforward or fixed. What does "a lesbian" look like? Was "lesbian" a gender identity that meant the same in the Midwestern United States as it was deciphered in Costa Rica and, for that matter, as separate from "straight" identity as she imagined? How was her heterosexual subjectivity bound up with self-perceptions of her "tourist [lesbian] body" and with her interpretations of other people's readings of her body?

Her desire to avoid sexual attraction, managed through bodily adornment, shifted for her when she arrived in Puerto Viejo. As I show, the management of her body eventually extended beyond what she wore, to becoming "a slender body" (Bordo 1993).

Several days after her arrival, Ember had sex with a security guard she had met at the guesthouse while looking to buy some marijuana. Ember fell for what are easily detected as a hustler's pick-up lines – "I knew you were mine from the moment I saw you," he had told her. When he offered to give her a massage, as Ember put it, "off go the clothes" and they had sex in her hotel room.

Subsequently, Ember decided to stay put in Puerto Viejo rather than move on to another destination. Her casual sexual liaison turned into a three-month affair, which ended badly. She discovered that he was married, which had not stopped her at first. Ember had enjoyed the sex with him too much, she told me, to end things too quickly. Eventually, her entanglement with him became overly complicated as she began to run into his wife, a German expatriate, around town and she discovered that he was sleeping with multiple women.

After ending that relationship, Ember had several more casual sexual relationships with local men, purposely avoiding American, Canadian, and European tourist men and foreign residents as sexual partners. As she explained, "I have not been with a white guy, a European or anybody with fair skin, since I left the States." In Chapter 4 I focus on the role that race and blackness played in tourist women's sexual desires. Here I highlight the way race is linked to the apparent "vibe" of the place. As I will show, the special mystical qualities of Puerto Viejo were manifested in a set of material elements. The men's physical attributes and their lifeworlds, in terms of their household situations and economic realities, were enfolded into her perceptions (and misperceptions) of the town as a place for corporeal experiences of many different kinds.

For Ember, the town was like a stage where flirtatious, charming local men were the only social actors. This is the borderzone described by Bruner, where tourists arrive "with already formed images in their heads of the primitive peoples they will see" (Bruner 1996: 158). Her tourist gaze was aimed at the town's "buff players" as they went about their daily business – the surfers who used the outdoor shower next to the guesthouse where she worked, baring the skin of the tops of their buttocks and groins, and the young men who cycled lazily through town looking cool on their red, gold, and green-painted bicycles (the Rastafarian colors representing the Ethiopian flag) (Figure 3.1).

But it was not only the men's bodies that occupied these spaces. Her own body also was central. Puerto Viejo was a place where women were watched, and also regulated, by others (including local men), but also where women, to some degree, could be in control of their bodies. It was a place where her corporeal, fleshy, heterosexual, gendered, and raced body, as Bordo (1993: 321) calls "the useful body" that "corresponds to the aesthetic norm," was reshaped.

While Ember had worn her "lesbian uniform" in order not to be harassed by macho men as a white-skinned *gringa* traveling solo in a Central American country, in Puerto Viejo this changed. Her local lover had impressed upon her a very different understanding of her body than the one she had previously known back home with American men.

As we sat in a café one bright sunny morning in 2007, Ember described her physical interactions with him:

> Oh, yeah, it was just very physical, I mean, you know, I hadn't been pleased with my body since I was twenty. And this guy's over here, you

Figure 3.1 Resident men spend time on a main street corner in Puerto Viejo, visible to tourists, as are the signs behind them advertising surfing lessons and rooms for rent. Photo by author.

know? Holding on to this, going, 'I love this!' You know, my fat. Some things that had disgusted me, well, I had always tried to cover this. I would never wear a shirt tucked in. I would never let my belly be exposed. And he, he made me feel good about, I didn't feel bad about being fat … American culture says you have to be skinny to be attractive – and that [i.e. her lover grabbing her flesh in appreciation and desire] is what made me feel good. That I could be heavy and still be pretty, still be a woman.

Her description of herself as fat was contradictory to the "American blonde" that was sitting with me. As her story unfolded, I learnt how she soon shed the "men's pants" and oversize shirts as she began to notice how local norms of gender aesthetics included a variety of body types, including "larger" women. This realization of different cultural ideas about what constituted "a sexy body" had, in her words, "opened up" sexual urges that she had repressed during what she described as her passionless marriage of several years.

"You know, here I've got all of this sexuality inside me that has been suppressed, made to feel guilt, made to feel shame, made to feel it's not right, whatever. And then you know? This person is drawing it out of me," Ember told me.

Her interracial encounters in Puerto Viejo (she had not had sex elsewhere on her travels) were powerful experiences for her that helped to assuage deeply entrenched negative messages about her body. When she told me, "I couldn't go anywhere without being hit on. I couldn't go to the beach. I couldn't go to the bar. I couldn't go to the restaurant. Any place men were, I mean, they were everywhere, I would have guys just come and sit down at the table, you know?" – she was conveying positive experiences. Being "hit on" was novel. She experienced desire and desirability in new ways, through her changing body. In contrast to avoiding men's unwanted attention, as she had done in San José, she liked to be looked at in Puerto Viejo because the men there made her feel good about her body. She had quickly traded her loose T-shirts and long pants for short shorts and skimpy tank tops, and wore her hair long in an upsweep exposing her neck rather than tied tightly in a ponytail.

In spite of the self-affirming experience of being desired by local men for the sexiness of what she felt was an "extra-fleshy" body, Ember began to lose weight. She went down from one hundred and fifty pounds to just over one hundred pounds in a few months, a huge loss in body weight. What brought on this dramatic shift in her bodily appearance?

While a partying lifestyle played a role, transcultural heterosexual gender politics also affected her change in weight.[2] She began to witness the power dynamics at play in local men's targeting of overweight women either as vulnerable and therefore "easy" or as possibly lesbian and therefore a conquest to prove their manliness. She witnessed men's shrewd appraisals of overweight women's bodies and, in Ember's view, their manipulations of the women's self-esteem. Recognizing a hierarchy of desirability for tourist women, measured by a range of factors including beauty, wealth, and country of origin, Ember altered her body from a khaki-wearing "overweight," "butch lesbian" to a "big, beautiful woman" and then, another transformation, to a super-slim American *gringa*.

In unraveling her story for its clues about the body, sexuality, and travel, it is important to note that her radical bodily transformation was not as "liminal" as it might at first seem. Ember had left the United States for a three-month "trip of a lifetime" to celebrate the end of what she described as a "frigid" marriage. Prior to her divorce she had begun a program to change her life. She ate healthier foods and went to health spas. She started to lose weight, and to read about spirituality. She arrived in Costa Rica on her birthday, a fortuitous sign to her, with condoms in her backpack and aspirations for spiritual connections and other life-altering experiences. When she met female tourists who recommended Puerto Viejo to her, Ember had scribbled the name of a hotel on a napkin and put it her pocket, determined to get there.

When I interviewed her she had been in Costa Rica almost a year. Describing her arrival story, Ember explained, "They're [the other women travelers] like, 'You've gotta come to Puerto Viejo! You've got to.' And I was like, I'll spend a couple of days, maybe a couple of weeks. When I got down there, [I realized] I was totally, totally, the typical woman that would come here."

Ember used "typical woman" as an allegory of negative characteristics of femininity – older, overweight, unhappy with their bodies, and with low self-esteem. While I found this not to be the case (in that the majority of interviewees were attractive women who invested time and effort in taking care of their bodies, as I will explain), I agree with Ember's point about the centrality of the bodily in women's experiences. "The" body was central to how she traveled. She variously inhabited, and created, a "lesbian body," a "fat body," a "sexy, thin body."

When people travel, their bodies are imbued with sexual meanings that, in turn, influence the kind of people that they will meet, what they will do as tourists embedded within local social networks and economies, and where they go in terms of gendered mobility. But bodies are constantly changing, not fixed entities. Tourists may already have embarked on bodily transformations before they leave their home country; vacations offer the promise of intensified renewal, as Ember's experience suggests.

Her description of the area as a "twilight zone" is illuminating:

> Something draws women here that we don't even understand. For me, it was just word of mouth – "You've got to come down here. You would so like it" – and it was. So something brings us women here to, I call it, the "twilight zone." It transforms us. It transforms, most women do not leave this place unaffected. Whether it's a seed planted now or that continues to grow, or the transformation happens here.

Ember used "twilight zone" in her imagining of the Costa Rican-Caribbean tourist town as a place for transformations and as a "women's place." Ember had actually been transforming her body for some time before her trip to Costa Rica, and therefore it was not a matter of her transformation being limited to there. Her perception that sexual relations with local men were more accessible and more "clean" and "good feeling" than sexual relations back home with American men, or elsewhere, led her to at first accept and even celebrate her fleshy body. Later, she controlled her body, by shedding pounds, so that men could not demand money from her or otherwise take advantage of her.

Materiality of a destination: flows of solo women tourists

How do tourist places become places with "special energy"? How did Puerto Viejo come to be constructed by tourist women as a "twilight zone"? Who occupied its sunny, humid, lush green, pulsating, sociable spaces such that Northern women felt safe and alive and compelled to engage in intimate and sexual interactions, as well as material–erotic exchanges, with local men? Its materiality as a destination, captured by the concept of "vibe," has been shaped by the presence of solo women travelers that goes back thirty years or so.

February 22, 2006   Fieldnotes I rode my bike a few miles down the road to meet up with Danielo. He met me at the bus stop, expecting me to arrive on the bus. He laughed when he saw me get off the rusted beach cruiser (a ubiquitous type of bicycle in the area, with wide handle-bars and a metal basket in front that many places rent out to tourists). "You like to ride your bike," he teased me. We began our interview shortly afterwards, near the sandy beach under a shady mango tree. When I asked Danielo about his attraction to foreign women, he told me that he first became interested in foreign women in the late 1980s, when he was in his early twenties. It was because of the Wildlife Refuge, he said, that was created in 1985, that a road was constructed.[3] It was at that time when things started to change. Danielo told me, "It was amazing how many women come. Men growing their dreadlocks [because] women think they're really cool. It was the start of the system [back then] and so many [numbers of] women come."

Constructed in the mind's eye of a long-time resident as a place where "so many women come," the social–sexual contours of the area have long been influenced by tourist women's presence. A brief and partial history provides a sense of this influence.

As I pieced together from stories told by local and foreign residents, after the road from Puerto Limón was extended to the smaller settlements in the south in the 1980s, women from Europe and North America were among the first influx of surfers, Peace Corps members, scientists, and former peace activists from the Nicaraguan revolution, along with nascent ecotourists to make their way to the remote and relatively under-developed communities. Some stayed to eke out small-scale livelihoods and native lifestyles envisioned as "simple" and in harmony with nature. Some foreign women started up the first ecotourism businesses. Others practiced midwifery and massage therapy, which, for the local people, were new ways of healing bodies and making money from bodies.

A backpacker from Europe, Gretta arrived in Costa Rica in 1983 when she was in her early twenties. As part of the early trickle of Northern women she contributed to the transformation of Puerto Viejo into a "place with a special vibe" and a mythical-and-material place for predominantly heterosexual women.[4] In her forties when I met her, the years of outdoors, yoga, and bike riding had clearly shaped her athletic and trim body. A self-identified "world traveler" in her youth, she was amongst the first foreign women involved in transcultural romances with local men. She had been attracted to the Caribbean side of Costa Rica because of the Caribbean culture that stood out as different from the dominant Latin American culture of white Costa Ricans. From the moment she arrived, a discernible "gut feeling" deeply affected her decision to stay.

When we spoke together on a warm afternoon in the summer of 2005, Gretta had generously invited me into her beautiful open-air living room in the house she shared with her Costa Rica husband of more than twenty years. Settling on the sofa across from me as I fiddled with the tape-recording device, once the light flickered in the "on" function she began to recall those earlier years and her initial travels to the southern Caribbean:

> At the time, Puerto Viejo was the end of the road. Right away, it was attractive to me because I'm someone who likes to go the limits. So right away, that was my aim – Puerto Viejo. I think in my case what made me stay here was something like destiny, following destiny, following something like an inner call, not knowing really what it was. When I arrived here, I knew it was my place. All my life, I was born in Europe, I had been living in many, many different places, other countries, and I never felt any roots.... I was feeling like a world citizen, always traveling. That was my passion, to travel.... [The day when] I got to Puerto Viejo, you reach that crossing there, and I saw that tiny little village there, it was the afternoon sun, it was magic touching me. It was like feeling home, I'm coming home.

Her meaningful identity as a "world citizen" was acquired by seeing other places and accumulating a long list – Mexico, Belize, Guatemala, and eventually Costa Rica. In those heady days in the late 1970s and early 1980s, a growing cohort of Western women were traveling independently en masse, engaging in travel partly as a means to comprehend the world and their place within it (Fullagar 2002).[5]

Gretta's journey was driven by a desire to see ever more remote places. In Belize some Swiss backpackers had suggested Costa Rica. By the time she arrived in Costa Rica she knew that she would head straight to the Caribbean side. With her crumpled map in hand she had looked for the spot on the map that was furthest away from other tourists. She was supposed to meet up with the Swiss women in Cahuita, an established tourist town known then for its hippy parties. But she bypassed it for Puerto Viejo, exactly the kind of "off-the-beaten-path" place that excited her.

Once there, she found the area resonated with spirituality, with possibilities to lead a lifestyle where, living close to the ocean and jungle, physical activity and communing with nature were daily certainties. Gretta soon started a small ecotourism business, and settled after years of non-stop travel. The undoubtedly complex reasons as to why she felt at home there, situated in the wider history and political economy of immigration in Costa Rica as well as her own biography, are beyond the snippet of her life presented here.[6] But her story hints at the gendered underpinnings of travel, embodiment, and home. As Fullagar (2002: 71) suggests: "The feeling of being at home (or not) with oneself (and one's cultural baggage) is heightened through gendered experiences of travel."

Arrivals are corporeal, sensual encounters (Crouch and Desforges 2003). Bodies are "active site[s] of desires which move the subject in ways that are not self-evident" (Fullagar 2002: 65). Gretta's interactions with local people and with the physical environment were mediated through her body – as suggested by the pleasurable corporeal sensations that her narrative invokes. Upon first entering the village, the afternoon sun was "like magic touching me," she said, vividly recalling an event had taken place twenty-three years ago. Tourists engage in sights with their whole gendered and sexualized body and not merely with "a tourist gaze" (Urry 1990), as Jordan and Aitchison (2008) suggest.

Despite Gretta's construction of Puerto Viejo as "completely remote," other foreign women had also arrived in those early years. Their Western womanly bodies, exuding exotic fleshiness, made an impression on local townspeople. One example that stands out has to do with swimming practices. While local customs linked to gender norms of feminine propriety dictated that women wear regular clothing to swim in the sea, Euro-American practices were different. It was a scandal amongst Afro-Caribbean townspeople, Gretta told me, to wear a bikini at the time. But she and her foreign women friends did so without reservation. When Gretta was pregnant, as she recounted to me, "We wouldn't hide our bellies. We would expose those bellies. I didn't see any reason why I shouldn't go to beach anymore, shouldn't go for a swim. This was at a time when women would still bathe in their clothes."

It was not only swimming practices but "techniques of the body" (Mauss 1950) surrounding sexual practices that Gretta saw as rooted in cultural differences. Gretta suggested ways in which her and her friends' Western middle-class attitudes towards their bodies, nudity, and sexuality – "about being open about your body" – influenced local gendered sexual practices:

> Foreign women would bring new ways of making love here. There were many things that maybe only a whore would do, [which were] so normal and natural for foreign women. Men would talk in between, amongst themselves. "Ah, she does this and that, ah, I'm going to approach too...." That would make also again local girls envious, although they would pick up fast! They learnt something from foreign girls, in these ways!

> That had some impact, but also just being so natural about our bodies. Not being at all, not having any malicious thing attached to nudity, we weren't even nude. I was always respecting ... I wouldn't expose myself even if that would be my nature. Still, going to town, I would wear a pareo, I would never walk just in a bikini. I was respectful. I was sensitive for that, so that was for me. And then we also were the first women to do home births.

Their bodily practices and gender performances that set them apart from local women contributed to the corporeal materiality of social life and to new and contested forms of transcultural sociality in Puerto Viejo. The ways in which the early wave of ecotourists and backpackers used tropes of "nature" to construct "natural" and "normal" bodies suggests, too, the historical contingencies of bodies. Unlike Ember, whose self-perception of her body seemed to require a constant making over, the bodies of foreign women in the 1980s, at least according to some accounts, were ideal "as is" in their seemingly "natural" state. Nevertheless, across the two generations women's narratives underscore their perceptions of local men's appreciation of foreign women's pale bare-skinned flesh-exposed bodies.

As Gretta's story shows, foreign women's bodies – gendered, racialized, and naturalized – affected the local community and also influenced future generations of women tourists. In tangible, and intangible, ways they have come to embody "the special vibe" of the place.

Getting off the bus: embodying place

> I've known Filipo and Markus since they were old enough to go to the bus stop to look for tourist women. They were some of the first boys in town to start.
>
> (Anna, foreign resident, August 2006)

By 2005, the central bus stop remained an important site of tourist–local interaction in town. Taxi drivers stood by for passengers disembarking the San José bus via Limón. Touts led weary, perplexed passengers to hotels in the side streets, to earn a small commission. Owners of small establishments waited for their guests. Youths rode their bicycles past or watched the activity from a distance. The ways in which local men checked out foreign women at the main bus stop was common knowledge amongst townspeople.

Mariella, a Spanish expatriate, first told me this. We were walking together on the beach exchanging news and gossip one summer day, when the subject of tourist women came up and how easy it seems that local men can control them. Mariella's theory was that the men tracked tourist women's movements from the moment they arrived in the town.

"How does that work exactly?" I asked her.

"Susan," she explained to me, "You will see. It happens all the time! The men go to the bus stop to look for who's coming from San José, and by the time she's settled in to her hotel, had dinner, and is out on the streets checking out the town, they already know about her. And she is oblivious to this!"

An Afro-Caribbean Costa Rica man in his late twenties, Filipo, recounted his teenage years checking out foreign tourist women coming into town. "You hang back, and watch," he explained. Seldom approaching right away, older youth and men observe women so they might later approach them. Men take notice of travel companions (preferably the woman is alone), the woman's clothes, and the accommodation they have selected (budget hostels or expensive guest houses, for instance). Hearing Mariella, Filipo, and others tell similar stories, I began to see how, just as tourists are attracted to "a vibe" in the town, local men, too, take stock of tourists' "vibe." They accomplish this within key spaces, the bus stop being one of many potential contact zones.

The local economy had transformed from the nascent ecotourism years by the time I showed up to conduct research on women's sexual tourism and transnational desires. While the first foreign women coming into the community were undoubtedly noticed by local residents, by 2005 Euro-American women had

come to signify economic possibilities bound up with sexual and romantic opportunities. "The system" invoked by Danielo emerged within a period of rapid
social and economic change, where an accelerated transformation from an agricultural-based economy (mostly wage labor in banana production) to global tourism took place in the span of a decade or so. Caught in the midst of the uneven
shift, youth and other marginalized local people and labor migrants were dis-
placed from opportunities held largely by elite Afro-Caribbean families, *Ticos*
from the Central Valley, and foreigners. According to a 2006 study, Afro-Costa
Ricans owned fewer than 15 percent of Puerto Viejo's small businesses, a drastic
reduction from 30 percent in 1998, meaning that wealthier foreign business owners and expatriates increasingly ousted Afro-Caribbean locals in tourist relations
and economic profits (Vandegrift 2007). During a decade of intensified economic
and cultural globalization in the 1990s, Puerto Viejo had become "a town that
operated in the interests and tastes of white foreigners and affluent white Costa
Ricans" (Vandegrift 2007: 26), rather than in the interest of the Afro-Caribbean
families whose ancestors had settled the area, local indigenous people, or recent
immigrants from Panama and Nicaragua.

A land boom was in full force when I arrived, nearing the tail end of a decade
or so of "massive land sales as investors and enchanted tourists sought property
close to the Caribbean coast" (Vandegrift 2007: 126). Local families sold tracts of
land for ridiculously cheap prices on the basis of what they thought were friendships with foreigners.[7] "*Se vende*" ("for sale") signs could be seen everywhere.
Backpacker hotels and hostels, owned by American surfers and British entrepre-
neurs, competed with locally owned guesthouses. A handmade sign posted on an
empty lot near the main road where small groups of horses roamed advertised a
vegetarian restaurant owned and operated by an Afro-Caribbean family. Small
shops and tour offices on all corners of the small town sold a range of tours, from
jungle hikes, surf lessons, horseback riding, river and ocean kayaking to zip-line
canopy tours. The spatial organization of the village, spilling over chaotically from
the neat-and-tidy grid design of its core, reflected the interests and tastes of backpacking, health-conscious, adventure- and nature-loving, "alternative" ecotourists.
This transnational culture was undoubtedly part of the visceral enchantment of the
place felt by many tourists. The mishmash and multiplicity of Jamaican, Costa
Rican, and American, Argentine, Chinese-Costa Rican, indigenous, and many
other ethnicities and nationalities constituted a cosmopolitanism that was hugely
appealing to my interlocutors.

That local men watched women as a form of economic hustling mixed with
sexual adventure suggests how borderzones in Puerto Viejo held multiple, contested meanings. Bruner (1996: 158) has suggested that for tourists what "is a
zone of leisure and exoticization, is for the natives a site of work and cash
income." While I disagree with such a binary in that local people find leisure and
the exotic too, just as tourists find work and cash income (Kantsa 2002), tourist
women understood their encounters with local men quite apart from the current
material–economic realities facing many people in the community, a point I
return to in Chapter 6. What I emphasize here is how within places of arrival,

Figure 3.2 A blur of three tourist women cycling along the road with beach gear in the bike baskets, heading in the direction of the southern beaches – a common sight. Photo by author.

bodies marked by gender, sexuality, race, nation, and class are interpolated immediately within a particular context of hospitality and sociability. Foreign women, often unknowingly, were regarded as "white girls," "*gringas*," and "*extranjeras*." Tourist women were "not able to help but notice," as many told me, the striking presence of "single" and sexually available local men hanging around town and on the beaches.

Because the men were often alone or with other men in the public spaces they inhabited, their ties to local women were obscured from plain view. Bracketed out of the picture were local men's girlfriends or wives and their mothers, sisters, grandmothers, and aunties. Local women – Afro-Caribbean, *Ticas*, migrant Panamanian, Nicaraguan, and indigenous women – tended to be obfuscated in tourist women's visions of the town (except for housekeepers at hotels and other service workers) as a place embodied by particular social actors.

Tourist women, too, were noticed by townspeople as potential links to fulfilling a range of aspirations. Local men "marked" incoming tourist women, who became potential "targets" for sex but also for food, commodities, and cash (or a ticket to Europe, Canada, or the United States), the topic of Chapter 6. Newly arriving tourist women entered into local practices of sociability where their own bodies held social currency in relation to other women's bodies. Predominating the social landscape were heterosexual cross-cultural eroticized and sexual relations between foreign women and local men, rather than between foreign men and local women such as in other tourist areas of Costa Rica. Euro-American tourist women were thus situated within a social world and erotic economy where bodies accrued meanings based on appearances (the skin, color of hair, weight, clothing) and actions (where they stayed, how they traveled, what they ate). Tourist women's bodies co-constituted "the vibe" of the place. Transnational sex necessitated, and shaped, particular embodiments. To demonstrate this point further I turn to the experiences of Kelly.

Kelly: "It's more heterosexual here"

Kelly, a twenty-nine-year-old backpacker from the Midwestern United States, noticed local men. Dressed in loose colorful cotton clothing, her tousled hair tied behind her head in a floral scarf, she looked the nature-loving, New Age, "eco-hippy" that she identified herself to be. When I met Kelly in 2006, she was traveling solo on her second visit to Costa Rica, specifically the southern Caribbean. In recollecting her first impressions of the town for me, she said, "I knew it [Puerto Viejo] was on the Caribbean coast obviously, but I didn't realize how infested it was with Caribbean culture."

The use of "infested" to describe Caribbean culture is undeniably an unfortunate choice of words. Like many other tourists, Kelly was likely blithely unaware of a discourse in Costa Rica that constructs minority groups, from Afro-Caribbean nationals to Nicaraguan immigrants, as "threatening" and "dangerous" by virtue of skin color and other attributes of difference vis-à-vis dominant white Costa Rican society (Sandoval-García 2004). Another meaning of "infested," however, connotes a sense of corporeality and extraordinary permeability, as Taussig (1992) might say, like "a nervous system" overwrought with the tactility and palpability of a place. It is an apt metaphor for traveling bodies constantly on the lookout for bodily risks. Physical adaptability is a requirement of international travel because "world travelers" must be culturally and somatically flexible (Molz 2006). Bodies are equipped and prepared (with sunscreen, bug repellent, inoculations) to face the seemingly inevitable risks of foreign environments, especially in developing countries (Molz 2006: 8). "Infested" is therefore a provocative metaphor for thinking about the affective power of host bodies as shaping forces on traveling bodies. As Johnston (2001: 196) states, "tourists and hosts become (re)sexualized through touristic events."

Considering Kelly's enchantment with Caribbean culture, which closely intersected with a transnational consumer and leisure culture consisting of restaurants, bars, and music, her sexual encounter with a local rasta was not surprising. Yet Kelly's bisexuality raised a new puzzle for me regarding women's transnational sex. Why did she choose men here and now? She had said to me, "Puerto Viejo was more heterosexual." Inferring a comparison with the United States where she was generally open about her bisexuality, Kelly associated "the vibe" of Puerto Viejo with heterosexuality.

Bisexuality is not necessarily more "fluid" than other sexual subjectivities (Wosick-Correa 2007). However, because bisexual women in practice "live their sexual and emotional lives as lesbians or heterosexuals" mired within the normative "mono-sexual" binary, "their identities shift according to social context" because "passing" as either lesbian or heterosexual is most often a social imperative (Wosick-Correa 2007: 51). Therefore, Kelly illuminated for me the gendered bodily politics and management of feminine bodies that are played out in heterosexual sexual practices, that is, in straight culture. Her local boyfriend interpreted her body, how she acted, the way she danced, and her sexual "vibe" as a straight woman and not a lesbian or bisexual woman.

Kelly gave meaning to her embodiment in Puerto Viejo through her own interpretations and tourism discourses of "Caribbean" culture (Anderson 2004). The friendships that she formed with other foreign women were also central to the connection she formed with the place. Through mutual interests, including an appreciation of reggae music, West Indian style of housing and food, and New Age spirituality mixed with environmental and social justice proclivities, she got to know Puerto Viejo. It was in spending time with women in the local transnational community, many of whom were involved with Costa Rican men, that she eventually pondered the possibility of becoming involved sexually with a local man.

As she explained:

> When I came back I knew that I would hook up with a rasta, a black man, whatever.... I knew that I would be here [again], and I would want sex in that period of time, and that it would be [with a rasta]. It would happen easily. Because last time, you know, I didn't do it but there were several opportunities. There are always opportunities. And since then I've learnt more about my sexual power, and knew that there would be lots of opportunities. I knew that ... [based on her awareness and knowledge of her women friends' experiences]. There would be lots of men hitting on me all the time, that sort of thing.

Intent on a "rasta experience," her narrative contrasts with other tourist women's experiences of sexual spontaneity. It captures the way in which women's bodies were noticed, and how "opportunities" for transnational sex were seemingly readily accessible. Like Ember's "twilight zone," Kelly regarded the place in terms of attainment of "sexual power." She articulated a bundle of things that she liked about the place and people and wanted to experience in terms of "vibe."

In her story of meeting David, her idealized "rasta black man," she makes repeated references to "the vibe":

> I met David the first, the first day I was here. He sold me my first bag of weed, like "off the bus kind of thing," you know? And he was, like, "We'll dance later." And I was, like, "All right, we'll dance later." And just whatever, you know. Many boys flirt with you and say they'll dance later. So, I didn't really think anything of it....

I actually went away for a week, and when I came back a week later, he was still there. Like, "let's dance, I like you, your vibes are nice, I feel your fire." You know, the rasta things that mean "I like you." He did that for a good two weeks before I would do anything with him. I was still kind of scouting out the town, and seeing, you know, trying to figure out the vibe. I knew that once I started sleeping with someone, I wouldn't sleep around. That's just not my, just not my style. I don't have anything against it, of course, but that's just not me.

So then I decided, yeah, I really like his vibe. So we hung out after the disco several times during those two weeks and, finally, I was like, "All right, let's, you know, do this!"

As Kelly talked in more detail about their relationship, it became clear that her choice of a sexual partner was fairly restricted. She was attracted to David because he embodied her image of a "rasta." Her preference in the United States for, in her words, "African Americans, or black, or Caribbean" suggests how racialized, exoticized, multiculturalized bodies shaped her erotic desires before she arrived in Costa Rica. His *machismo* masculinity, however, was paramount to the heterosexual experience she sought, although her complicity in the power dynamics was complicated.

The sex acts Kelly desired were those involving what she called "straight up sex," meaning vaginal–penile intercourse with little foreplay except kissing, and absolutely no oral sex. Kelly felt that, in her words, "a climate of homophobia" within the local community prevented her from seeking sexual relations with a woman.[8] Concerns about homophobia were also why she hesitated to (and never did) tell David that she sometimes slept with women. (It did not occur to her that he saw her as anything other than straight.) Yet this was not a simple matter of Kelly feeling her sexuality had been oppressively regulated or policed. Rather, *machismo* shaped the sexual practices that she purposively sought out, in that her Costa Rican male lover did not demand oral sex, which aligned with her own dislike of fellatio. His preference for "straight up sex" was satisfying to her. She also felt that anti-LGBT sentiments, vocalized amongst David and his friends in their taunts to one another and to other men, did not detract from the homosocial contact between the local men and what she saw as "more ability to touch one another in Afro-Caribbean culture." As a "great cuddler" at the same time that he was hyper-masculine in his sexual practices, David was appealing to Kelly in terms of sensual pleasure (his looks, the touching, the places where they had sex) captured in the concept of "vibe."

However, Kelly's sexual interactions with her rasta boyfriend were also very limiting to her. She grew exasperated by their constant conflicts over condom use – he practically refused to use them – and his hopes to impregnate her. In spite of the enjoyable aspects of sex with David, she soon found it tedious and she bristled when he tried to control what she did in bed. When he began to ask her for money – small amounts to buy clothing and food, mostly – she refused his requests and their sexual relationship ended soon after (although she was leaving for Honduras shortly anyway).

While many complications are worth unraveling, Kelly's management of her body as a bisexual woman who engages in heterosexual sex while on a holiday in Costa Rica underscores the shaping factors of tourism. Kelly saw herself as someone who could go "either way." Her decision to "go with the vibe," that is, with a local man performing the rasta identity, entailed a reflexive awareness of her body as desirable in the eyes of Afro-Caribbean men. In this regard, her most highly feminized body parts according to local gender codes for the "sexual body" (Donnan and Magowan 2010), such as her long hair, full-figured breasts, and pale skin, became emphasized. Able to maneuver outside of standards of beauty in the United States where she had, in her words, as a "larger woman" suffered body-image issues, Kelly had felt sexually empowered in her transcultural interracial sexual encounter, insofar as she "passed" as heterosexual. Her desires for experiences of Caribbean culture as a backpacker seeking cultural immersion affected her desire for black Caribbean men.

Lesbian or bisexual spaces did not appear to exist (publicly) in Puerto Viejo. Under these conditions, did Kelly "go with the flow" of a local "vibe" or did she, under conditions of opposition, take control of her body? As Hemmings points out, "there are enormous dangers in bisexual subjects' assumptions that they are not constrained by sexual, gendered, and raced oppositions" (2002: 4). The palpable history and culture of sexual relations between foreign women and local men and a well-established community of foreign women residents in the town had clearly shaped her sexual desires and subjectivity. Kelly's sexual preference for black Afro-Caribbean men versus other men was played out in spaces of touristic desire for racialized exotic masculinity, which I discuss further in Chapter 5, and also within local and transcultural sexual cultures of heteronormativity and homosociality. Discourses of "the vibe," while eclipsing power structures including racism, sexism, homophobia and the political economic underpinnings of transnational sex, were generative, affective forces. Kelly's negotiation of bisexual subjectivity within these spaces and discourse challenges any assumed heteronormativity. Bodies, sexual practices, identities, are not straightforward.

Bodily practices and tourists' bodies

January 2006   *Fieldnotes* I sat on a futon on the floor while the torrential rain made loud pinging sounds on the metal roof. Iris, an Italian woman, long-time resident, and amicable host, had invited me to her small apartment, nestled deep in a dense overgrown wild garden, to talk about my research. Sitting across from me she puffed on her cigarette and intently spoke in hushed tones, as though someone might overhear her above the thundering downpour. Her astrology books stood in stacks spread around the small candle-lit room. Iris told me how foreign women are drawn to the area to learn lessons about sexual relations with men because the place contains special magnetic and biosocial qualities. Without all the distractions of technology and commercialism in Northern metropolis living, she explained, when women come here they are forced to face new challenges. Iris said, "This is how they discover their strengths as women. This place has special powers ... special energy."

The vibe held the promise of transformation, to become a different woman, to attain a "more pure lifestyle," or to learn "lessons" about heterosexuality. Puerto Viejo was a place resonating with opportunities, within the local and transnational economy, to become thin, tanned, to practice yoga where the heat made bodies more limber and the natural surroundings of the ocean and the rainforest, and the magnetic qualities of the earth, purified bodies, to get a massage, walk the beach, hike in the jungle, consult with a healer, drink fresh fruity drinks, and learn about medicinal plants. Women brought projects of bodily-and-self-making with them, rooted in Western notions of gender and middle-class aspirations of self-development and personal growth through consumption and bodily discipline, and in a bodily oriented "carnal" tourism.

"Bodily practices" were salient to women's experiences and constructions of Puerto Viejo and, in turn, to their orchestration of sexual relations with local men, in two main overlapping ways. First, my interlocutors focused on bodies and wellbeing in their professions and through recreation. An Afro-Caribbean man once asked me, "What is it with white women and yoga?" Some women were yoga teachers or massage therapists. Other women were consumers of the plethora of bodily healing services offered by foreign residents, who posted their signs on bulletin boards all around town (see Figure 3.3). Yoga tourism was emerging. Spas were springing up, advertising their services as "100% body," for instance, run by foreign women who had moved to Costa Rica after a vacation there. Women sought to experience nature through their bodies too – the mud and mushy leaves in the dense tropical forest, the howls of the howler monkeys, and the smell of ginger. Several women had worked on small-scale farms for their holiday, while others had taken part in environmental-based volunteer tourism.

Second, their bodies were loci of transformation. Women arrived with one body (a "fat body," a "lesbian body," a "bisexual body") and left with another. Women wore clothes that exposed more skin than they considered appropriate to wear in North American or European cities. They lost weight, and sometimes gained weight. But it was not always physical changes in terms of pounds or inches or suntanned pale skin, for instance, but self-perceptions that changed. Many women felt sexier in Puerto Viejo, partly because local men appreciated their bodies in ways that they did not experience in their communities back home, and also because other women noticed them (Frohlick 2008b).

Figure 3.3 Sign advertising multiple ways for tourists to participate in bodily practices –
yoga, massage, and surf classes. Viva el Momento translates to "Live in the
Moment." Photo by author.

The concept "bodily practices" brings attention to the creation of heterosexual
desire in one specific touristic borderzone. Sex "just happens" in Puerto Viejo.
Ember interpreted her sexual experiences as unbridled heat-of-the-moment passion
with local men who desired her "as is," at the same time that she radically modified
her fleshy body. Kelly "passed" as a straight woman, distancing herself from the
"bisexual" label, in order to "feel the vibe" of a local player as part of her
"Caribbean holiday" experience. Desire was located "in" material corporeal bodies
but not a singular or "natural body" (Lock and Farquhar 2007). Rather, bodies were
made through material–social relations and cultural practice in specific spaces.

Feminist scholarship has "turned away from the commonsense body" and
instead considers how "dynamic, intersubjective, and plural human experiences
of carnality … can no longer be referenced by the singular term 'the body' (Lock
and Farquhar 2007: 2). Travel practices are a prime instance of how bodies are

"made" fit (Molz 2006). At its most primary level, as Desmond (1999) aptly states, "travel is about the movement of bodies through space." But we must ask: Which bodies? Which embodiment? Bringing flesh-and-blood bodies into analyses of travel and tourism challenges universalized disembodied theories of tourism and instead acknowledges the "multiplicity of differences, sex and sexuality in tourism" (Veijola and Jokinen 1994: 12; Johnston 2001).

By drawing out tourist women's interest, and investment, in the bodily, I demonstrate the ongoing processes of sexual subjectivities as lived through bodies, which come about in social praxis. Feminist poststructuralist theories of the body and embodiment suggest that tourist women are not "docile bodies," as per Foucault (1977), that is, merely oppressed victims of regimes of power, nor merely surfaces like texts that are read and inscribed upon. Yet, nevertheless, their bodies can be seen as "sites of struggle" (Bordo 1993).

Small's research on the body in women's holiday accounts suggests that travel to a foreign place can be seen as a moment "during which the body and bodiliness are questioned and lose their self-evidence" and where the body's "finiteness, limitation, transience, and vulnerability" is revealed (2007: 88). "No holiday can be understood without reference to the body since it is through the body that the holiday is experienced," Small states (2007: 88). At the same time, as her research indicates, women left out female bodily processes such as menstruation, pregnancy, breastfeeding, or sexual behavior in their accounts and, instead, carefully constructed a "disembodied sexuality" (Small 2007: 88).

For the women I interviewed and spent time hanging out with, a common understanding of their bodies was closely linked to healthfulness and a notion of Puerto Viejo as a "healthy place." Women partook in activities such as going to the reggae bars, soon after arriving, apparently without need of rest and recuperation.[9] Although women's experiences with dengue fever and tropical diseases such as papalomoya were talked about in terms of risk and also as a kind of traveler's social status, other kinds of deleterious and "messy" bodily processes were often absent in their stories. Concerns about exposure to sexually transmitted illnesses and HIV were muted. Only two women explicitly talked about getting an STI (chlamydia). But women experienced a range of bodily inflictions and also sexual assaults – realities that I became aware of by living in the community. The way in which some aspects of the body were underscored and other aspects were absent or obscured suggests how women's experiences of transnational sex were mediated by discourses and embodiments of health and also power, knowledge, and control, which relates to gendered dimensions of heterosexual subjectivity.

Women's narratives and experiences reveal the contradictions and tensions of heterosexual subjectivities that were played out in Puerto Viejo. Embodiment of female heterosexuality "entails both exercising and losing control" as "women are socially constrained to control their own bodily appetites and suppress their own desires, since these are deemed 'unnatural' or at least unseemly" (Holland *et al.* 1994: 27) A certain kind of body is an imperative of female heterosexuality, where "ideal femininity requires radical bodily transformation" (Holland *et al.* 1994: 27). Women manage their bodies to make them socially acceptable, so that messy, smelly, hairy, bloody, bodily fluids are unmentionable and to be controlled, in situations where cross-cultural knowledge is partial and often tricky to decipher.

The anthropologist's body: feeling the vibe … ?

May 9, 2007   Excerpt from my fieldnotes Angelika and I sat in the jeep, outside the Sea Breeze Café. It was late afternoon. We had spent three hours together catching up on her life since I spoke with her last time, nearly two years ago.

Saying good-bye, she turned to me and said, "I don't want to tell you how to do things but I do want to say that the best thing is to experience this yourself."

I smiled. So many times I heard that advice. "Experience it yourself." "Feel the vibe." "Walk the beach, look at the ocean, feel the energy of the place."

She went on, "You need to feel this place through intuition and body rather than through your brain and intellect. Put the book away for a while and just live this place."

Laughing, she pointed to her forehead and said, "Turn your mind off."

Then she pointed to her crotch and told me, "And open this up! Laugh about it. It's the only way."

February 14, 2006   Interview transcript

ILLONDRA: My whole theory about the men here is that it comes from a lot of sexual abuse. I think there's a lot of chakra issues here. There's a lot of energy stored up in the second chakra.

SF: Can you explain that to me?

ILLONDRA: The second chakra is the reproductive chakra. It has to do with emotions, sensuality, sexuality.… Like, basically, there's certain, there's a balance that you're supposed to have.… I think that having to have sex all the time is an imbalance in the second chakra, and also I've encountered a lot of people, I would say, maybe, three or four of the lovers I've had here, have had really excellent, mind-blowing kind of almost making love but not being in love, really kind of transcendental sex, and I don't see them for three weeks later. They are so freaked out by it.… I feel that a lot of guys here have a problem making love as opposed to just fucking. They can have really good sex, but making love is a different thing.

These fieldnotes and interview excerpt highlight two overlapping stories widely circulated amongst tourists, foreign residents, and locals. They speak, in different ways, of how various energy forces (chakras, the earth's magnetic force, astrology, vibrations) are seen, variously, as the causes of the sexual attraction and tension between foreign tourist women and local men. Women talked about how the place wakes up inner states of consciousness and about feeling alive. They recounted visceral feelings of connection, passion, sexual desire, openings, closings, and a sense that not only "good things" (like mind-blowing sex) but also bad things (like generations of abuse) happen here too. "It is a karmic and power-ful place." "Women don't choose to go there but, instead, arrive there." As Angelika advised me, "The best thing is to experience it." In other words, allow the body to win out over the rationalizing, over-analytical, skeptical mind?

My data speak volumes about my own (in)capacities for understanding what was going on around me. A *Tico* friend admonished my fieldwork style many times.

"Slow down, Susan," he would say as I zipped past him on my bike or rushed on foot with my notebook in hand heading to another interview, with barely a wave.

"Slow down, and you'll learn more," he said, gently chiding me. Sometimes, to make his point ever stronger, he would add, "You're a typical woman from the States!"

These are complex data to sort out, especially Illondra's interpretation of her sexual experiences with what she understood as emotionally and spiritually dis-connected Costa Rican men in terms of a Westernized Eastern system of healing and the body. Here I want to address the perplexing things said to me by people whose experiences I was trying to comprehend in order to make a point about their import as "formative moments" (Beatty 1999: 7) to me, the researcher.

What does an anthropologist do with claims to mystical experiences and being attracted to a place through destiny and higher powers? These ideas rang in my ears at times like nonsense – the "irrational" use of New Age cosmologies to explain political economic, late capitalist, and neo-colonial underpinnings of tourism – and other times, particularly when I was immersed (bodily) in a plea-surable fieldwork activity such as listening to reggae music on the beach under the stars, or watching the contours of the dense jungle fade in the falling dusk, as entirely plausible. In one of many discussions about the push-and-pull factors of Puerto Viejo for tourist women I was recapping to Illondra the theory that another friend, Iris, had espoused about the apparent magnetic characteristics of the land and air that draws women to the area in a kind of natural force to teach women about their sexuality. When I asked Illondra what she thought, my skepticism must have been written on my face.

She responded with a well-deserved stinging critique of my epistemological angst: "Why can't anthropologists just believe their subjects?"

Ouch. Believing in our subjects? Ewing notes how, for reasons to do with the disciplinary taboo of "going native," "anthropologists tend not to seriously enter-tain the possibility of entering or believing in the world of the people they meet during fieldwork" (1994: 571). Such stances continue to uphold epistemological divides between our subjects and us, so that certain knowledge (ours) is valued more than others (theirs). But feminist tourism researchers urge an embodied methodology in order to move beyond "methodologically precise and statistically impeccable but otherwise disembodied" accounts of tourism experiences (Johnston 2001: 181). Such accounts, ideally, help show how tourists try to comprehend and make sense of often confusing and overwhelming events through cognition, as well as by the senses, affect, and embodiment. Did I doubt the existence of the magnetic energy fields that my interlocutors felt so strongly? Or, was it more an issue of getting outside of my head long enough to "feel" "the vibe" and chakra energy as theories of sexuality?

Fieldwork "is necessarily an embodied activity" (Coffey 1999). The ethnographer's body affects the content and analysis of fieldwork. Also, fieldwork is a site where bodies are managed and produced (Coffey 1999: 60). As "central rather than peripheral aspects of fieldwork, both the physical body of the fieldworker and its cultural significance" are implicated in the messy, confusing, overwhelming, stifling hot, exhausting realities, and in the micro-negotiations of a researcher trying to fit in inconspicuously, with social adeptness, ethically, and productively in multiple situations each day and night in the field (Coffey 1999: 75). In recognizing the many challenges in inhabiting our "fieldwork bodies," which can be easily misinterpreted, feel pain and bruising, and are, as with all bodies, vulnerable, the question of "belief" is brought into relief. Simply put, I found it challenging to "just believe" my research subjects and to "feel the vibe" for a variety of reasons – yet it was not simply a matter of complete disbelief or complete lack of feeling the vibe. My personality and also duties as a parent when my daughter was with me did not allow me to venture too far into what I call the "wilder" parts of some tourist women's social worlds, such as after-hour parties. Nor did I read the same books on New Age spirituality, or did I engage as fully as they did in yoga and meditation, for instance. I did indulge in yoga tourism and other health and wellbeing services offered in the community by foreign women, which was one of the reasons I was drawn to this area as a field site. These shared activities also allowed me access into the everyday lives of the women whose experiences I was studying.

While I fell short of "feeling the vibe" as much as Angelika and many interlocutors had inspired me to do, I will say that the most productive fieldwork, in hindsight, came out of the times where I did participate more fully. I also want to say that "second chakra" and "feeling the vibe" are both expressions that relate to how the body and embodiment were central to the meanings these particular women gave to their experiences in a particular time and place. In this way I translated the frameworks of my interlocutors into a feminist analysis that pays credence to how "certain places have different energy" (Kantsa 2002), where energies are situated in social relations, history, and economics.[10]

Conclusion

> This is a town full of female tourists.
>
> (Interview with Ember, May 2007)

Over the years the presence of European and North American women and their ("natural," "Western") bodies have significantly affected the social contours of the town. The flows of women tangibly contributed to the charting of Puerto Viejo as a particular spot on the tourist map, not only through the constantly changing population in and out but also through the businesses and social networks and economic transactions. It was not only the presence of local men that made the place attractive to Northern women. The companionship of other foreign women greatly appealed to some tourist women like Kelly. Other women complained about "too many female tourists" and wished instead for a better mix of men and women. Ember made the comment above when she was telling me that for "months and months" it had been predominantly female guests staying at the hotel where she worked and how she was ready for the surfing season, which would bring the male tourists back. Regardless of whether "a town full of female tourists" was regarded by my interlocutors as an aspect they enjoyed or disliked, it was clear that homosocial relationships between foreign women were important to the transnational sex that played out. Puerto Viejo, like all tourist spaces, was transformed "by the presence and practice of bodies" (Crouch 2002: 214), more specifically, those of heterosexual and bisexual Euro-American female tourists.

In this chapter I have drawn out some of the gendered underpinnings of complex transnational sexual encounters, and indicated some of the power dynamics of gender, money, and sex entangled within the spaces of a salubrious and magical vibe, a "place with special energy." In the next chapter, I delve deeper into the meanings of love, sex, and intimacy experienced by Euro-American women as an outcome of their embodied encounters with Costa Rican men, who seemingly, from the perspective of a British expatriate who joking around once told me half-seriously, "spent an extra hour every day exchanging information about tourist women."

4 Intimacy

Sleeping arrangements

> What do I know of this person's sleeping arrangements?
>
> (Wolcott 2005: 71)[1]

> Everything here is so intertwined.
>
> (Interview with Chelsea, February 9, 2006)

Chelsea sat across from me on the patio of my rented beach cottage. It was late morning. The sea was loud from the storm the night before; waves pounded across the stretch of beach in front us. She was perplexed.

A few nights ago, Nigel, a sociable, outgoing Afro-Caribbean surfer with many international friends, had slept on the extra bed in her hotel room. She had heard that he had been "couch surfing" since his Austrian girlfriend had returned home, so she invited him over. "Like little kids," Chelsea explained, they spent half the night talking and laughing. He stayed over again and eventually joined Chelsea in her bed to cuddle. Nothing sexual happened, she told me.

Chelsea was confused. The physical intimacy of sharing a bed with him and the domesticity they were engaged in (they had been cooking and listening to music together) were acts that she felt were, in her words, "intensely intimate." Unsure where the boundaries of their friendship had been crossed, the domestic intimacy they now shared baffled Chelsea.

She pulled her long dark hair behind her neck, and looked down at the line of huge cutter ants moving across the cement patio floor. "Look," Chelsea explained to me:

> I'm sharing my space with him, which, for me, is sometimes kind of difficult, but with him, it's not at all. But it could get to be, but I don't want that. I'm not sure where it's going, if I [even] want to sleep with him. So it's really strange. He hasn't even tried to kiss me, so I don't know what that is. And I haven't really given off that either. He hasn't

tried anything yet. I don't know if he's interested. I think he's attractive. But all my girlfriends are, like, "Oh, you're hanging out with Nigel." But, I'm like, "Yeah, but we haven't even kissed."

Chelsea's story was surprising to me because it presented a new narrative disrupting the hegemonic *Tico* and especially Afro-Caribbean hypersexual masculinities reproduced by local men as well as foreign women. Danielo once told me how Caribbean men believe that if they are with a woman then they should be having sex with her. He explained, "We even criticize the Spanish culture because they are kissing and touching. We are not like that. We get horny and want to have sex ... we could never give a massage because of the touching." With these notions of local masculinities in mind, I voiced my surprise to Chelsea over what she was implying.

"I haven't got the sense yet, from other women's accounts, that these guys are capable of platonic friendships with foreign women," I ventured, "But from what I'm hearing from you, you know at least two [local men who have friendships with her], and, possibly, others as well?"

Chelsea nodded in agreement then continued her story:

We'll spend hours lying on the beach, talking about everything. About falling in love! Talking about everything! For me, that's more important. But then the part that is kind of off, like right now, in the situation that I'm in, if we slept together and I enjoyed it, what would it be – Would we live together? Whoa. "You're one of my best friends." "You live with me." Like, what, "Instant Relationship"?

"So, this is different than going out to the clubs and going home with a guy?" I asked.

"Yes, with that, there's nothing to lose. With this situation, it's potentially really messy ... because I value his friendship more than anything else," Chelsea went on to say, "Everything here is so intertwined."

Chelsea had some insight into why Nigel wanted to share her bed: As a local guy with available women all around him pretty much all of the time – she told me, "He could have a different woman every night if he wanted." This meant that he was not used to being alone, nor did he like sleeping alone. He had been sleeping alone since his girlfriend had returned home two weeks ago.

For him, like "a lot of guys here," Chelsea explained, "That's a really big deal." I asked her, "How many nights is a 'really big deal,' like, a couple of nights?"

She laughed and replied, "A couple of nights is a big deal! I mean – a week? A month is unheard of for these guys! I have another friend who, literally, went crazy when his girlfriend left – after five or six days!"

Tourist women puzzled over the meanings of their interactions with local men and questioned their assumptions about what constituted "intimacy." Did Nigel best fit the "best friend" category or had he become an "instant relationship"? Who became intimate with whom, and why? What did it mean to share a bed and cook together in the same living quarters and not have sex? What did it mean to be invited to a local man's family home to meet his grandmother after knowing him a few days? Euro-American women confronted these quandaries through the course of their holidays, extended backpacking trips, volunteer work, return visits, and migratory tourism in Puerto Viejo.

Women often reflected on how local men did not normally "take women out," that is, according to Western dating practices. They contrasted the ways local men "romanced" women to norms back home, such as going out to nice restaurants or to movies. Recall in the Introduction the situation where a woman threw her sandal at her local boyfriend out of anger over him refusing to take her out on a "proper date." Tourist women confronted confusing differences in courting practices. Being taken to men's homes almost immediately after meeting them was a new and sometimes pleasurable experience, as I will explain. At the same time, that local men did not "take them out" raised women's suspicions about men's motives for intimacy and brought to the fore the cross-purposes of transcultural sex.

Bodies and intimacies in new places

> Since tourism involves travel, a cross-cultural … encounter is inevitably produced, and it is the social transactions involved in this encounter that provide a key to the anthropological understanding of tourism.
>
> (Nash 1981: 462).

Anthropologists are interested in sociality encountered by tourists in places away from home. "Transformations in intimacy," argue Donnan and Magowan, "have occurred as cultures touch and brush against one another, traveling further than ever before" (2010: 157). While global tourism enables connections between people from different countries and cultures, the notion of cultures "touching" and "brushing against one another" suggests a rather free-form meeting of strangers, which glosses over the particularities of tourist–local encounters. While being perhaps chaotic, touristic borderzones are nevertheless socially organized, as I demonstrated in the last chapter. According to Harrison, "The meeting of tourists and locals is a complex phenomenon … that engages histories, ideologies, cultures, personalities, race, gender, class, and age differences, as well as situational contingencies" (2003: 65).

Intimacy is complex and, even, as Berlant (2000) indicates, illusory. Looking at the contemporary United States, Berlant argues that in spite of the "traditional promise of intimate happiness to be fulfilled in everyone's everyday life" intimacy is something "virtually no one knows how to do" (2000: 2). The "modern, mass-mediated sense of intimacy" – wherein desire, self-reflection (therapy), and legitimated attachments ("the relationship") are cornerstones – has come to stand for "the only one plot [that] counts as a 'life'," Berlant opines (2000: 6). She alludes to the marginalization of queer people, single people, and others outside of normative heterosexual "love marriages." Such critiques of conflations of intimacy with marriage, home, and family are useful for examining intimacy in the context of contemporary travel.

Rather than illusory, however, anthropologists regard intimacy as an affective dimension of human life embodied in material relations, that is, how people practice intimacy cross-culturally. Intimate relations, Constable posits, are "social relations that are – or give the impression of being – physically and/or emotionally close, personal, sexually intimate, private, caring, or loving" (2009: 50). As social relations, intimacies are in flux and engendered by principle discourses, such as those pertaining to heterosexuality and modernity, and undergo change through global capitalism, neoliberalism, and commoditization (Appadurai 1996, 1997; Padilla *et al.* 2007).

Under conditions of globalization, mass mobilities, and dislocations of people through migration and tourism, intimacy does not cease to exist, in spite of what was predicted more than a decade ago when Appadurai offered a bold statement: "globalization marks the end of any sort of space of intimacy in social life" (1997: 115). He questioned, "How do small groups, especially families, the classical loci of socialization, deal with these new global realities as they seek to reproduce themselves ...?" (Appadurai 1996: 43). Such concerns about the apparent "end of intimacy," feminists demonstrated, reflect masculinist nostalgia for sanctuary-like notions of home and nuclear family rather than the "resolutely local" practices by which intimate ties continue to be forged within a range of power relations (Visweswaren 1994). The problem, as reformulated by Appadurai, is to consider how mobility affects (rather than destroys) intimacy:

> However far people may travel, however porous the boundaries between cultures, however mobile the values and meanings of the world in which we live, human life still proceeds through the practices of intimacy – the work of sexuality and reproduction, the webs of nurture and of friendship ....
> (Appadurai 1997:116)

But yet when travel is seen as antithetical to intimacy, the relationship between tourism and intimacy is further complicated. Travel is often seen as an escape from the refuge of home – "the" site of legitimized intimacy (Frohlick 2006; Puar 2002a) – and therefore represents the "cosmopolitan" antithesis to the "binding" "constraints" of domesticity, nation, and "the baggage of home or family" (Kaplan 2001: 224). Women's travel is often equated with freedom from domestic ties historically afforded to men (Enloe 2000; Kaplan 2001). A popular idea, therefore, is that travel prevents intimacy or, conversely, transcends everyday intimacy to foster a kind of sublime intimacy (Harrison 2003: 83).

Ethnographic research with tourists, however, indicates otherwise. Neither sublime nor deeply private forms of intimacy necessarily unfold during travel. In her study of middle-class Canadian travel enthusiasts, Harrison shows how they "seek intimacy through worldliness" (2003: 51). The international tourists she interviewed found meaning in "touristic intimacy," meaning experiences of intimate relations, of connection, and physiological arousal that arise through "unpredictable chance encounters" where tourists are vulnerable to the exigencies of their most basic bodily needs and to the public sociality necessitated by international travel (Harrison 2003: 51). These connections are lived through bodies that are gendered, raced, classed, and sexed.

Desire is central in discussions of how globalization is changing the meanings and practices of intimacy: Povinelli and Chauncey (1999: 440) posit that various movements of people have "affected the sexual practices, subjectivities, and politics of the immigrants' homelands and host nations." As Padilla and colleagues (Padilla *et al.* 2007: x) show, material practices of sex and love are bound up with transformations in "the most intimate aspects of one's life" due to "escalating population mobility," related to globalization, including global tourism. By showing how international travel to Costa Rica transforms intimate sociality for heterosexual tourist women, I build on these theories. I proceed with the story of Alex and the way her ideas about intimacy changed over time as she transformed from a "new tourist girl" to, by some measure, belonging in the community.

Alex: sex with "the street boys"

April 4, 2006 Notes after talking to Alex today She came to the World café as I was eating lunch today. Hung over. She told me a bit about her night last night at the Lion Disco ... too drunk, didn't remember how she got home, maybe Danny drover her? She vaguely remembers getting into his car and asking him to take her home. Vaguely remembers being joined in the bathroom with a "Carlos" (one I don't know) who wanted to do it with her, either there or later ... they made plans for later, she said, but then she got bored and just went home.... The guy she nearly slept with last night, and slipped up on her plan, was someone related to the guy from Cahuita she told me about ... more about this (her staying off men), more about her feelings of guilt over sleeping with a married man, but it was more about her getting bored with him and wanting someone to be able to look at her when they meet on the street, she says. Then she told me about how the husband of a foreign woman (who had just returned from several months back home in Europe) had one night been grinding up against Alex, rubbing his beer bottle up her back, which she didn't appreciate.

Alex traveled to Costa Rica from Canada as a volunteer on a community development project, an ambition of hers since she was a young girl. Transnational sex "just happened" through a series of contingencies. Her enchantment with Puerto

Viejo while on a brief holiday at the end of her tour on the Pacific coast had spurred her last minute decision to stay. She then met a local man while out dancing one night. Their domestic lives very quickly became entangled. Alex's relationship with Fernando, a twenty-six-year-old mixed Afro-Costa Rican man lasted nearly a year.

In the year of their shared domesticity Alex had thought of herself as "a nice little housewife," she said. Hardly a static arrangement, it changed over time. At the beginning, Fernando insisted that Alex not work and that he provide for her. He washed her clothes and cooked their meals. At first it was Fernando who provided Alex with a dwelling, sharing the family home with his siblings.[2] She had been firmly committed to what she considered in retrospect to be a fantasy, that they were "a monogamous couple living under one roof."

When I first met Alex, she was grappling with what she viewed as the cultural underpinnings of his infidelity, associated in part with Euro-American stereotypes of Latino *machismo*.[3] On a July day in 2005 while sitting under the shade of a sweeping mango tree on the patio of a local *soda*, Alex explained to me:

> My boyfriend's generation – their parents, none of them are together. Culturally, in Latin America, I don't think people stay together. I have spoken to quite a few of his friends here who have children. Two, three children, different fathers. "Why are you like that? Why don't you want to wait? Don't you want to be married? In my culture, it's about longevity, about having a partner for life, thirty, forty years, like my parents." To them, that's a foreign concept … I mean it doesn't always work, but it doesn't seem here that the intention is here. In Western society, I mean, many, many couples split up but you kind of hope that it's going to work out.

In spite of these cultural constraints, Alex remained hopeful. Her understanding of sex, love, and marriage was based on an assumption of "a sexual relationship [as] the one truly important personal relationship" (Budgeon 2008: 302). As Alex aspired to longevity in spite of what seemed to be highly improbable odds that any marriage would last, her boyfriend's resistance to a long-term monogamous partnership, rooted in cultural difference, as she explained, was a hurdle she hoped she could overcome.

Six months later, Alex's beliefs were shattered. She kicked him out of the house they were renting (by then she was paying most of the rent), fed up with his party lifestyle and his habitual cheating. Her aspirations for "true intimacy" took a radical shift afterwards, which I trace here.

Alex promptly set her sights on the town's "street boys," a term she used to categorize the young men who are visible in the public spaces interacting with tourist women. When I interviewed Alex in 2006, she was in the throes of attempting to "beat the system." I asked her what this meant exactly. Alex reasoned she would act differently than both local women, who normally "looked the other way," and naïve tourist women, who were "clueless." In her words:

It tends to be the men that pursue the women, whereas we [referring to herself as a savvy foreign woman] are far more the pursuers. We know what we want and we go out and get it. We might let them think it's their idea but we're in control. There's a lot of nice girls [the new tourists], having a nice time, and men approach them. More traditional way of meeting. They're not aware of the game. They tend to believe the crap that comes out of these boys' mouths. The typical, naïve girl who just arrived. I've done it. They fall in love. They believe the lies. There's a whole section [in the bars and clubs] like that .... Yes, tourist people who come here through no fault of their own are completely clueless as to what's going on. And it takes a long way of living here before you realize, and it requires a readjustment of the head to get used to a completely different set up.

Rather than remain "the typical, naïve girl," Alex emulated the strategies used by the town's "street boys" that she carefully observed in the bars and other hook-up spaces.

One of the key cues in the local sexual culture Alex picked up on was practicing discretion rather than publicly "flaunting" her sexual availability, a sure marker of a "fresh tourist girl," as she explained:

I'm careful about who I let rough me up in the disco. I might want to sleep with this guy. I might be sleeping with this guy, [but] it doesn't mean that I'm going to dance with him. It's pretty obvious, if I'm dancing with a guy a certain way, everyone is going to think I'm sleeping with him, whether or not I am. Even this whole thing might be going on, you're working it, you go outside and have a chat, you're going to the toilet, you go by and he gets a little grope. The thing is on even if you don't leave the disco together. For all intent and purposes, no one knows about it. I try and keep it down.

Alex did not want to be seen leaving with one of the local guys, otherwise her chances of hooking up with the others might be deterred because they had grown up together in the small town and as mates shared information about tourist women. Moreover, as Alex saw it, because of "the whole *machismo* thing," calling up a ubiquitous stereotype about "all Latin American men" (Gutmann 2003: 18), she was acutely aware of how being labeled a "*puta*" ("whore") could derail her sexual pursuits. Being "a nice girl" and remaining sexually passive was an important reputation to uphold, in the eyes of local men. Yet Alex refused to acquiesce to sexual double standards. By guarding the privacy of her sexual encounters, she strategized to avoid being seen either as a "town slut," as she put it, or, on the other hand, a "typical naïve girl" who allows herself to be taken advantage of by local men.

By resisting being compartmentalize in one category or the other, she was, to her mind, "playing the men at their own game." Alex said:

Some people, it's that whole *machismo* thing, they don't appreciate my behavior. You get the little chats. There are some guys you give it all, then when I explain how I am, it's scary for them, that I can be aggressive about my sexuality or so open about it. They want to be in control and have their nice little girls. They can't have it both ways. "You picked me up in a nightclub." What do they think?

Alex kept track of the men she slept with in order to avoid having sex with a lover's brother or cousin. In part because the men went by multiple names (nicknames, English names, Spanish names) and also because, since she did not have much social contact with local townspeople under ordinary daily circumstances, it was difficult to learn about the social organization of the men's lives, including kin relationships. Through her sexual activity, however, she discovered a lot about their lives. For Alex, hearing about their families and relatives, and about their childhoods and growing up in Costa Rica, and seeing where they lived and the inside of their homes, was a new and gratifying experience. Since she was a young girl, Alex had wanted to learn about different cultures. An unexpected outcome of her casual sex pursuits was the access she gained into the private worlds of local men, an intimacy in contrast to being Fernando's "woman," where he kept her at a distance from his social world.

While sexual pleasure was an important reason she sought out the street boys – Alex clued in to which men gave oral sex, for instance – becoming a player on her own terms was also spurred by other motivations. She wanted to disrupt what she saw as the domination of foreign women by local men in the town, and to avoid being "played" (lied to and cheated on). She also wanted sexual relations that were more physically safe than her previous relationship. With Fernando she had assumed that he was faithful. When Alex discovered that he had been sleeping around, she was livid that he had exposed her to risks of STIs and HIV infection. In contrast, with the town's players she avoided the deception and therefore felt safer: Condoms were mandatory, although a constant source of power struggle and negotiation. Moreover, without a man sharing her apartment, her privacy was no longer jeopardized. Alex explained, "[It's safer] to have sex with the cute, nice boys and then not let them into that part of my house because that's where they'll do damage. Not let them into my house when I'm not here, stuff like that, because you can't trust them." For Alex, a conjugal union was more perilous than casual sex with multiple lovers, as sharing domesticity with Fernando had turned out to be risky.

Alex's shift in sexual practices was related to her desire for intimacy defined by familiarity with men's personal lives and the local culture. Hooking up with men involved erotic acts in public (being groped, furtive glances, chats outside of the clubs) that she enjoyed, as well as the intimacy that materialized in spaces otherwise off-limits to her – their domestic spaces, phone conversations, and stories of family and growing up. But also, when she spotted former hook-up partners in town she liked the way they nodded at her in discreet gestures of

recognition. Such exchanges signaled to her a savvy knowledge of local socialities that she had earned through her own tactics. For Alex, the shared glances or
furtive gropes were meaningful forms of intimacy, contrastive to local men's
public and overtly sexual interactions with new tourist girls.

Homegrown notions of sex and love (and race)

> One of the positive aspects of all these multicultural relationships is that we
> bring our culture.
>
> (Interview with Alex, July 2005)

Tourist women interpreted their encounters based on cultural notions of gender,
sex, and love, although these notions changed over time. Women were also pow-
erfully influenced by local practices, such as the sleeping arrangements with
Nigel and "the game" that Alex joined in on. Women's ambivalences about transnational sex were triggered by norms of Western femininity and heterosexuality.
One reason why women wanted to participate in my research was to discuss the
uncertainty they felt about their relationships with local men.

Several dominant cultural beliefs shaped tourist women's notions of sexual
intimacy. These included what Ingraham (1996) calls the "heterosexual imaginary," which upholds a monogamous heterosexual relationship as necessary to
women's well-being, the axiom that women ought to "marry up," that is, choose
their partners from higher social and economic status groups, and also lingering
taboos against interracial dating and marriage even within countries as Canada,
the United States, and Britain with high levels of immigration (Frankenberg
1993; Poovey 2000; Rosenfeld and Soo 2005). Transcultural relations thus
encompassed crossing racial as well as class boundaries, since heteronormativity
in middle-class white Western society continues to condemn interracial unions
(Rosenfeld and Soo 2005: 541). The meanings women gave to their interracial
sexual encounters were filtered through how they understood white femininity
within hegemonic discourses of racial privilege and exclusion and discourses of
normative heterosexuality (Deliovsky 2006, 2010; Frankenberg 1993), as the following examples illustrate.

Raised in a large city in the northeastern United States, Micaela was well traveled and cosmopolitan in her taste for ethnic food, world music, and indigenous
art. She referred to herself as a "rasta chic," and had fallen for her Afro-Costa
Rican boyfriend, Antonio's, patois accent and vibe. They met when she was
shopping at the artisanal stalls, where he sold trinkets. Shortly after they hooked
up she moved into the small house that he shared with his brother. When she
returned to the United States at the end of her two-week holiday she promised
to return soon, and they stayed in touch via phone calls and emails.

When I met Micaela she had just returned. She was excited about her relationship with Antonio but had some nagging doubts. She wondered about his fidelity while she was away. An issue of money had recently surfaced. She worried, too, about how an Afro-Costa Rican black man might clash with her life back home as a middle-class white North American urban professional from a fairly conservative Catholic background. A story hints at these underlying tensions. In her words:

> Yesterday he went to Limón [city] to see his grandmother. The previous night he had said that he was going, "I don't think it would be fun for you." Basically telling me not to come. So I didn't know how to take that. It felt, like, I don't know. Maybe he would want me to meet his grandmother. Because, if the situation were reverse, I would want him to. No, maybe I wouldn't. My grandmother would probably have a heart attack. She did see a picture of him. My grandmother is ninety-nine. It's difficult for her knowing that I'm with a black guy. She's actually come a long way because when I went to visit her I showed her a picture and she didn't say anything except that he had a beautiful smile. My mom goes, "Do you know how difficult that was for your grandmother not to say something very racial and prejudiced?"

Micaela felt shut out of what seemed to her an opportunity for her to forge ties to his relatives. However, while reflecting on her assumption that her boyfriend was being unfair she suddenly changed her mind. Recognizing how their relationship went against the grain of her family, especially her grandmother, Micaela retracted her accusation of gendered double standards that she had leveled at Antonio. The racist overtones of Micaela's European-American grandmother's intolerance of interracial dating and adverse reaction to Antonio, couched in the backhanded compliment on his smile, contributed to Micaela's sense of uncertainty about the relationship.

During the interview and in subsequent conversations she vocalized her reluctance to help him with obtaining a visa to live and work in the United States, even though he was pushing her to do so, because she doubted that she could bring him home to meet her family without feeling stigmatized and looked down upon.

Moral discourses against interracial dating, a legacy of anti-miscegenation laws and beliefs entrenched in American history and racial politics (Frankenberg 1993), as well as in Canada and some European countries (Kitossa and Deliovsky 2010), mediated women's concerns that they would be judged as white women for their choice of partners. As Deliovsky (2010: 56) has shown in her research in Canada, white women who date or are intimately involved with men of color experience stigma related to their "association with a negatively racialized individual" in ways that their male counterparts do not.

Local men's masculinities were constructed around blackness, a topic that I return to; however, foreign women's femininities were also racialized. According to Frankenberg, "white women who choose interracial relationships are presented as sexually 'loose,' sexually unsuccessful, or (at the least negative) sexually radical" (1993: 77). Such discourses, including prevalent "slut" name-calling, undeniably affected women's decisions to become involve in transnational interracial relationships. Some women struggled with feelings of uncertainty stemming from growing up in racially homogenous communities. Illondra, a woman I introduce below, said, "What were there? Maybe three black men in [the town she was from]?" Some women, exposed to discourses of racial "tolerance" and, for instance, anti-racist education at university, hoped to distance themselves from whiteness and white privilege. A continuum of "taboos" against interracial intimacies thus triggered tourist women's decisions to cross racial boundaries set up in part by their parents and communities back home in the United States, Canada, Italy, and other Western countries. Christine's situation illuminates such dynamics.

Christine became a good friend. My daughter and I met Christine and her daughter when the girls were young, and we spent many days together on our trips down from Canada. On one visit in 2006 after I had known Christine for over a year, we spent an evening at their house, talking late into the night. After the girls fell asleep, with the sound of crashing waves in the background, Christine recounted her experiences as a young woman off to see Central America straight out of college in the Midwestern United States. After living in Puerto Viejo for many years she tried to avoid the rampant gossip about people's private lives, which meant that she did not often speak to anyone in the community much about her past. Her story, about her attraction almost twenty years ago to black Caribbean men whose charm had led her into one rebellious liaison after another, came spilling out in the humid tropical night like a crescendo. She reflected on how she had acted, in her words, like a "stupid white woman," gossiped about by townspeople for being overly emotional, for wanting only sex from men, for choosing inappropriate men as boyfriends, and other traits associated with tourist women.

She described what she felt North American and European women commonly believed:

Well, I was one of those "stupid white women," maybe I still am. I arrived here with this idea that the local black men would make better lovers than North American men, that they are different in every way including in bed, that I wanted to be part of the Caribbean. This mythology breaks down, but not as quickly as I wish it did.

Throughout her childhood her father had told her, "Black people have different souls than white people," a racial stereotype that had triggered her aspiration to overcome racism through international travel. Looking back on earlier days, Christine made sense of her interracial sexual experiences in terms of rebelliousness. Rebelling against her family's conservative, racist intolerance of black people and interracial sexualities, racial stereotypes shaped her erotic desires. As a young woman in the 1990s, when she first arrived in Costa Rica, her own cultural misperceptions and fantasies about black masculine hypersexuality influenced her sexual liaisons and intimate relationships.

Micaela and Christine's stories convey how transnational sex was made meaningful through cultural assumptions and tacit rules about sexual propriety and intimate sociality, based on gender discourses bound up with race and class. There were many tensions and contradictions in women's experiences and narratives. Intimacy with Costa Rican men, through shared domesticity or sexual intimacy, was, for some women, a cultural transgression. Racial difference, the focus of the next chapter, was linked with education and socio-economic status. The levels of men's formal education (often not having finished high school) mismatched those of the foreign women's (who held post-secondary degrees and/or professional certificates in massage therapy, and other healing arts). Such disparities created boundaries, which were exciting to cross but also created conflicted feelings related to Western heteronormative discourses about hierarchies of preferred intimate partners.

However, belief systems about sexuality and gendered expressions of desire and intimacy are neither completely fixed nor unyielding. Constable posits, globalization "offers new opportunities for defining new sorts of relationships" and for meanings of intimacy to be reworked in the "ongoing tension between more complex micro-level patterns of power and agency and broader macro patterns of global inequality" (2009: 58). As short-stay, long-stay, and migratory tourists and temporary residents, foreign women arrived with Western beliefs about intimacy and they were also exposed to new ideas about intimacy and different practices of intimacy unfolding within a transnational tourism economy and increasingly heterogeneous Afro-Caribbean community.

Two further examples – glimpses into the lives of Illondra and Bethany – illustrate the reworking of intimacy at the micro-level that transpired in Puerto Viejo.

Illondra: "I reach you sometime"

Illondra was a twenty-three-year-old journalism major from the northeastern United States who moved to Costa Rica after college. She ended up in Puerto

Viejo because it had been recommended to her as a "really cool place." Shortly after arriving, she became involved with a middle-class *Tico* that she met through friends. In her words:

> I moved in with him in his place in town and never paid for anything. We were really, it was, I mean it was unusual [compared to] North American standards because, you know, we moved in with each other really quickly. Relationships here seem to be as soon as you sleep with each other, unless it's a one-night stand, you basically are married. You move in with each other. You spend all day together.

They spent time at home, cooking meals with his mother and siblings, who felt "like family" to Illondra. That relationship ended after he slept with another foreign woman. Soon afterwards, one night out dancing, Illondra hooked up with an Afro-Caribbean man, Bryan, who she described as "straight up local." He was younger than Illondra, had little formal schooling, and was from a poor family. Those differences were part of his intrigue. Drawn to "his nice pure vibe" and what she thought was a mutual emotional connection, Illondra was mistaken in believing that they had an exclusive relationship. Finding out that Bryan had multiple girlfriends was a blow to her but several months later, once again, Illondra fell into a close relationship with another local Caribbean man, only to find out that he, too, had multiple girlfriends.

At that point in her story I turned to Illondra to ask her, "Did you see another guy after that?"

She responded, laughing, "Yes, for sure! You never learn. What's that saying? If it happens once it won't happen again but if it happens twice, it will happen again."

She went on to explain how North American and other white men were not of interest to her, largely because intimacy played a significant role in her choice of men. "Intimacy is the big thing. It's really easy to be intimate here," was how she put it. In reflecting back on her first relationships with local men in Puerto Viejo, she said:

> It kind of fulfilled, what I noticed about all the relationships I've ever had here, because they are intimate so quickly, and you live with them immediately, and you do all the day-to-day things [together], it kind of fulfills the fantasy that we have. I don't know if it's a Canadian, American, or woman thing, if we're socialized that way, but it was really fulfilling, the playing house kind of thing. I loved it! Waking up, sweeping the floor, cooking breakfast, going to the beach…. It happens here all the time because people are broke. I don't think I'm the only one who's like that. I would want to live with someone if I was dating them. I have never run across a North American man who's interested in that.

Her first encounter was meaningful to her because of what she called "instant intimacy," the close proximate relations with her boyfriend's family and shared domesticity. The downside, though, was the incongruent meanings she and her boyfriend held about the entanglements of their lives, stemming from gender and cultural differences and also from the circumstances of tourism in which men had access to a steady stream of new tourist women. Over time the implications of the local practices of "instant intimacy" became apparent. The dream of living together and sharing domestic intimacy receded, and the desire to hook up for occasional sex was of greater interest to her.

Months after living in Puerto Viejo, Illondra continued to believe that intimate relations were easier to find and quicker to manifest in Costa Rica than in the United States. But her belief that "true intimacy" came about through domestic arrangements changed over time, from an interest in being part of a couple living under the same roof to an interest in casual sex with local men.

Illondra recalled the time that a young Caribbean man she had known for a couple of years had once said to her when they came across each other by chance in the street, "I reach you sometime." His utterance had made her happy because it signaled her understanding of the communication of local codes and practices involving spending time in private spaces. "Moving in" lost its appeal to Illondra, because she resisted the power dynamics that arose in each of her "live in" relationships. She turned to particular local men, those who did not "hunt" foreign women, for meaningful sexual intimacies. While Alex liked the "street boys" who dated tourist women, Illondra sought out sexual intimacy with local men who were guarded in their relations with foreign women. Yet both women, in their shift from tourists to temporary residents, were influenced by local practices of sexual intimacy.

Bethany: domesticity

Bethany, a twenty-eight-year-old American woman, hoped she might find what she referred to as "heartfelt" connections with others on her trip to Costa Rica. In the first few weeks in the Talamanca area, she worked as a yoga teacher and planted trees on a permacultural farm. One night away from the farm out dancing in town she met Harris, a local man in his thirties. His quiet "down home" personality appealed to Bethany. Days later she moved into the house he shared with his parents, adult sisters, and nieces and nephews.

Bethany felt fortunate to have been invited into his home life. His family home, where he had lived since his childhood, was the nucleus of a world that revolved around taking care of his nieces and nephews and playing soccer with his mates. He wanted to build his own house one day, preferably on the family plot. Bethany appreciated that he allowed a relative stranger to share his private life. She enjoyed the intimate daily activities they shared – eating with the family, and watching him tend to his young nieces and nephews. For Bethany sharing a house with a man from a low-income family and a household organization that was so different from the American household she grew up in (a middle-class, nuclear family, where she moved out of the house in her late teens) was alluring.

Intimacy has been defined as feelings "born of the complex relations of every-day life," that is, domesticity (Goodfellow and Mulla 2008: 258). While diverse forms of domesticity occur, "home" and "family" as legitimated intimate rela-tions are often associated with domesticity and serve as desirable modalities and feelings of intimacy (Goodfellow and Mulla 2008: 258). Bethany found home life with Harris to be an almost heady desire, as it replicated her ideal of a close-knit traditional family, yet was exotic in its sounds, smells, and tastes. These experi-ences meshed closely with her touristic desires to experience emotional connec-tions with others from cultural backgrounds different to her own. Such a positive feeling, however, dissipated for Bethany when she discovered something about Harris that jarred her image of domesticity bound up with sharing a life – and a future – with someone.

One day they traveled to Limón city together so that he could help her open a local bank account. She required a statement from him that they were a couple. When it came time for Harris to write the statement to give to the bank teller, in an awkward and perplexing moment Bethany became acutely aware of Harris's low level of literacy in comparison to her university education. As she explained:

> I realized when he had to sign ... the lady was saying, to him, that you have to write a letter that you are officially saying that she lives with you. He pushed the pen and pad to me. I was thinking, okay, I can write it, just tell me what to say, talking to the woman and to me. He had to sign it at the end. He could hardly write his own name. That threw me for a little loop. I had seen him reading a newspaper. It hadn't really come up. I assumed of course he knows how to read and write. I know that he reads, but I don't know to what extent. I constantly read my books on the beach and he doesn't. It's not a part of his life.... That sort of bothers me. But I realize that's not everyone's cup of tea.... But anyhow, the fact that it was like a six-year-old's handwriting ... his own name! I haven't broached that topic with him. I'm not thinking I'm better than him ... it presents different opportunities, so that you're not stuck. A big part of my life is not wanting to feel stuck, and wanting to feel free, and that's hugely important.

Her discovery that Harris could not read or write very well was an unanticipated consequence of her everyday intimate relations with him, and it jolted her into a less romanticized perspective on their rapidly intertwining lives. She poignantly recognized that her multiple aspirations to form a "nuclear couple," to be part of an Afro-Caribbean family, and to "feel free" as a North American well-educated middle-class woman and world traveler were competing desires. Domesticity was hugely attractive to Bethany at first but ultimately she withdrew from Harris's life because, in a sense, it was too intimate, too close for comfort. – Another way of putting this is that the "regulatory processes of kinship" (Goodfellow and Mulla 2008: 259) enfolded her in material relations in which she came to feel "stuck" by virtue of her nationality, gender, socioeconomic class, and aspirations for an equitable partnership. Domesticity, when it was a kind of touristic enchantment, aligned with Bethany's desires. But the subjective and geopolitical realities of Harris's familial space and domicile, marked by a lack of education and therefore opportunities, in Bethany's mind, stopped her from becoming involved in a committed relationship.

"Because they are strangers"

> My husband speaks German to the children, I speak English and Spanish. We want to provide them those opportunities. Most of my family [members] are married to strangers. With Greek, English, American. My brother [is] with a Swedish [woman]. My brother speaks Swedish perfectly. He lives in Sweden, since maybe fifteen years. My uncle is married with a lady from England. His daughter lives in England. My other uncle married with a lady from Germany; his son lives there. My other uncle married with a lady from Greece, and she lives there so the little boy speaks Greek. So, finally, it's complicated.… When strangers [foreigners] come here they have good communication with Afro-Caribbean people, because of the language.
>
> (Interview with Miss Helen, May 2010)

I return now to Nigel, the affable, tousled-looking surfer who was "couch surfacing" with Chelsea. Like other young men in town, as Chelsea reasoned, he "could have a different woman every night if he wanted." The practices of local men co-inhabiting very quickly after meeting foreign women were common – and were related to the structuring of time since the women were visitors.

These "instant intimacies" aligned with women's broader hopes and aspirations for particular experiences in Costa Rica. Tourist women sought up-close "immersion" experiences of integrating into the local culture and community, rather than an all-inclusive resort "detached" holiday experience. The area held the promise of the opportunity to mix in with local people, to see them go about their daily lives, and to live out their own fantasies of meaningful connections with locals.[4] But these are not one-sided relationships. For tourists to realize these kinds of proximate relations, local people must, to some degree, also want intimate sociality, although the history, culture, and practice of "intimacy" may not be the same. Nigel's interest in shared sleeping arrangements is situated in a wider context of economic resources (did he have his own place?), masculinity discourses (is it an expectation that men spend the night with a woman every night of the year?), local and translocal social organization (what was the spatial configuration of family, marriage, kin?), and the role of tourists in shaping these practices.

Globalization affected Puerto Viejo by the "present absence" (Giddens 1990) of those who were away. Kin worked or attended school in San José and other

Figure 4.1 Wood frame houses in a residential neighborhood in Puerto Viejo. Situated close to tourist lodgings and other tourism businesses, tourists regularly pass by the private homes and gain a "glimpse" of everyday life, in contrast to an "enclave" type of tourism that keeps tourists segregated from locals. Photo by author.

parts of the country, worked on cruise ships out of Puerto Limón or in construction on the Pacific side, or lived overseas with girlfriends in Germany, Canada, the Netherlands, and many other countries. Transnational migratory patterns, in place for decades, linked Afro-Caribbean Costa Rican families with kin in Bocas del Toro, Panama and Bluefields, Nicaragua as well as places in Jamaica (Lefever 1992; Madrigal 2006). This "stretching out" of relations across the country and across nations meant that townspeople experienced everyday an ever-changing and expanding spatial orbit of social life within wider Caribbean and Costa Rican diasporas (Bourgois 1986).

As kin members and sexual partners left, tourism and leisure-oriented migration brought new people daily into residents' spaces. Tourists lived among the residents in the various lodgings situated in residential neighborhoods. Tourists ate in neighborhood *sodas* owned and operated by Afro-Caribbean women and their families. They shared the semi-public televisions fixed high on the walls that blared out images and sounds of world soccer (*fútbol*) or Costa Rican soap operas (*telenovelas*). As foreign women stayed rather than returning home from their vacations they negotiated their roles in the local community and therefore their identities as "tourists" or "locals" as well as *"novias"* (girlfriend) or *"mujeres"* ("woman" or wife).[5]

In her research, Vandegrift shows how global tourism has restructured women's lives in Puerto Viejo, including foreign tourist women who decide to extend their holidays or to become temporary or permanent residents:

> Living in a locale focused on providing relaxation and escape means that women needing social services or childcare find few institutional resources they can turn to. Even the most privileged transnational migrant experiences gendered disadvantage when negotiating childcare responsibilities or difficult marriages. Tourist towns develop for the pleasure of visitors; neither childcare nor battered women's shelters are abundant. Women staying in Puerto Viejo over time struggle after the birth of a child or the end of a marriage.
>
> (Vandegrift 2008: 786–787)

While Vandegrift aims to show how Costa Rican, Nicaraguan, and Northern women are affected unequally as laborers engaged in the highly gendered and racially segmented "flexible" tourist economies, I raise a related point. The presence of foreign women, and foreign men, as potential, and desirable, sexual partners, has resulted in not only what one local woman referred to as "fiesta tourism" and casual sex but also has resulted in many international marriages and bicultural families in local communities. As Miss Helen indicates above, her family includes marriage partners from Sweden, England, Germany, and Greece.

The reasons why *extranjeras* make desirable sexual partners for residents are undoubtedly complex, partly rooted in beliefs and practices of exogamy. A young *Tica* in her twenties, Janelle, who grew up in the area, gave me some insight in this regard. Janelle was a teacher at a public primary school and I picked her up from school one day at the end of her workday, as I had offered to drive her home. She had agreed to speak with me about youth and children's sexuality in the local communities.

As I pulled into the earthen driveway at Janelle's house that she shared with her mother, older sister, nieces and nephews, and her own two school-age children, dogs barked and chickens squawked, wings flapping. Before climbing out of the car, Janelle sat for a few minutes to share her reflections on growing up in a small rural community in Atlantic Costa Rica. During her childhood she had many friends, including close friendships with boys. But as she grew older the boys that she had grown up with made for, what she described as, "inappropriate intimate relations." She explained that many of her friends avoided the problem of turning childhood friends into quasi-incestuous sexual partners by turning to tourists.

"Why do you think tourists are so interesting to people here?" Janelle explained, "Because they are strangers."

Her remark provides important perspective on Euro-American women's putatively "wild" erotic desires for local men. For decades, local sexual culture has incorporated tourists and other foreigners, including Nicaraguan migrants, as well as *Tico*s, into the mix as far as desirable sexual partners. In her study of the demography of Afro-Caribbean people in Limón, Madrigal (2006: 184) notes that "very frequent exchange of mates between the Afro-Costa Rica and Hispano-Costa Rican communities in Limón" took place in the 1970s as the area opened up via agriculture then tourism. By 2005, the grandparents of local youth who had foreign girlfriends had witnessed the continuation of inter-ethnic mixing, as well as many changes, in the social sexual organization in the community.

Men such as Philippe, who grew up in Puerto Viejo, talked about the ways in which local people learned about sex during their childhoods, factors that influenced their acceptance of transnational sex. Philippe told me it was common for young children to watch their parents having sex because the houses were small – thin walls and close quarters, rooms separated by a thin curtain. For practical reasons, sex was not so private. He watched his older brothers making out with their girlfriends late at night just outside the open window shutters. Philippe's and other local men's recollections indicate how ideas about sex, sexuality, and intimacy were transmitted across generations. Historically, public discourses on sex have been muted in Costa Rica (Arroba 2001), dominated by a "vision of sexuality" defined by the Catholic Church (Schifter 2000: 2). Public sex education in the school system has been limited (Schifter 2000). Men learned about sex from the anecdotes of uncles, older brothers, and grandparents, and from what they could see in the public/private spaces within the small community of extended kin relationships. Miss Gladys, an Afro-Caribbean mother of several grown sons, told me how in raising her boys she did not talk to them about sex, nor did she care to, because sex was a taboo subject that only men talked about. "They go out on the street for that," Gladys explained, echoing what men told me about their experiences.

Luis, a Caribbean man in his twenties, grew up in a large extended family. When I asked him about when and why he became interested in tourist girls, he told me, "You listen to the men's stories and how they used to have sex on the beach. The old men. Then you start to think of that. Maybe I can take a walk on the beach with this girl. Then you see this girl, and then you try it." His earliest sexual experiences as a young teen boy were with local girls (*Ticas* and Afro-Caribbean girls) but once he acquired some confidence in his late teens, his interest shifted to the pursuit of foreign women.

Luis said, "When you start to feel like a man, you can get the tourist girls, when the shyness goes away.... By the time I was nineteen, I started to see so much tourist girls.... You get your confidence up and soon the boom girls come hitting on you."

Young people growing up in the early tourism development era in the Talamanca coast had been influenced by the increasing presence of tourists (Palmer 2005). Since the Limón region historically was socially and physically separated from the rest of the country for reasons to do with racism, as I mention in the Introduction, local youth grew up amidst rapid social and economic changes as the area shifted from an agricultural-based enclave to a tourist-based enclave. Mediated through discourses of masculinity, sex for local male teens and young men was linked to the intimate spaces of home and domesticity, as well as to public places of recreation such as the beaches and dance halls (Frohlick 2007). Tourist women – *extranjeras* – came to embody "new blood," insofar as sexual intimacy between childhood friends within the small community was generally undesirable.

"Exogamous" practices, referring to the selection of marriage partners from outside of one's cultural group, which largely began with the arrival of increasing numbers of white Costa Ricans in the 1950s, according to Madrigal (2006) and Purcell (1993), and continued into the 1980s and 1990s when foreign tourists arrived (and were valued as unrelated strangers) were commonplace in the mid-2000s. Nevertheless, cross-cultural intimacies were not easily negotiated. However common mixed unions between tourists and locals had become, friction between the two groups was also common.

"Research buddies": intimacy and ethnography

May 11, 2007   Fieldnotes Christopher called me up today out of the blue, wanted to meet with me. I was on my way to drop Breck off for the day at a friend's place on Black Beach, so we stopped by en route. He was in a surly mood. "Stop snooping around," he snapped at me. Turning to Breck [who was eight years old at the time], he uttered a facile claim, "Your momma knows everything about everyone." I tried to calm him down by reassuring him that was simply not true. I was only learning Spanish, so how could I know "everything," I reminded him. He smiled when hearing that, and we joked about my floundering attempts at learning the local language. Christopher, a local man in his forties who had become a good friend, backed off a bit after this exchange but the issue re-surfaced over the course of my fieldwork and our friendship.

The nature of fieldwork as "a deeply bounded, prolonged, personal experience" (Coffey 1999: 88) necessitates intimacy. Living within a locale for extended periods of time means that an ethnographer is "intimately part of the place and people that are being studied" (Coffey 1999: 89); and, also, ethnographers rely on the fostering of closeness with their research participants and informants for ensuring valid data. As Lovell indicates, "The ethnographer's ability to penetrate the secrets of his or her subjects becomes a major stake in the ethnographic quest" (2007: 56). This view of ethnography as inherently intimate, that is, that which seeks "the innermost" of its subjects' lives, is reflected in the comments of my friend, Chris, when he voiced his concern over me transgressing a precious line between private and public knowledge: "Your momma knows everything about everyone." Knowing everything, or the aim to, is a form of power that he perceived to be vested in the anthropologist who constantly asked questions that in his view ought not be asked.

In some respects, my friend's criticisms were valid. People divulged aspects of their lives that held implications for other people, such as extra-marital affairs or custody disputes involving young children, and that could potentially tarnish people's reputations. Agonizing personal revelations, such as a boyfriend's inability to write his own name, a grandmother's racial slur, or a sexual attraction to poor young black "bad boys," were made in the context of privileged dialogue between an anthropologist and her research subjects. "Informant" is both a problematic and accurate name for people with whom researchers have an "interested" relationship, including the friendships that inevitably develop in the field. People recognized it was the nature of what I was doing that I would be told many personal things.

In my capacity as an anthropologist, therefore, I came to know about individuals' lives beyond what Chris, and others, felt was culturally and socially appropriate. Intimacy does "unfold" in the field – but not because of the confiding of innermost, previously undisclosed secrets but because of how intimacies are produced in time and space in ethnographic research. The ethnographic situation itself, insists Lovell (2007: 58), not solely what is brought into the ethnographic encounter as a pre-existing personal experience, "produces the contours of what is 'personal'."

A notable example of this was my experience with Iris (mentioned in Chapter 3), an Italian woman who became a close friend, when we initially met at her small bungalow for an interview. It was a stormy evening. I had been concerned about getting back home to my daughter safely on my bike in the thunder and lightning, and Iris had been nervous about disclosing too much of her knowledge about the community to a stranger that she had taken an instant liking to. Those factors, combined with the dramatic elements of the darkness and torrential rain, created a heightened sense of camaraderie. Afterwards, Iris asked to withdraw her information, for it felt to her as though she had unwittingly crossed a boundary and told too much; more like "gossip," she said, than an interview where she would be more careful about she said. It was not that she had told me things she had not already told many of her friends. In fact, some of the stories were common knowledge (that I heard subsequently from other sources). While I complied as I would with any research informant, with Iris I felt doubly compelled for we had formed a friendship. It was not "revelations of secrets" I was after, I assured her. Yet I *was* interested in her telling me stories that were meaningful, truthful, and within the limits of what could be re-told. At a later time and place, where she felt less emotionally vulnerable than she had in our initial meeting, I re-interviewed her.

This story hints at the production of intimacy in fieldwork and the politics at play, where the power that the anthropologist holds vis-à-vis her informants presents dilemmas regarding what is said and, also, what is done with what is said. However, the power dynamics are rarely, if ever, only one-way. Chris had thus imbued much too much authority and capacity in the anthropologist, and his accusations were unfounded. After all, while anthropologists seek the truth about their informants' personal lives as a matter of disciplinary epistemology, the telling of intimate truths is contextual, dialogical, and political (Metcalf 2002). As Lovell suggests, not only is what "constitutes 'innermost' or the most private domain of existence" unclear, in that subjects' ideas of what counts as "private" may differ from those of the anthropologist, but, also, intimacy is always a matter of self-preservation in which people resist giving out personal information or they measure it out strategically. In other words, that our informants do reveal intimate details about their lives does not indicate a total lack of agency (Lovell 2007: 61). Metcalf puts this slightly differently: "There is nothing self-evident about why anyone would bother talking to the would-be ethnographer – assuming they do – except perhaps for polite platitudes.... they select what to tell and how to tell it" (2002: 1).

Chris was worried about what I would do with the information I collected through the methodology of immersion as a kind of "deep hanging out" we do within communities we study (Clifford 1997). He cared deeply about the privacy of community members, whose interactions with tourists had led their lives to become exposed, to some degree, by my research. He wondered, "What will you tell?" Other townspeople, too, asked me about the "secrets" that I might reveal in my book. What, then, about the traffic of ethnographically produced intimate knowledge?

My daughter came up with a useful appellation one evening near the end of a particularly intense period of fieldwork, when I was saying good-bye to a woman with whom a friendship had developed. We were both sad but trying to keep the mood light by joking back and forth about what category she now belonged in vis-à-vis me. Was she a "friend" or a .... How could I possibly refer to her as a "research subject" or, worse, "informant"? When Breck chimed in, "What about 'research buddy'?" we both laughed. When she drove out of the hotel parking lot with the fading light of dusk on her lime green scooter, from that moment on the moniker stuck and is now a shared joke between the three of us.

While methods textbooks offer sage advice about maintaining a careful distance from research subjects, in actuality these lines between our lives and theirs become blurred. I agree with those who believe that close relationships, including friendships, cannot only enhance research findings but also help discern how boundaries should be drawn over what is written about and what is not. Such intimacies helped me to comprehend the subjective elements of the time and spaces where women recreate and talk about men and their sex lives, which shaped the research outcomes (and how the analysis became focused on heterosexuality) – and also helped resolve dilemmas over representation. "Research buddy" aptly points to the tension between research and friendship, which is a productive tension ultimately because it brings the subjects acutely into the analysis in ways that a "stranger–subject" relationship might not, such that it was easier to decide what was written about. Such relations in the field also enabled me to get a glimpse of the ways foreign women were mired in gossip and also took part themselves in the machinations of rumor mills. I learnt how gossip, as an embodied practice, draws people closer and establishes intimacy, and was also a means of social control.

In spite of my friend's warnings to me that I "knew everything" (and therefore too much) about people's private lives, I came to know firsthand how impossible that was, even if it had been a professional goal, which it was not. People I came to know and who knew me, people I "brushed up" with as an anthropologist and as just another tourist dancing in the reggae bar at night or staying cool in the shade at Miss Lydia's Soda, managed their stories and identities as much as I did mine (Coffey 1999: 55). They "used" me when it suited them and participated in my research and fielded persistent questions when they wanted to, even if sometimes it was a matter of "friendship."

Nevertheless, remaining critical of methodologies that depend on the exploitative extraction of secrets and also on the potential capitalization of friendships to produce credible accounts is at the forefront of navigating research relationships in the field. For such relationships remain "real," and, as such, should not remain naturalized as a power-free zone (Whitaker 2011). Friendships, even those between women, which are often essentialized through gender discourses as idyllic and harmonious, are fraught with tensions, as Whitaker (2011) has pointed out. It is in recognizing this tension, encapsulated in the term "research buddy," that I see intimacy as part of the solution to dilemmas rather than merely a problem to be avoided, which is unrealistic in the best fieldwork.

"Doing intimacy" in transcultural touristic spaces and places

> It took a long time to realize I was operating from a different manual.
> (Interview with Illondra, February 2006)

> These foreign women, they come say to me, "These guys don't take me out."
> (Interview with Miss Helen, May 2010)

Complaints about local men who "don't take me out" suggest the ways in which tourist women encountered unfamiliar "ways of doing" intimacy (Berlant 2000). Experiences interpreted as intimate, in turn, shaped Euro-American women's "ways of doing" heterosexuality. As feminist and queer theories underscore, heterosexuality and intimacy are closely intertwined. In thinking of marriage as "society's container for intimacy," Kipnis (2000: 41) recognizes intimacy as an aspired achievement of marriage and therefore related to sexual identity. McGlotten, too, argues intimacy is a powerful "cultural metanarrative about heteronormativity" (2007: 125). As VanEvery (1996: 41) contends, a defining norm of heterosexuality is the sharing of living space by monogamous partners. Although in North America and elsewhere in the twenty-first century "dating" is a social practice that now extends into hook-up culture and cyber-mediated intimacies (Frohlick and Migliardi 2011; Kalish and Kimmel 2011), a normative trajectory of romance and courtship prior to a committed relationship nevertheless exists as a powerful credo.

Many foreign women arrived with romantic cultural notions about what they felt constituted "true intimacy," associated with the legitimized heterosexual domestic relations and social institution of "love marriages" (including common law marriages and "living together" arrangements). From a Western perspective, intimacy also requires the "healthy" sharing of and disclosure of innermost feelings (Illouz 2007), socialities that tourist women enjoyed with local men who had the time and interest to talk about their lives with foreigners. Such ideals, however, did not always align with the local social organization of intimate relations that were shaped as much as by cross-border movement and flux (the coming and going of tourists) as by co-present kin ties and conjugal bonds. During an interview when we were discussing her surprise and feelings of betrayal when she had found out each time that her boyfriends had all cheated on her, Illondra articulated this tension. She said, "It took me a long time to realize I was operating from a different manual." Domesticity did not equate to intimacy, as she understood emotional closeness to be bound up with heterosexual monogamy. Intimacy remained an attractive element of relations with local men, but its meanings and modes shifted.

Globalization gives rise to multiple, complex, transgressive, and transformative ways that intimate relations are "understood, formulated, or prohibited within and beyond local and global spaces" (Constable 2009: 58). Intimacies of many kinds are re-worked in the touristic borderzones within Puerto Viejo. Tourist women held strong desires to be close to people from the local community, living with them and becoming familiar with local ways of life. The chance to meet and get to know someone from another culture was exciting. Gender is central in touristic intimacy deriving from "unpredictable change encounters" related to "the exigencies of bodily needs and public sociality that international travel requires" (Harrison 2003: 53). Local men looked for foreign women to sleep with, literally and figuratively. Foreign women sharing living spaces with local men and, often, their family members too, experienced "instant intimacy."

Yet, "living together" in Puerto Viejo did not carry the same meanings as living with a partner in a common law or boyfriend–girlfriend arrangement of sexual exclusivity that many women associated with the practice of domestic intimacy and being a couple back in Canada, the United States, England, Italy, Austria, Germany, and other home countries. "Instant intimacy" was organized around time and pragmatics rather than romance, although many women spoke of how romantic their local boyfriends were. As Chelsea indicated, social life in the village entailed fluid sleeping arrangements based on who was "outside" (away from Puerto Viejo) and who happened to be around. Moreover, sometimes drugs and alcohol were part of men's daily existences and shared spaces with their foreign girlfriends, which women found challenging or in which they also partook. While I do not go into this issue in the book, the existence of "pharmaceutically [marijuana, crack cocaine, cocaine, and alcohol] mediated relationships" (Goodfellow and Mulla 2008: 267) was a common experience for the women I interviewed.

Spontaneity was a key lens through which newly arriving tourist women mediated their cross-border experiences. However, when they remained in Puerto Viejo beyond the bounded temporality of the holiday, the meanings of their sexual relations with local men changed. Unhappy with cultural norms of men's "hunting" for *extranjeras*, some women aimed to distance themselves from "fresh tourists." By steering clear of domesticity and *machismo* control of women, they negotiated some measure of sexual agency. When women grew aware of the sexual secrecy by which practices of multiple girlfriends was sustained, they turned to casual sex. Thus, intimacy was a cross-cultural set of ideas, desires, and practices that were simultaneously appealing and confounding to tourist women. Racial and economic underpinnings were central, and I turn to these in the next chapters.

5 Difference

I can see how a white person would come down and go, "Oh, a black guy. I met this black guy, you'll never believe it!"

(Interview with Annabella, April 2006)

Imagining the other

Annabella and I sat together one morning in a café along the southern beach road. A tall, athletic, fair-skinned young woman in her mid-twenties, Annabella was on a two-week holiday from Canada to visit a Canadian friend. A truck drove past us carrying a group of men, construction workers on their way to a job site, standing on the flatbed with their bare torsos exposed. Annabella gave a long look at the truckload of semi-naked men until they disappeared from view. She turned to me and grinned widely, exclaiming, "These guys are so hot!"

We enjoyed our breakfast of fresh fruit and granola while the tape recorder whirred, recording the interview. When I asked Annabella what it was that she found sexy about the local men, she replied:

I find myself to be a little bit shallow because the body does really matter to me. They are beautiful [with their] sun bleached hair and they are gorgeous. Oh god! I have been an athlete all my life and ... athleticism is hot. It is really attractive. I like sport.

She was especially attracted to the way that local men and older boys danced, how their bodies moved, and how they enjoying dancing amongst themselves. "They enjoy being together and actually dancing with each other like girls do in the States. It is so funny. I love it," she told me.

When I asked Annabella if she was attracted to tourist guys or any of the foreign residents, she was emphatic in her reply. Twirling a piece of papaya on her fork, she said:

> Tourists, no. If I wanted to be with a Canadian, I would [date them] in Canada. I like the exotic. It is like experiencing a bit of the culture [because] they can show you things. They can. They grew up here. They know the place really well.

I saw Annabella several times after our interview since her friends were women I spent time with too. She liked to stay out late at night dancing and hooking up with different local men. In our discussions of casual sex between foreign women and local men in the town, she had made her views clear. She was "boy crazy," as she put it, and she felt she could, as she put it, "do what I want." Figuring out which young man she would sleep with was itself a source of pleasure for Annabella.

One day my daughter and I ran into Annabella walking barefoot down the rough road, her rubber *Havaianas* sandals in hand and shielding her eyes from the sun, making her way slowly to her friend's house after a long night out.[1]

Cycling alongside her for a moment, I teased her: "Hey, chica, what are you doing up so early?"

"Oh, wow, Susan," she replied, her face broke into a big smile, "I had a great night... "

I could not help but recall what Annabella had said to me earlier in her interview. Still grinning after watching the truckload of men go by, she had effusively stated, "Walking around with all these beautiful men everywhere, I am, like, I want this one and this one!"

Many travelers search for "sex, bodily pleasures, intimacy or erotic excitement" as "acknowledged motivations" in their travels overseas to different and exotic countries, and not only those who seek paid sexual encounters (Frank 2007: 164). In this regard, travel is an important yet under-examined process in the formation of hetero-sexualities and straight culture (Waitt *et al.* 2008). Queer, gay, and lesbian tourism is a burgeoning area of scholarship that considers the expanding ways in which same-sex sexualities and identities are produced, and differentiated, through tourism (e.g. Cantú 2009; Howe 2001; Johnston 2005; Kantsa 2002; Murray 2007; Puar 2002a, b; Rushbrook 2002), but less has been said about how heterosexual subjectivities and desires are formulated through myriad processes of pleasure travel.

Yet, as Annabella's story clearly shows, a youth backpacking trip to Costa Rica "produced circuits and flows of power and desire through which new forms of otherness and exoticism arose" (Grewal and Kaplan 2001: 673; also see Alexander 1994). "I want this one and this one!" she exclaimed, referring to the "hot" bodies of local men who were, in her eyes, "gorgeous," "hard," and "beautiful." In her "boy crazy" antics she was unabashed in her expectations to have sex with whatever local guy caught her attention. Racial overtones are clear in her stories of travel sex, including stereotypes about "black guys" as naturally skilled dancers and athletes. The local men are objectified as hers for the picking as she and her friends go out on their nightly jaunts to the town's hot spots to seek out the sexiest local "hotties."

Women's notions of race and ethnicity shape expressions of heterosexual desire, a point raised in the last chapter. More than anything on her visit to Costa Rica, as a young, white Euro-American woman, Annabella wanted a "Caribbean experience." In previous chapters I have shown how sexual and emotional intimacy served as a "way in" to access local culture, as Annabella's narrative elucidates ("They can show you things," she explained). But heterosexuality entails more than intimacy, even though gendered norms of femininity closely link meanings of sex with emotional closeness and monogamy, as I explain in Chapter 4. On their travels, my interlocutors were looking for sexual pleasure as much as they were hoping for romance and a "relationship" marked by exclusivity. Women found that along with tasting Caribbean food, dancing to reggae music, and seeing and touching the exotic local flora and fauna, the idea of having a sexual liaison with a local man was an appealing cross-cultural experience.

"Travel sex" can be between tourists; for instance, amongst Northern university students on a "spring break" in Cancun (Maticka-Tyndale and Herold 1997), backpackers in Canada and Australia (Egan 2001; McNulty *et al.* 2010), youth at singles' "Club 18–30" resorts in the Mediterranean (Pritchard and Morgan 1996), and couples on honeymoons and sexual leisure vacations (Frank 2007). In Puerto Viejo, tourist women undoubtedly engaged in "travel sex" with other tourists – reputedly "rampant" amongst young backpackers and surfers, according to local gossip. For the women I interviewed, however, sex with tourist men was not of much interest (although perhaps initially when they first arrived in town, as Ember's story in Chapter 3 shows).

For most of my interlocutors, Puerto Viejo panned out to be a place where cross-border sex with local men was preferred over "endogamous" travel sex.[2] Many interviewees were quick to point out that they did not want to hook up with North American or European tourist or expatriate men. "I like black men," said Mariella, a Spanish woman who had a local boyfriend. Her declaration sums up a common demarcation of a "different" exoticized "black" masculinity vis-à-vis (white, brown, black) masculinities back home, an orientation shared by some but not all European and North American women. While I have indicated throughout the book that Afro-Caribbean-ness was seen as particularly sexually appealing to tourist women, this chapter focuses on the particularity of this "difference" and at the same time its fluidity. "Black," "Caribbean," "rasta," "creole," "mixed," "Costa Rican": Each of these terms was used by women to refer to men who captured their interest. I trace the mediating discourses and imagery through which these erotics were imagined and the boundaries that fueled the erotic charge between foreign women and the local men.

The man who lived in the tree

One late night under a sparkling sky, I stood with several women outside of a bar. Nestled amongst a strip of small shops and restaurants that ran along the front road facing the ocean, including an ice-cream shop run by an Amish woman and an American-owned free-trade coffee café, Mango Bar attracted a mix of locals, expatriates, and tourists. It was reggae night, and patrons were dancing on every available floor space and out onto the street. I had accepted a friend's offer to serve as a kind of local guide on a field trip to see and interpret the evening's action. Around two o'clock in the morning people spilled out from the cavernous club onto the pot-holed street parallel to a narrow strip of beach. Illondra and I joined several other foreign women on the beach, admiring the unusual pool-like surface of the ocean for that time of year and chatting for a bit before heading our separate ways home.

Standing just a few feet from us was a group of tourist women vying for the attention of a dark-skinned, bare-chested man. Wearing baggy surfing shorts that sat low on his waist, his long, black hair knotty and tangled, he was easy to distinguish, or so we presumed, as a "local." He walked towards a picnic table on the sand set up for restaurant patrons during the day, his balance off as he wobbled to sit. Three white women dressed in blue jeans and halter-tops snuggled close beside him on the narrow, rickety bench. Their arms encircling his shoulders, they smothered him with public displays of affection, while he silently worked at getting his cigarette lit. The smell of ganja soon filled the air, mixing with the earthy salty scent of wet sand after the downpour earlier in the evening.

An American woman named Maddy, a massage therapist at one of the local spas, stood beside me. Entertained by the performances taking place within an arm's reach, she blurted out to the group of us, "That is hilarious. Even 'the man who lives in a tree' scores with tourist women." Turning directly to me, Maddy added, "Put that in your book, Susan!"

Some of us had noticed his presence in the town over the past few weeks, because he had made his home in an old tree along the shoreline. At the opposite end of town to Bar Mango he was often perched in a smoothed-out rounded nook on the trunk of the tree. I passed by him on numerous occasions as he slept in the middle of the stifling hot day with a straw hat pulled over his face. I heard from others that he had drifted into the village from another part of Costa Rica without friends or relatives in the community. Rumors circulated that he sold "a bit of herb" and that he scored his meals from tourist women. Gossip spread about how on occasion a "fresh tourist girl" would take him back to her hotel room to spend the evening – perhaps one of the women we saw him with that particular reggae night.

"The man in the tree" shows how exotic difference was highly valued by European and North American tourist women, yet also how "difference," to some degree, was a matter of perspective. It also shows how "local" was a fluid category. While Maddy found a dark-skinned man, basically a vagabond, unappealing, other women found him exotic and considered him a "local."

Her stinging remark and our complicity with it thus shows how boundaries were created, how boundaries enflame a sense of taboo and erotics, and how women's sexuality is regulated through such boundary making. By leveling an accusation at "tourist women" for (stooping so low as to have) sexual relations with (by all appearances) a homeless black man, a particular category of Euro-American femininity is homogenized, stereotyped as "loose," indiscriminant, and "stupid," and rendered sexually deviant. While the exercising of sexual power over a vulnerable person vis-à-vis economic disparity is indefensible and not outside the practices of some Northern women in their sexual relations with local men (and an issue I return to), another issue here is the moralizing over Western women's sexual "codes of conduct."

When class and racial boundaries are transgressed, in other words when women do not organize their opposite-sex sexual desires and practices within the confines of endogamy (staying with the same class and racial group), social sanctions kick in. Maddy was correct in that within Puerto Viejo it seemed that it was easy for all men who fit a particular category of "local," no matter what their personalities or backgrounds were, and without much being known about them, to find sexual partners amongst the numbers of Northern tourist women coming into the town on a regular basis – an ease that other men did not experience, notably Euro-American men. The question this raises for me is how the contempt shown towards foreign tourist women who were seemingly indiscriminate in their choice of sexual partners fixes on sexual pathology, located in an individual's psychology and body, and brackets out the social processes by which "difference" is created and regulated.

To judge women's tastes in men or rate the men's caliber as sexual partners befitting foreign women serves to uphold normative prescriptions for female sexuality, that is, how women ought to behave, and also "normative expectations of 'white' culture" (Deliovsky 2010: 10); in other words, that the best sexual partners for white women are white men. Rather, I want to underscore the point that tourist women do place local men within racialized categories of desirability and "sexiness," as reggae night helped me to understand, and that these categories do not come out of thin air or out of individual women's physiological or hormonally induced impulses. Men's skin color, their hair, the clothes they wore, the language they spoke, and their physical mannerisms and ways of interacting with each other and with tourist women were the material-symbolic resources by which tourist women emplaced Latino, Afro-Caribbean, and men of mixed ethnicities in categories of "local" and "exotic," and therefore sexually desirable. While the category of "black Afro-Caribbean" masculinity was especially valued, in actuality women often found the categorization confusing – and how (on what basis) men were placed in the racial–ethnic category varied from woman to woman.

Women shared their confusion with me over how Costa Ricans, distinct from Afro-Caribbean-Costa Rican nationals, were considered "white" when, according to North American discourses of race, Latino people back home in the United States and Canada, for instance, were considered "black," "brown," or "of color." Indigeneity was also complicated, and not all that visible to most of the women I spoke with.[3] To further complicate the "colorism," a term Lancaster (1992: 216) uses to describe the way in which "people put color into discourse in a variety of ways," there were multiple names for "Atlantic coast natives of African heritage" residing in the area, some who were from the Atlantic regions of Nicaragua and Panama – "Afro-Costa Rican," "Afro-Caribbean," "Caribbean," "black," were used by English speakers more or less interchangeably, for instance (see also McIlwaine 1997).[4]

Bethany, a woman I introduce in Chapter 4, in describing her local boyfriend, articulated a sense of ambiguity over the racial–ethnic lexicon: "I don't know what to call him. He's 'black.' He's 'creole.' I know the blacks in this area are descendants from Jamaica, but there's been over the years mixing of cultures. He is a lighter skinned man." Blackness, linked to "Caribbean-ness," was visibly obvious to tourist women in ways that other racial and ethnic dimensions of masculinities were not; yet, as I show, was also fluid.

Crucially, it was not only foreign women but also other social actors within the town's diverse population who co-constructed cultural and racial difference that gave meaning to and shaped interracial erotic tension. In this chapter, I further develop my argument that European and North American women's erotic desires for local men were shaped by tourism as a quest for the exotic, to experience alterity, and "to have" particular experiences, notably to submit to the "naturalness" of Costa Rica. More specifically, I focus on how desires to have experiences in the "wild" and "primitive" spaces of the Atlantic region cleaved off by its "blackness" from the rest of Costa Rica and dominant white/*mestizo* society (McIlwaine 1997; Sharman 2001) shaped women's erotic practices. The production of interracial cross-border heterosexual desire can be situated within national discourses and global tourism media co-complicit in racializing and eroticizing black masculinities in Caribbean Costa Rica. I turn to these specific discourses after first establishing an example of what Taussig might call "the erotic fetish-power of borders" (1992: 150).

The "aura" of black

> There's all these strong, virile, attractive men that has [sic] *an aura* about them, and it makes them really attractive.
>
> (Interview with Alex, July 2005)

It was my friend, Alex, who first used the expression, "the aura of black men," to articulate the "erotic fetish-power" (Taussig 1992) of Caribbean alterity and masculinity in Puerto Viejo.

On the morning of my interview with her, I easily spotted Alex and her boyfriend. As I approached the tiny café on my bicycle, they were sitting side-by-side under the shade of a sprawling mango tree in the *soda* "Love and Peace." An attractive man in his mid-twenties, sporting short dreads, surf shorts and no shirt or shoes, Fernando smiled up at me from his plate of food. Alex pulled up a white plastic chair for me to join them. As Fernando finished his breakfast, a large plate of rice and beans and scrambled eggs, we made our way through a brief conversation peppered with laughter. In a mixture of my poor Spanish, his few words of English, and Alex's gracious attempts to translate for us, we managed to figure out the basics – where he was from, who his family members were, where I was from, why I was in Costa Rica, and whether I was married, single, or had a boyfriend.

He was eager to tell me things about his life. I learned that his father had grown up in Limón city, and his mother, a white *Tica*, was from Guanacaste. Fernando had several siblings. "Too many to count," he joked. His mother and two sisters shared a house in Puerto Viejo, all trying to support one another because his father had moved away with a new woman. With a receptive audience, Fernando entertained us with stories about his childhood, as the pampered little brother of older sisters. He played with girls' toys, because there were no other toys, he explained. One day when his mother went to work, she left the older siblings with a small amount of money to buy milk or other food for the day. The sisters sent young Fernando off to the store. When he returned, to their surprise, he had bought, not milk or rice, but 1,000 frozen *bollios* (ice milk in a little plastic bag)! Fernando grinned as he recalled putting all the *bollios* in a bucket to enjoy them one at a time throughout the day, popping them in his mouth while his big sisters glared at their sweet little brother with exasperation.

By the end of that story, Fernando's friends were waiting for him across the road by the bike repair shop. As they called to him, he politely excused himself, waving a friendly *adios* as he headed off.

Alex and I remained on the patio to conduct the interview, where she talked mostly about her relationship with Fernando, which had begun several months previously. At one point Alex referred to some of the "imbalances" in their relationship, meaning the discrepant levels of schooling, and differences in language and cultural backgrounds. I wanted to know if such imbalances were irreconcilable, such that they might eventually "push" her towards dating men from her own socio-economic group, that is, other tourist men.

But Alex refuted my speculation. First, it was the sheer number of local men that was a draw to foreign women, she explained. Second, because it was, in her view, local men with Jamaican and other Caribbean island ancestry who flirted with and approached tourist women, their bodies were genetically superior to all other men. In her words:

> I think the [tourist] women tend to stay more than the men do. If they're [the men] surfers, they come for the surf and they stay. I see a lot of guys come for several months every year but it's the women who tend to stay more. For various reasons …. You don't find hoards of local women going out and getting it on with the local guys. You do find hoards and hoards of local men going out to get it on with the tourist women. So that attracts women here.

> I've been with different color men. I don't say I only want to be with white men or I only want to be with black men. But I do like black men. If you look at them, physically, because of their heritage, the slaves coming over from Africa, most of them didn't make it. The ones who made it to Jamaica and those islands are super fit. So there are generations of that. Then the strongest and the fittest of them came here to work on the railway and the banana plantations. So these guys here are born with six-packs. They might lie in a hammock all day long, do no exercise and they're ripped.

> Physically, they have strong genes, and very nice physiques. I think that on a very base level, what attracts men to women has to do with the gene pool. You're attracted to someone on a very basic level; it's not something you're conscious of. So there's that. There are all these strong, virile, attractive men that has [sic] an aura about them, and it makes them really attractive. I think a lot of girls come for that. I think that there are a lot of attractive reasons to be here, much more for girls than for foreign boys.

"There is *an aura* about them," is what Alex said to explain Northern tourist women's erotic desires for Costa Rican Caribbean men. The meanings that are inscribed onto Fernando and other local Caribbean men by virtue of anatomy and genetic make-up construct difference in a particular way. In Alex's narrative there were many aspects of her boyfriend's personality, background, and lifestyle that Alex felt were attractive – he was a good brother and a loving son, he was funny, he was curious about other people and different cultures, and so forth. There were also many aspects that were culturally distinct, in her view, such as kinship, social organization, and religious beliefs. Foreign women were often fascinated with these differences. Yet the narrative most often utilized when tourist women talked about their attraction to local men was the fixation on their bodies, the surface inscriptions of muscles, hair, and skin color, and their inexplicably emotive and sexy "vibe."

How does exoticness come to hold particular meanings in local sites of global tourism? Racial and ethnic boundaries are inherently changeable, and also continually mobilized as "expressions of value" (Bhattacharyya 2009). Within Costa Rica, the borders around "whiteness" are regulated such that an us/them binary maintains distance between white *Ticos* and the rest of the nation. As Sandoval-García explains, "national belonging involves not only recognition of certain identities, but also misrecognition and nonrecognition of internal others, for instance, indigenous peoples, blacks and peasants" (2004: 3). Geographically and socially removed from the capital city, the site of modernity and "desired nationhood" (Sandoval-García 2004: 2), in the transnational Caribbean spaces of Puerto Viejo the markedly heterogeneous population is a virtual "minefield" of ethnic and racial fluidity (McIlwaine 1997: 37). Vandegrift points out how the shifting, multiple identity terms used by people living in Puerto Viejo contradict the state's division of the country into three tidy categories – "*negro*" (or "*afrocostarricense*"), "*indígena*," and "*ninguno*" ("non-ethnic") (2007: 1125). Moreover, in spite of the demographics in Puerto Viejo whereby less than one third of the residents in 2000 had identified as "*negro*," the "Puerto Viejo tourism Chamber of Commerce highlights the ethnic differences of Afro-Costa Ricans and the cultural uniqueness of the Southern Coast to draw tourists" (Vandegrift 2007: 126).

It is within this clash of plurality and hybridity, on the one hand, and singularity and purity, on the other hand, that the decidedly attractive "aura" of "black Caribbean" men was imagined. Representations of the southern Caribbean in local and global tourism discourses provide important clues as to how alterity in this region of Costa Rica is produced and thus, in turn, how cross-border erotics are mediated through such "borderland" representations.

The "wild side" of Costa Rica: zone of otherness

Tourist sights become only marks of alterity.

(Goss 1993: 686)

The tourist has long consumed the other in marginal districts and liminal spaces, visiting zones of deviance and excess to transgress social norms.

(Rushbrook 2002: 185)

[G]eographies of difference ... define the North as 'civilized' and the Caribbean as 'unreal'...

(Sheller 2004a: 35)

Undeniably, the southern Caribbean area of Costa Rica is marked by marginality and alterity in tourist discourses (Anderson 2004; Rivers-Moore 2007; Sharman 2001). The "remote"-ness (measured by distance from the Central Valley) of the Talamanca region and its locale as home to the country's most culturally distinct ethnic minority populations make it a "frontier" for touristic adventure and discovery:[5] For, according to the rhetorical prose of travel media, not only can indigenous peoples be "found" in the reserves in the mountains but "*los negroes*," the country's black Afro-Caribbean population, await to be "discovered" on the Atlantic coast – "out of the ordinary" and "a world away," states an advertisement for the area appearing in the "bible" of travel guidebooks, the *Lonely Planet*.[6] Another tourism website proclaims, "It is without a doubt an experience that you can't get anywhere else in the country."[7]

In contrast to the ways that sex tourism websites proliferate for the dissemination of information to men about everything from the costs to where to go to find commercial transnational sex in Costa Rica (Bishop and Robinson 2002), tourist women were not influenced in their travel trajectories by explicit advertising about the "traffic in men" (Ebron 1997). However, Northern women were manifestly influenced by local and global images of "Caribbean culture."

"The Caribbean" has long been a world tourism brand (Cartier 2005) and an idealized place for "natural hedonism" (Sheller 2004b). The "Caribbean" that exists in Costa Rica is a mere sliver, though, as it is geographically and ideologically located on the peripheral edges of the (proper) Caribbean region and thereby constitutes what Anderson refers to as "the outer limits of 'the Caribbean'" (2004: 25). This slice of "outer" Caribbean is demarcated from other tourist regions of Costa Rica as a "zone of otherness," a term I borrow from Rushbrook who uses it to articulate ethnically and racially segregated spaces produced and promoted for "whites' [tourists] consumption of the exotic" (2002: 187). More than a century of "spatial incarceration" (Appadurai 1988) and concomitant "Afro" and "Caribbean" identity formations of West Indian inhabitants has led to the racial enclave of the Limón province (Harpelle 2001). This enclave, in turn, has been further sliced up and offered as a niche-marketed commodity for tourism capitalism, as one local resident explained to me, by a government that previously disregarded the area "as a mosquito infested swamp." As Mr. Duncan put it, speaking ardently against the co-optation of the Caribbean for the use of the nation:

> Since the Costa Rican government now finds out that we are one of the most beautiful beaches in Costa Rica, okay, well, now "this belongs to Costa Rica." Suddenly they claim Limón and, you know, when we came here, it was too hot, too much mosquitoes, too much malaria, so only blacks could live in this place.

While nebulous, many images indelibly marked Puerto Viejo and the surrounding area as an "exotic world" in its distinct racialized, ethnicized "vibe." Crucially, however, tourists perceived Puerto Viejo as not only different (vis-à-vis the homogeneous white/*mestizo* culture of dominant Costa Rican society) because of its localized culture, a borderline brandished in national and local tourism imagery, but also because of its international flavor and cosmopolitan Caribbean culture. Heralded as a "multicultural" place, tourists felt that alterity – Otherness – could be brushed up against in many forms (Caribbean but also indigenous, Argentine, Chinese-Costa Rican, Panamanian, Italian, and many other nationalities and ethnicities). Because a boundary was constructed between the Caribbean region and the rest of the country, tourists interpreted travel to Puerto Viejo as an adventure-some boundary-crossing where the possibilities of cross-cultural interactions with exotically unique (yet cosmopolitan) English, patois, and Spanish speaking Afro-Caribbean men and women were embedded in a widely advertised "Caribbean experience."

In order to show how boundaries shaped tourist women's interracial erotic desires, I recount two scenarios where particular images suffuse the place and its people with marginality and exoticness. The first scenario demonstrates how notions of "wild" and "untamed" are deployed in tourist women's narratives, and the second scenario shows how a tourist postcard "sells" the beguiling faces and bodies of three Afro-Caribbean men.

End-of-the-world place: "the traveler's guide"

Hannah was a twenty-five-year-old backpacker from England. Bored with her restaurant job, on a whim she took off for Costa Rica. After two days in San José, she and her travel companion bolted from the hot, stifling city to explore more promising prospects of a Caribbean seaside holiday. Once they arrived in the beach hamlet of Puerto Viejo, they decided it was worth staying longer than a few days.

Hannah explained how her decision to stay in Puerto Viejo came about: "We were only going to stay here two weeks and we ended up staying the whole three months here [the duration of a tourist visa]. We had big plans to travel all around Central America, like Honduras and Belize and every-thing, and then we just came here and got stuck really."

"Wow," I responded, "How did you find out about Puerto Viejo?"

Hannah paused, thinking back and trying to remember.

"Umm," she ventured:

I think it's one of those places that kind of is on the traveler's guide. You know, you stay in the hostels and everyone talks about "Puerto Viejo." I was actually thinking about going to Limón and staying there but then everyone said, "No, that's such a big town and it's not as nice. If you carry on going you get down here and it's a lot nicer." And I guess it really is.

Continuing her explanation, Hannah said, "There was just a feeling about this place, you know? I suppose we got sucked in, you know. We could just stay and relax. It's just, the vibe here is just really, like, I don't know. It sucks you in."

Another woman in her mid-twenties, Ashley, was making her way back to Australia after working in Europe for several years. Her mother and sister met her en route in Costa Rica for a family vacation. Puerto Viejo was their first stop. After her mother and sister left, Ashley elected to stay for another two weeks, which was when I met her. We played with the resident puppy in the guesthouse where Ashley was working, while she talked to me about coming to Puerto Viejo. "I kind of read a little bit about it in the *Lonely Planet Guide*," she explained, "Then when we got to San José, we read in a book about a place people had gone and written stuff about it. So we decided to come here first."

I prodded her to tell me more about what impressions had influenced their decision to travel straight to Puerto Viejo, "What kinds of things were written about it that were really enticing for you?"

Ashley could not remember clearly but she offered, "Something about how beautiful the Caribbean coast was.... I wish I'd actually written it down because I can't actually remember why we had chosen it."

"But it grabbed your attention anyway?" I suggested.

"Yeah, it was a bit unusual, off the beaten track, I guess. We wanted to be someplace different."

"Someplace different." Tourist women's decisions to travel to the beach communities in the southern Caribbean were based on information gathered from travel media, including the canonical *Lonely Planet* guidebooks, and also from vague but remarkably powerful imagery about the "special vibe" of the place. The promise of an experience of "difference" served as a kind of "place seduction" (Cartier 2005).

In the "Where to Go" section in the 2001 *Rough Guide to Costa Rica*, the country is divided into seven distinct zones for touristic exploration and consumption.[8] In this ideological mapping of the country, Puerto Viejo is located in Zone 3, "Limón Province and the Caribbean Coast." A passage describing this zone reads:

> Limón province, on the Caribbean coast, is the polar opposite to traditional ladino Guanacaste, home to the descendants of the Afro-Caribbeans [sic] who came to Costa Rica at the end of the nineteenth century to work on the San José–Limón railway – their language (creole English), Protestantism and the West Indian traditions remain relatively intact to this day.
>
> (McNeil 2001: ix)

Further along in the guidebook, the author embellishes on this sense of remoteness, writing:

Hemmed in to the north by dense jungles and swampy waterways, to the west by the mighty Cordillera Central – an effective wall that it cost at least four thousand lives to break through during the building of the track for the Jungle Train – and to the south by the even wider girth of the Cordillera Talamanca, Limón can feel like a lost, end-of-the-world place.

(McNeil 2001: 155)

In this framing of the nation, while Guanacaste in the northwest is referred to as "the home of Costa Rican folklore" and "cowboy culture" and Monteverde, the cloud forest, is depicted as "the country's number one tourist attraction," the Atlantic region is presented as a "world apart" from the rest of the six apparently more homogeneously "non-ethnic" zones of the country.

Described as "polar opposite" to the rest of Costa Rica and situated at the "end-of-the-world," this imagery abounds on the Internet, billboards and signs throughout the town, and on posters that constitute a national tourism campaign. I describe in Chapter 1 the branding strategy implemented by the Costa Rican government in the 1990s, the "No Artificial Ingredients" logo, which weds images of purity, greenness, and nature with the nation. A series of advertisements isolates different "scales of experience" or "micro-sites" for the consumption of nature.[9] Couples, or families, appear in most of the images that serve to market these regionally "distinct" offerings of nature. Solitary white heterosexual couples are emplaced within green nature – standing on balconies amidst a canopy of green foliage, steering kayaks along a green-blue river, and plunging into a cascading waterfall. In each of these scenarios, romantic love, associated with monogamous, endogamous, mono-racial heteronormative desire, is emphasized.

But a poster for the Southern Caribbean area (see Figure 5.1) offers something different – a dreadlocked black man dances on the beach, his head down, presumably in rapture, in the company of an equally enraptured white tourist woman, while her white tourist husband looks on from the distance. Invoked here is the iconic Caribbean, where "Edenic" encounters with sexually excessive "sinful" natives are "coded into the representation of Caribbean landscapes and the tourist pleasures to be found there" (Sheller 2004a: 19). In Anderson's analysis of the recent marketing of the "Caribbean" in Costa Rica, she calls attention to the role of Afro-Caribbean men, and more specifically, "the Rasta," in the production of Caribbean-ness. Anderson contends, "the racialized sexuality of the 'Rasta' body is the most central aspect of the 'Caribbean' ... 'a cultural marker,' the grand signifier of 'the host culture'" (2004: 35).

But Anderson's analysis focuses on Cahuita, a community twenty kilometers further north and said to have a "completely different reputation" than Puerto Viejo. (Recall in Chapter 3 how Gretta had avoided Cahuita in the 1990s and traveled further down the road instead to Puerto Viejo.) Even within the "micro-site" of the Southern Caribbean region, therefore, ever more zones of difference are created. Not only different from all other tourist regions in Costa Rica, the southernmost Caribbean beach-and-surfing utopias and cosmopolitan villages close to the Panama border were a distinct borderland at the crossroads of international,

Figure 5.1 A poster from the "No Artificial Ingredients" campaign for the Southern Caribbean region features the figure of a rasta man and a white Euro-American woman as key elements in a transnationalized "Caribbean" landscape.

Caribbean, indigenous, Panamanian, *mestizo*, and Costa Rican cultures. In the minds of many backpacking, yoga-loving, long-haul female ecotourists, Cahuita was ruled out because of what one woman referred to as "the 'dirty rastas' who hang about the streets."

"Puerto Viejo," on the other hand, was invoked as a cosmopolitanized place – its reputation promised a safe, or at least safer, adventure than, for instance, the notoriously "dangerous" "black city," as Puerto Limón is known (Sharman 2001). While Puerto Viejo remained characterized by urbanites in San José as a treacherous backwater destination (I was often warned by rental car agents against traveling there alone or with my young daughter), within backpacker hostels and *Lonely Planet* guidebooks its reputation was positive, although tinged with peril, which gave it its "edge." Its history as a surfing Mecca for Western surfers and its recent surfing tourism cottage industry and culture lent it a globalizing feel (Maksymowicz 2010), as did the dozens of foreign-owned businesses that offered yoga, meditation, and massage therapy to foreigners.

Yet while "rastas" had in many ways gone "out of style" by the time I conducted my fieldwork, the image of smiling, hospitable, and sexy Afro-Caribbean men, transformed from rastas and "beach boys" to "jungle boys," "street boys," and surfers, nevertheless continued to signify, in diverse ways, "the Caribbean experience," as the poster (Figure 5.1) and the postcard/business card (Figure 5.2) described below suggest.

Rastas on the beach: a postcard/business card

One day my sister and I hiked a long trail that parallels the ocean for several kilometers. We were caught in a torrential downpour along the way; our feet were sore and blistered and our clothes drenched by the time we emerged at the end of the trail, where we spotted an inviting poolside café. Striking up a conversation, the Italian owner asked us the usual questions about how we liked Costa Rica and what kinds of tourist activities we were interested in. At the same time that he was checking us out, we were assessing his leather shoes, his gold chain, and the "pin-up girl" and World Cup soccer (*fútbol*) posters tacked on the café walls. When I told him I was an anthropologist conducting a study on sex tourism in Costa Rica, he gave me a bemused look.

"You want to study sex tourism?" he sneered, "Maybe you want to come here, I think, *for* sex tourism."

Without waiting for my response, he went on to say, "Let me tell you about 'the boys' here."

With that, he pulled a postcard out of a stack from behind the bar and held it out for us (see Figure 5.2). The image featured a photograph of three bare-chested rasta men sitting in a line on a driftwood log on a white sandy beach. The man in front is holding a green coconut, placing it close to his crotch as if to offer a comparison to his anatomy. All three are smiling, looking straight into the camera with friendly faces. The dark-skinned men's decidedly "Caribbean" identities are effectively established through a visual framing of brightly colored drawings of bamboo, a hibiscus flower, a butterfly, and a monkey that form the edges of the postcard.

We stood in disbelief while the Italian bar owner proceeded to name each of the men, presumably for our benefit. When I asked him if I could buy the postcard from him, he happily launched into a lengthy story about women

Figure 5.2 Postcard, widely available in local souvenir shops, that was sold to the author in 2004 by an expatriate bar owner.

who come to Puerto Viejo to be "pleasured" by local black men. "Even my [own] sister!" he exclaimed, and then informed us how she had been "converted" after her first encounter with a local Afro-Caribbean "stud." In an avuncular gesture, he boasted about the reputation of the local men for their sexual prowess and their "willingness to please" foreign women for "nothing" in exchange "but a good time." Unless, he cautioned, "the women are bad lovers and then maybe they should pay the men something for their time."

I dutifully wrote the men's names on the back of the postcard and in doing so transformed the tourist postcard into a business card. As an anthropologist, the postcard and the men's actual names were useful information and a form of empirical evidence of "women's sex tourism." For the Italian expatriate, it seems he was providing two middle-aged Canadian women with both the imaginative resources to fantasize about black hypersexuality as a distinct cultural feature of the area (a local commodity) and the material resources we needed (names and phone numbers) to pursue a "Caribbean experience" readily available, only a phone call away!

These scenarios suggest the delineating processes wherein the Caribbean region is represented as a space not only geographically segregated from the urban metropolis and central regions of Costa Rica but "a world apart" in terms of its ethnicity and, by extension, sexual culture. Rushbrook describes how "zones of otherness" are produced by cities and other tourist destinations emphasizing their ethnic diversity in order to "stake a claim in cosmopolitanism ... a desirable form of contemporary cultural capital" (2002: 183). The Caribbean experience set up by these images is similarly invested in cosmopolitanism as a kind of "attraction for and identification with otherness" or what Nava (2007: 8) has referred to as "visceral cosmopolitanism," where intimacy with locals is at least the promise. The Caribbean dancing man on the beach in the national tourism board poster is a prime example of this. I extend the idea here to how "Costa Rica" is a place imagined by tourist women as a space for the spontaneous discovery of "pure," "green" nature and safe adventure.

How do tourism media affect gender and sexual subjectivities? As Goss (1993: 663) argues, "Destination marketing is ... simultaneously implicated in the construction of place making and the constitution of subjects who experience that image in specific ways." While there is no singular way in which tourism advertisements and guidebooks are interpreted, images are intended to trigger "the social insecurity or ambition of readers" so that they connect with the place and activities depicted in the media (Goss 1993: 669). Desmarais (2007: 215) argues that domestic advertising too, such as television ads in hotel rooms and posters on hostel walls, "plays a key role as an agent of cultural pedagogy in the process of acculturation tourists go through when visiting a country." In other words, powerful images that align with people's values and desires serve as imaginative resources from which people fashion identities, experiences, and travel trajectories. As I show, women talked about their sexual experiences in such a way that Costa Rica as "pure" "nature" was incorporated into tourists' imaginations of a place where they can emplace their bodies and enact heterosexual desires and sexualities (Frohlick and Johnston 2011: 1103). More specifically, Caribbean tropes that dovetailed with women's aspirations for the bodily and for cosmopolitan and anti-materialist travel experiences were deployed in their interpretations and articulations of their cross-cultural sexual experiences as "different."

"He was the rainforest"

A volunteer tourist working on a farm located in the coastal rainforest, Rayne hooked up with a Caribbean man in his early twenties who had been pursuing her for a few weeks. Not attracted to the "street boys" or "surfing boys" in town or the indigenous men who lived in inland communities in the hills, Rayne was deeply attracted to this particular local man (whom, she found out later, was born and grew up outside of the area) because he was, in her words, a "jungle guy."

When she described her sexual experiences, her words reflected her own identification as an environmentalist and nature enthusiast. She articulates the tropical rainforest as a meaningful eroticized space, cordoned off from all other spaces. In her words:

> For my body, there is something about Sebastian's spirit that is the tropical rainforest for me. There's something about any person living anywhere that

is close to the earth that takes on characteristics of their environment, takes on actual personality of the environment. The humid, lush, tropical rainforest has to be the most sexual place on earth.

As someone who aspired to life "off the grid," Rayne found the dark-skinned young Afro-Caribbean man to be irresistible because he embodied the mythical and material space of "the jungle," the local term for the coastal forest. Her interview narrative is peppered with ecological words and phrases like "lush rainforest," "his energy was grounded," and "something deeply spiritual [about him]." Her sexual experiences with Sebastian are expressed as "intense," "the sharing of souls," "my body reacting to his presence," and "pure pleasure."

Rayne was Sebastian's girlfriend for several months. In time, the complexities of his personality and background (he had been raised in a poor household by an alcoholic father and abusive step-mother) became evident to Rayne. While it became apparent to her that he grew up in a tough inner city (and not the jungle) and that the independence he had shown at first was contradicted by what Rayne called the "dog pack mentality" he displayed with his city friends, she nevertheless continued to associate him with the tropical rainforest. In Rayne's eyes, it was when he was "on his turf," that is, living and working in the jungle, that she had fallen for him, a space where she had formulated her identity as much as Sebastian's and where her aspiration for a particular experience had been played out. Their relationship shifted from an idyllic love affair in the forest to a transnational interracial romance that could not endure the challenges of long-distance separation when she returned to the United States to work, his infidelity with other foreign women, her distrust of him around her money and things, and his lifestyle of partying and alcohol when he was not working as a guide in the jungle. Their break-up was bitter (they are the couple depicted in the Introduction, fighting on the beach) and involved violence on both sides. But yet Rayne's bittersweet memories of her attraction to Sebastian were redolent of the sights, sounds, and senses of the space in which they first met.

"Jungle sex"

Thirty years old and from a metropolitan Canadian city, Carolyn traveled to Costa Rica to work for a few months as a yoga teacher at a resort. Single for several months, after a rough break-up from a long-term relationship, she had hoped to hook up with someone while away from home. In Carolyn's words, she was looking for "any kind of contact." She ventured into the town by herself on her evenings off to dance at one of the reggae bars, and one night she met a local man she described as a "really beautiful rasta, just really pretty." She accepted his invitation to leave the disco with him, "throwing caution to the wind," as she put it. He took her to a small apartment on the second floor of a cement house in the back streets of the village, where she stayed with him for two nights and days, which she described as occupied with sex and "only stopping to eat and sleep."

After that liaison, on another night out dancing she met another "pretty rasta" she described as a "really cute kid," and, again, she went home with him. In the morning when they were talking about siblings and family, she found out, to her surprise, that he was much younger than the twenty-something she had assumed. Just nineteen years old, his age had made Carolyn feel uncomfortable but she "had no regrets about the sex." For Carolyn these encounters were memorable and enjoyable sexual experiences. She told me:

> They are really amazing in bed. Not in a giving way at all. Not like they're going to perform oral sex for an hour to you. No. They're in really good shape most of them. A lot of them surf so they're strong through the middle. Powerful, passionate, crazy sex. Crazy wild jungle sex.

I prodded Carolyn to explain, "What about the idea of this 'jungle sex'? How different are they as lovers, from Canadian guys?"
  She explained:

> A lot of women don't like to admit it, but I think they like to be manhandled, not have to be in charge, not have to initiate things. It's macho …. The two that I had sex with, they're just powerful. More animalistic. None of this, "Are you okay?" None of them are ever going to give you a massage. None of them are going to give you oral sex. It's just powerful.

Carolyn's story illuminates how she interpreted a number of events and acts as sexual taboos – going home to a complete stranger's house, not letting anyone know where she was, hook-up sex with a stranger, sex with a teenage boy, sex with black men. Prior to her encounter with the "pretty rasta," she explained, she "had never been with a black man before." Her confessional tone insinuated that what she had done was beyond the propriety of Western femininity and norms of gender equality. By engaging in what she articulated as "jungle sex" she had both crossed a border (of what was proper for a Euro-Canadian heterosexual woman) and was complicit in the production of a border (black male bodies as hypersexual and primitive).

"Totally roots"

It was not only the men's bodies that were viewed as erotic vis-à-vis other categories of men (*Ticos*, immigrants, Canadian tourists) but other dimensions of the encounters were also part of the eroticism. Linda was a young backpacker in her early twenties from the northwestern United States. A returnee tourist, she had first traveled to the area on a humanitarian tour several years earlier. Becoming aware of the public street culture of the towns' players, the surfing boys and boys in the discos on her first trip, she returned in hopes of meeting some of these guys. Linda connected easily with a town youth, a young Afro-Caribbean man who wore short dreads, sold ganja, and went by a number of different names, all elements of the usual "street boy" performance. They hooked up at a club and started sleeping together shortly afterwards.

A particularly memorable experience for Linda illustrates how the transcultural encounter was infused with tactile and sensual components that constituted a quintessentially Caribbean experience and therefore one marked by a highly valued difference.

Her boyfriend had invited her to his home, a wood-framed shack with Bob Marley and Marcus Garvey wall hangings on the outside, a brightly painted lime-green front door, and weathered stairs and shutters. He cooked her a local specialty called "rondon," which she was impressed by for not only did he make it himself but it was also a family recipe. After dinner, she had to dash outside in the pouring rain for lack of an indoor toilet. The following morning, they were lying together in his bed when she heard chickens and roosters crowing right near her head, inside the room. This particular aural sensory experience strongly resonated for Linda because, in her words, "It was 'totally roots.'" For Linda, this was a moment where she fulfilled her desire to "experience the culture, and get as close to the insider [experience] as possible" (her words).[10]

The house, the sounds of roosters, the excitement of having to dash outside in the rain at night, the noises of the family right next door, her boyfriend's natty dreads, the fish soup he cooked over a one burner stove, and the posters on his walls, in other words, the multi-sensual spaces of exotica, were all vital and heady components in the overall "place seduction" (Cartier 2005). Linda's quintessential moment, when she heard the rooster crowing from inside the house, was an accomplishment of several converging touristic desires. As a budget long-haul traveler, an ecotourist, a cultural tourist, she had been looking for an intimate connection with a local, a non-monetary slice of everyday life in the local community, to witness and participate in alterity, and "to have" a "roots" experience. Her sexual pleasure derived not simply from the dark-skinned virile body of a local black young man but the physical-sensual space in which their bodies interacted was integral. The dwelling space with its chickens and tin roof, along with the sounds of children playing in the yard, were iconic "Caribbean roots" to her, and she was pleased to have been able to cross a number of boundaries (racial, cultural, sexual) to acquire that experience.

Border mobilizations

> Well, you know you are in a low pool when you start having sex with a tourist.
> (Interview with Annabella, April 2006)

One day as I walked out of the yoga studio towards my bike, the yoga instructor and I carried on the usual kind of exchange between two foreigners who meet in Puerto Viejo.

> "Are you here for a vacation?" he asked me.
>
> When I replied that I was a cultural anthropologist researching sexuality and tourism, he nodded his head in recognition.
>
> "Right, I heard that someone was doing a study on *that*. I'd really like to speak with you sometime about your research" he continued, finishing his sentence with a not-so-surprising zinger, "because I find it very odd, kind of sick, to see these women so interested in these men."[11]

Tourist women actively participate in the construction of borders in their sexual practices, through the naturalization of black men and their bodies as sexually skilled and as belonging to atavistic spaces of the jungle and simple dwellings, for instance, and also of white men as belonging to the "lowest pool" of desirable sexual partners. Other tourists and residents in the community construct borders as well. On countless occasions during my fieldwork, expatriate and tourist men offered commentary like that uttered by an American yoga instructor about how troubling they found it to see Western women "so interested in these men."

Such comments reflect what is seen in the community as widespread and objectionable sexual boundary crossing between foreign women and local men, as Maddy also picked up on with her quip about the man who lives in the tree. My American friend, Brandon, was a business owner who provided work for local men but also competed with them for tourist girlfriends. Like many foreign residents, he kept tabs on relations between tourist women and local men. It was Brandon who described to me what he referred to as a "totem pole" of hierarchical masculinities, wherein groups of men were ranked according to their success in sleeping with tourist women: Black Afro-Caribbean men were on the top rung because they were the most exotic to tourist women and therefore were "pretty much always" successful, followed by lighter-skinned but still exotic Latino Costa Rican men because they were sometimes successful, and then, third, tourist men, who might be lucky on occasion. Last, local indigenous men were placed on the very bottom rung because, as Brandon explained, they very rarely "score" with tourist women. This "totem pole" reproduces a range of ethnic and racial stereotypes about the supposedly innate sexualities of men and women. White Costa Rican men are the "hot, Latin lovers." Afro-Caribbean men are the ultimate in "big black dick." Indigenous men are feminized and "carry a low erotic charge" (Wade 2009: 185). White Western women are sexual liberated. Black, brown, and indigenous women are bracketed out of the picture entirely in a schematic where white femininity is the most prized.

Such stereotypes extend to the entire Latin American and Caribbean region (Brennan 2004a, b; Cabezas 2009; Kempadoo 2004; Wade 2009). Like all stereotypes about naturalized sexual proclivities, they rely on essentialized notions of race, ethnicity, and the body, that is, the notion about inherent fundamental differences between people traced to biological attributes such as skin color and anatomy (Nagel 2003; Wade 2009). Sexuality, bound up with gender, is closely connected to race and ethnicity where "difference" is located in the body, for race and sexuality are constituted one through the other (Butler 1993: 167). Nagel (2003) puts these ideas this way: despite the diversities in sexual practices and ways of being sexual that exist across human cultures, "particular bodies (male, female, black, brown, white) are sexualized in essentialized ways such that socially approved kinds of desires (for approved numbers and types of partners) and appropriate sorts of sexual activities (at appointed times and places)" are coded according to gender, race, and ethnic categories.

In Western discourses, "the naturalness of black and brown bodies has been equated with animality, in particular with animal-like sexuality" (Mascia-Lees 2010: 210) or what is referred to in anthropology as "primitive sexuality," an evolutionist notion linking blackness ("race") with primitivity and sexual alterity or "otherness" (Lyons and Lyons 2011: 30). As postcolonial scholars underscore (e.g. Brennan 2004a; Cabezas 2009; Kempadoo 2004; Piscitelli 2001; Wade 2009), it is such racialized stereotypes of exotic Others and of beauty and eroticism, and the attendant hierarchies of sex and race (which vary across cultures and regions), that serve to erotically charge and sustain the political economy of race and sex in Latin America played out in sexual tourism and cross-border intimacies.

Foreign men and others who participate in the judging and categorizing of sexual actors in the town in terms of racial stereotypes and a hierarchy of desirable masculinities are complicit in the reproduction of such erotically charged stereotypes. In conceptualizing these tiered layers of racialized men who are ranked for their presumed sexual attributes according to the erotic proclivities of white Northern women, the boundaries of white heteronormativity, that is, the boundaries between appropriate kinds of desires and categories of sexual partners (Nagel 2003), are mobilized. Foreign men projected their own meanings of interethnic desire onto the experiences of women, claiming time and time again that it is black men's well-endowed penises that turn on white Euro-American women most of all. A German expat and owner of a local tour business, married to a *Tica*, told me, "They're all crazy for any 'black dick.' They can't get enough." Lumping together all Northern women as "they," as well as reducing local dark-skinned men to body parts, the German man's lurid comment was not atypical of numerous similar observations about the erotic subjectivities of tourist women in relation to the men they chose to have sex with. In this casting of sexual actors, foreign women's sexual agency is objectionable, if not despicable, when they choose Afro-Caribbean men as their erotic partners, and foreign men are seen to suffer at the hands of biology and genetics, which does not bode well, they believe, for their white heterosexual bodies. Primitive hypersexuality wins out, is this story.

As Maksymowicz has shown in his study of foreign men's homosocial relations with local men in Puerto Viejo, "Western tourist men described feelings of confusion, sometimes anger, for embodying masculinities that they perceived as being more 'proper' with regards to their interpretations of hegemonic masculinity that did not align with the town's alleged sexual hierarchies of desirability"

(2010: 62). Tourist men spent considerable time compartmentalizing men into categories of "good" versus "bad" masculinities, where "good" masculinities were associated with Westernized traits such as "a strong work ethic, honest labour that did not involve stealing or hustling, monogamy, having a 'healthy' sexual appetite (in opposition to a hypersexual one), and not engaging in domestic violence" (Maksymowicz 2010: 65).

This compartmentalizing of masculinities according to erotic desires of heterosexual white women is emblematic of what Nagel (2003) calls "ethnosexual frontier crossing." Ethnosexual frontiers, as "sites where ethnicity is sexualized, and sexuality is racialized, ethnicized, and nationalized ... constitute symbolic and physical sensual spaces where sexual imaginings and sexual contact occur between members of different racial, ethnic, and national groups" (Nagel 2003: 11). In this regard, as a global "fiesta tourism" place-for-play with a history of inter-ethnic mixing, Puerto Viejo is made and re-made as a space for sexual contact across ethnic borders. Such spaces imagined as frontiers or "borderlands" offer up new sexual possibilities, whether transgressive in their rule breaking or a means to exert newfound power and domination (Donnan and Magowan 2010). But yet for borderland sex to play out, I argue, the borders are vital.

When race and ethnicity are fluid, as they are in Puerto Viejo, the mobilization of borders and the upholding of the values supposedly contained within those borders are essential. As Donnan and Magowan explain, it is in looking at "the everyday relations of these racial, national, and ethnic boundaries" that we can begin "to understand how sexual relationships are negotiated and regulated in a zone that is perhaps more often analyzed in terms of ... sex as colorful or spicy anecdote" (2010: 115). In other words, it is the assumption that sexual contact between those "who undertake expeditions across ethnic divides for recreational, casual or 'exotic' sexual encounters" (Nagel 2003: 14) is necessarily "colorful" or "spicy" that requires critical reflection – as much as the borderland sex. My point is this: Erotic desire based on racial difference is generated in part by the borders that are placed around people and cultural categories. The state of otherness is not "an essence" contained within particular sexualized bodies, as socio-biological explanations of race and sexuality would have it, nor is the supposedly physiological "black dick" lust that continuously scandalized tourist women contained within the women themselves (as a deviant expression of "natural" desire).

Taussig's notion of alterity is helpful (1992: 129): Not "a thing in itself," alterity is a powerful, visceral sense of difference that is transmitted or "emitted" through social relations. In this sense, the "aura" of black Afro-Caribbean men was derived from a "hierarchy of alterities" in which, as Taussig explains, "some alters [Others] exert positive, and others negative, charges" (1992: 144). In other words, the boundaries that created different masculinities, wherein men were placed into a virtual marketplace of black, white, and brown masculinities, and the policing of boundaries, where Northern tourist women were stigmatized for their "crossing" over to Afro-black men or *Ticos* as sexual partners at the expense of Northern men, were generative forces underpinning inter-ethnic desire between the notorious pairings of white Northern women and the iconic Afro-Caribbean "rasta" or "beach boy."

"I want this one and this one!" Difference and desire

> Degrading the virtue of women who cross the color line is a widely reported feature of the ethnosexual frontier ...
>
> (Donnan and Magowan 2010: 123)

Unlike foreign women interested only in dark-skinned men fitting a particular "Afro-Caribbean" look, a fixation that Illondra regarded suspiciously, she dated men from various cultural backgrounds. She told me about the time she dated a white American tourist and how townspeople looked at her strangely because she had already been categorized.

"As soon as you date one of the black guys in this town then you are considered 'one of these girls who only dates black men'," Illondra explained, "I didn't know that there was such a classification until then! I have never even had a boyfriend with dreads but I've had a lot of people, *Ticos*, tell me that, 'Oh, you like dreadlock boys.'"

But, in her words, "I like everyone. I've had San José *Tico* lovers. Whoever is interesting, I just follow the vibe wherever it takes me."

The trope of "difference" held significant meaning in Northern women's travel sex experiences. The Caribbean region of Costa Rica was a place where possibilities for erotic pleasurable encounters with "the Other" were coded onto the physical and social landscape, and where, in the eyes of locals and foreigners alike, tourist women were seen to "go wild for black dick." With its roots in Western capitalism, orientalism, and colonialism, tourism has historically been a quest to see, know, and imagine the "exotic Other." All kinds of touristic quests, including adventure tourism, ecotourism, and sexual tourism, are "tours of desire," and as such, "they tell us more about our society than about the society to be visited" (Bruner 1989: 440).

It is also the case, however, that "tours of desire" tell us about specific locales, which are discursively represented and are also tactile and sensual embodied places. My point is that tourist women's erotic subjectivities, including the choices of their sexual partners, are formed within particular contexts of "the exotic." As I explain in Chapter 2, desires are played out "in entire surroundings" (Lambevski 2005: 584). In different regions of Costa Rica, different masculinities appeal to tourist women, relating to the racial identities of local populations and also to social histories of tourist–local relations and local sexual cultures. In the rural town of Monteverde, Northern women tourists are attracted to the light-skinned "white" *Ticos* who are the ecotourism tour guides and men who like to dance salsa and *cumbia* in the bars at night (Romero-Daza and Freidus 2008: 178; also Puccia 2009).

Postcards, guidebooks, and posters framed the southern Caribbean region as the *most* remote and *most* culturally distinct of the otherwise seemingly homogeneous white society, where tourist experiences were valued according to scales of nature and wildness. Stereotypes flourished. Boundaries were mobilized between "good" and "bad" men for women to pick and choose from, between those with "vibe" and those who lacked, as Alex put it, "the aura." "Black" and "Caribbean" were central markers of difference that were generated by the tourism industry and wider discourses, which, in turn, generated a heady sense of exciting and adventurous erotics to women's pleasure travel experiences. Words and images that closely aligned with these markers of exotic difference were echoed in the women's narratives about their sexual experiences. Notions of a "Caribbean" masculinity shaped tourist women's sexual preferences for one category of sexual partner over others. Carolyn, Rayne, and Linda's narratives suggest how women interpreted their sexual experiences in terms of "jungle sex," "roots experience," and "tropical rainforest."

But not all women could be considered "Rastaphiles" by any means, as Illondra's comment above illustrates. Men were "rasta" but they were also "jungle guys," and "Caribbean men" with "vibe." Those who surfed and danced were particularly sexy – and many women avoided the rasta-type all together. Various women had different aesthetic preferences and "tastes" in men – and perceptions of blackness and Caribbean identity varied in women's stories of transnational sex. While the aura of Caribbean black men was an absolutely compelling draw, what constituted desirability in terms of skin color, hair, clothing, and other bodily inscriptions was fluid and differed across women. "Race" was a confusing terrain. The attraction of "difference" often had more to do with the worldliness sought by Euro-American women as part of a cosmopolitan Caribbean culture linked to global forms of music, food, and masculinities (see Figure 5.3). A surfing aesthetic was increasingly displacing an earlier rasta aesthetic.

I want to underscore that the "Caribbean experience" was not for every tourist woman. A New Zealand backpacker, Brittany, thought the men were "gross." Ashley, from Australia (mentioned earlier in this chapter), thought that the way that local Caribbean men kissed was completely off putting. She did not like the feel of their hair or the way that they dressed. While she thought that the physical environment of the coastal rainforest ("the jungle") was romantic, she was turned off by the pick-up lines used by the local men who worked at the farm where she was part of a volunteer tourism group. Both women explained how they could not understand why so many foreign women were attracted to the local guys because in their own view the men were "creepy" and "weird." They did not see the "aura" or feel the "vibe" that other tourist women talked about; rather, they saw the shortcomings in local men ("who could not even finish a sentence") vis-à-vis the Australian and New Zealand men they preferred by far.

This very brief glimpse into ways that some tourist women were ambivalent about the "aura" that other tourist women were so taken by points back to the issue about how other people reacted to tourist women's so-called sexual "appetites" for Afro-Caribbean men. Why was it that the sexual preferences of tourist women were so often regarded as one narrow stereotype? Illondra draws this out – "Oh, you like dreadlocked boy!" she is told even when she had dated men of a variety of racial identities.

Figure 5.3 A business in town owned by a foreign woman is evidence of the kind of cosmopolitan Caribbean culture expats and tourists are both attracted to and also actively produce. Photo by author.

In her study in Cuba of intimate relations between tourists and sex workers, Cabezas notes, "The transcultural liaisons that have attracted the most attention in sex tourism research are those that are marked by the most visible differences, people who are noticeably of different racial–ethnic backgrounds, age, class, cultural capital, and nationality" (2009: 167). The problem with a rigid focus on cross-racial sex for Cabezas is that it "assumes the exchange of sex for money is the most important and demarcating aspect of the relationship (2009: 167). It also has to do with the way that sex is involved rather than other forms of sociability or intimacy between tourists and locals. While I return to the money factor in the next chapter, here I stress the point that women's erotic desires are open to surveillance due to gendering processes bound up with race and sexuality. The image of white Western women "in the clutches of grossly stereotyped imagined ethnic others" has long functioned, as Donnan and Magowan cogently state, "more as cautionary tales about the perils of crossing ethnosexual lines than as a license and invitation to those who might be tempted to transgress in this way" (2010: 116).

Sexual intimacy across ethnic and racial boundaries, whether at home or away, is often looked at, by scholars and non-scholars alike, as "a potentially disruptive and perilous act that can endanger the structure and stability of society, unsettling the relations of power and subverting established moral codes" (Donnan and Magowan 2010: 131). In the United States, Canada, and the United Kingdom white women and black men involved in relationships continue to be victimized (Deliovsky 2006, 2010; di Leonardo 1997; Frankenberg 1993; Nava 2007). When, through travel mobilities, women cross national as well as race, class, and ethnic boundaries, their sexual behavior is especially suspect, often regarded with putative salaciousness. I have tried to show instead how the ethnic and racial differences that shaped my interlocutors' sexual encounters arose from complex social relations and boundary making. "Crossing forbidden frontiers is never just about a challenge to the social order, even if this is the interpretation that many academic analyses have a tendency to promote" argue Donnan and Magowan (2010: 131) but also about, for instance, "the quest for pleasure, relationship, and identity" (Ho and Tsang 2000: 317). Women's ethnosexual adventures were only one piece of a wider quest for "a Caribbean" experience, heterogeneous experiences made meaningful through tourism discourses bound up with racializing processes.

Women's attraction to Caribbean men (a fluid category) aligned with wider touristic quests for the exotic and with the particular representations of the southern Caribbean in terms of alterity and marginality. For this region of Costa Rica is a highly ambivalent space in the eyes of the nation. Momsen notes how the institutionalized racism in Costa Rica contributes to the role the government plays in discouraging tourists to visit the Caribbean coast, "spreading the word, erroneously, that it is an area of high crime" (2005: 211). Therefore, travel to Puerto Viejo is already set up as a "transgression" before tourists arrive. Furthermore, local processes, including a sexual pattern of "inter-ethnic mixing" in practice for decades (Madrigal 2006), served to create possibilities to experience difference intimately by crossing boundaries, which were crossable yet also carried gendered social stigma, into the coveted terrain of "Caribbean" masculinities. The man referred to as "the man who slept in the tree" was heralded for "scoring" tourist women, while the tourist women were denigrated for sleeping with a man who was seen as essentially "homeless." The desire for alterity in many forms, including the tropical "jungle" and "Caribbean" food offered up in the marketing of a Caribbean adventure, rooted in educational and national backgrounds where international travel is promoted as a cosmopolitan activity (Kaplan 2001), structured tourist women's erotic desires for particular local men over others.

That women hoped to find sexual pleasure in their quest for a Caribbean experience hints at the economic underpinnings of their relationships and encounters in Puerto Viejo. The so-called "taste for the Other" (hooks 1992) shows how tourism shapes women's sexual and erotic subjectivities. Being a white *extranjera*, an identity that was stereotyped by local men and held a particular currency in the local community, meant that sexual opportunities, while plentiful, entailed a negotiation. It was the "exchange" dimension of transnational sexual relations that was most troubling for tourist women, whose identities were associated with budget alternative travel and anti-materialism, the focus of the next chapter.

6 Erotics

I don't like to be a "sugar mama."

(Interview with Rayne, August 2007)

We don't make a lot of money. It's a whole thing that these foreign women need to learn about locals.

(Interview with Jackson, local resident, February 2006)

The (hidden) price of hedonism

In 2005, during the rainy season in January when tourists were starting to get antsy and not sure how to spend their time, my American friend and budding tour company entrepreneur, Brandon, circulated a pamphlet all around the town. The small handbill listed "10 Fun Things to Do on Rainy Days in Puerto Viejo." Listed as number one was: "Make Love! After all the Caribbean is very romantic, right? Don't let it go to waste. And what better time?"[1]

As I explain in Chapter 2, media affects the tourist imagination; that is, the imagining of the possibilities for a particular tourist experience, be it embodied immersion in "pure nature" (evoked by the "No Artificial Ingredients" branding logo) or the coveted spontaneity of a last-minute adventure to the "far reaches" of the "unknown" Costa Rican Caribbean as described in travel guidebooks. The Caribbean has long been imagined as the quintessentially romantic landscape, but more than romantic it has been constructed as a locale for hedonistic tourist practices, including "sensuous abandon and bodily pleasures," excessive eating and alcohol consumption, and taboo erotics with "'dark' Others" (Sheller 2004b: 31; also Kempadoo 2004). As Sheller (2004b: 24) has aptly pointed out, these historical imaginings of risk and desire, with which Caribbean islands have been so indelibly depicted in colonial representations, are "deeply implicated" in contemporary touristic hedonism, including sex tourism. The invitation in the tourism leaflet summoning tourists, always on the lookout for pleasure, to "Make Love!" thus both draws from past imperialist discourses and participates in new ways in "naturalizing hedonism" associated with Caribbean tourism destinations (Sheller 2004a, b), even those pushing the Caribbean's furthest geographical boundaries like Atlantic Costa Rica (Anderson 2004).

This is an important point because it should be no surprise that female tourists, like male tourists, might hope to participate in this well-established and highly celebrated touristic hedonism. Yet gender thoroughly mediates tourists' forays into "borderland erotics" (Ortner 1996) such as those that are played out between foreign women and local men in the spaces of pleasure seeking in Puerto Viejo. As Ortner suggests, "encounters and transactions in the borderlands [are] always gendered and eroticized, both in practice and in the imagination ... parties meet as gendered beings with gendered fantasies, anxieties, and desires (1996: 182). The role of money within these tempestuous practices remains cloudy, however. Culture, gender, and economics all intersect in how erotics are played out in transnational spaces and the sexual relations that unfold within these spaces, the topic I now turn to in this last chapter.

The powerful notion of the Caribbean as a site for bodily and sensuous pleasures, conveyed *ad nauseam* in a multitude of tourism media, undoubtedly gave meaning to Euro-North American female tourists' travel experiences in Puerto Viejo, as I have explained throughout the book. As I demonstrated in the last chapter, they actively participated in the exoticization and hyper-sexualization of dark-skinned and "Afro-Caribbean"-looking men, influenced by locally and globally trafficked iconographic images. Yet, in contrast to rumors that spread like wild fire around town, besmirching white women (*extranjeras*) and accusing them of "paying for sex" with local men, in my fieldwork I did not come across a single woman who boasted about, confessed to, or recounted to me that they had spent money for sexual services. While within local gossip circles fingers were pointed at certain foreign women believed to be exploiting, and exploited by, local men working as gigolos, in my conversations and interviews with tourist women they expressed ambivalence and confusion around the role of money in their transnational sexual relations. What became clear to me is that while tourist women did not partake in outright commercial sex they nevertheless did engage in pecuniary transactions with their Costa Rican boyfriends and hook-up partners that they had not anticipated. From the perspective of many women, as I learned in interviews and by hanging out with the women, a most troubling – and unexpected – aspect to their sexual relations with local men was the monetary dimension.

Erotics were heavily infused in tourist women's ways of talking about Puerto Viejo and also the activities they took part in. Many times women said to me, "this town is all about sex, sex, sex." Some of the erotics of sensual and tactile space that affected Euro-American women's sexual subjectivities were described in the last chapter. Rayne was turned on by the jungle and its sounds, and by the sultry humidity of the southern Atlantic tropical climate. For Linda, the rustic dwelling with chickens and wooden floorboards that epitomized a "roots" experience contributed to feelings of sexual excitement with her Caribbean lover. Along with the jungle and intimate spaces of people's homes, the beach and also the open-air nightclubs or reggae bars were central spaces to some of the most meaningful sensual and erotic experiences for tourist women, and I explore this here. I focus on how women came across and dealt with monetary requests and expectations from local men that came as surprises to the women and that changed the meanings of borderland erotics from no-strings-attached encounters to exchange relations.

How did the material underpinnings of cross-border encounters with local men shape Euro- American women's experiences of the erotic? What did material–erotic exchanges consist of and what did they feel like for the women involved in them? These are the main questions that I address in this chapter. As much as camouflaging the market is part of a global touristic fantasy and the historical naturalization of hedonism in the Caribbean, women came across realities of a local erotic economy in which they were complexly situated. Tourism spaces and borderland erotics, I argue, thus shed light more broadly on women's heterosexual subjectivities as ongoing processes of negotiation between meanings of erotics and the economic contexts in which sexual pleasure is played out, a key debate in feminist scholarship.

I begin by briefly sketching out the local context in which tourist women grappled with money as a complex social relation in their travel practices, before introducing Lucy and her experience with Thomas after an erotically charged night of dancing.

Tourism and money

> Money renders places placeless. It mitigates against the formation of rewarding relationships with those living and working in tourism destinations.
>
> (Desforges 2001: 362)

I return briefly to the tourism leaflet from my friend's local tour business. As well as illustrating the centrality of eroticism to how the area was imagined in foreigners' representations, it also reveals some important elements of how Northern tourist women were drawn to and encountered the economic structures of tourism in the southern Caribbean towns of Costa Rica. One central factor was the entrepreneurial nature of much of the tourist-based businesses, which were mostly small-scale and independently owned. Many but not all were owned and operated by foreign residents, like Brandon.[2] This meant that a mix of locals and foreigners defined and co-constructed the vibe of the place through the types of businesses they offered and also how they marketed them.[3] Another factor that the small handbill signals is the budget (and mid-range) economic scale of the tourism in the area as far as the types of accommodations, food establishments, and organized tourist activities that are available.[4] When I was doing fieldwork there was not a lot for tourists to buy except what could be found in the handful of souvenir shops, one surf shop, and an internationally known boutique art gallery, plus the numerous crafts and Marley paraphernalia from market stalls scattered along the town's main road and several gravel side streets.

As I showed in the last chapter, Euro-American tourist women were attracted to Puerto Viejo as a destination regarded as completely different from the rest of Costa Rica. This cultural difference extended to economic contours as well. Contrary to the political–economic and development aims of the government,

"Caribbean" trope in Costa Rica is not associated with high-end Caribbean resorts or all-inclusive mega-resorts typical of many Caribbean islands, such as Jamaica and the Bahamas, but rather with small-scale tourism development that promoted local culture.[5] The women I interviewed and spent time with were predominantly budget travelers and what I call "anti-materialist" tourists.

Drawn to the Atlantic with the promises of small-scale tourism development that contrasted with the Pacific coast towns where Americanized condominiums, time-share vacations, and other upscale holiday packages could be found, their budgetary practices were organized around what I categorize loosely as minimal spending – an exigency of long-haul backpacker travel for some women, for instance, but also, more importantly, a desired ethos. They liked the fact that the place consisted of independent businesses, vendors selling their own wares on the street, and a hodge-podge of commerce – from the "patty man" riding his bike through town selling Jamaican patties, to the old *Tico* selling fruit at the far end of town, the effervescent Afro-Costa Rican women offering her barbequed chicken outside the disco late at night, and young boys randomly selling *pipas* (green coconuts).

Minimal spending was conferred with a kind of social status; more specifically, "green" consumerism that aligned with ecotourism discourses (Butcher 2003) and "ethical" consumerism that aligned with cultural and immersion-type tourism quests were held in high regard. Patronizing a certain establishment, one that conveyed a transnationalized Caribbean look or, on the other hand, one that was cosmopolitan, like the popular "world cafés" and Italian and Tex Mex eateries, were various ways in which spending money was not simply an instrumental act but also the enactment of social relations and identities (Desforges 2001). In this sense, they were tourists who were drawn to the area because of possibilities they foresaw in realizing aspirations for "living off the grid," "simple living," (catchphrases used by the women) and non-materialism.

While money more generally was not a topic that I probed too deeply in my interviews, I nevertheless found a common attitude prevalent among many of my interlocutors, as well as among other tourist women I spoke with as I sipped my icy *batido* or chai latte in one of the several cafés in town frequented by tourists and foreign residents (and seldom local people). In his research with independent long-haul European travelers in Peru, Desforges (2001: 258) observed a similar attitude wherein particular experiences were valued by the fact that they involved paying little money – such as taking an extraordinarily inexpensive local train or paying a local discounted price for food or lodging. Desforges' (2001: 358) argument that such "consumption knowledges" align with the wider tourism notion that authenticity of a place and people is "imagined as lying outside the wider circulation of money" fits, too, with the spending practices of Euro-North American women tourists in Puerto Viejo, many whom were backpackers and independent travelers, as I have previously noted.

Basically, money was seen as the "antithesis to authenticity," as Desforges argues (2001: 358), but, I add, tourist women felt that it was not a facile matter of spending no money, which was impossible and undesirable, even. Rather, the

Figure 6.1 An establishment in town offering a "global" "Caribbean vibe" in its food and décor is a popular spot with many of the women tourists I interviewed. In this photo, local men congregate around the barbeque grill that cooks the Jamaican jerk-style meat. Photo by author.

issue was how they spent their money. Particular expenditures, in other words, facilitated a sense of authenticity and, specific to Puerto Viejo, of getting in with "the vibe." Anderson (2004) has pointed out the irony in which Caribbean restaurants that are advertised with global names rather than those with local names are the ones frequented by tourists, which holds partially true for what I observed (Figures 5.3 and 6.1). An additional irony was that while locally owned rice-and-bean *sodas* were undoubtedly cheap and authentic and held a certain cachet, at the same time free trade coffee and organic food, more likely to be found at foreign-owned establishments, were central to my interlocutors' search for meaningful experiences "outside of the circulation of money" (even though money, specifically, cash, was involved).

Monetary transactions thus played a complicated role in their connections with local people because, while bracketed out of women's imaginations of the place, at the same time they had to constantly assess the meanings and effects of money, since tourism is a form of consumption. Paying a young boy to crack open a coconut might be seen as an appropriate ethical expenditure whereas doling out spare change to those who panhandled outside of the *pulperia* may or may not be.

Like the travelers in Peru described by Desforges (2001), Euro-North American female tourists in Puerto Viejo were uncertain about what their spending practices meant to local people, such as tour guides, in as far as how they were being perceived and situated. Such constant judgments and concerns about the meanings and politics of money suggest the way in which monetary negotiations took place, irrespective of women's desires to keep the "business" of tourism (paying for food, hotels, souvenirs) separate from non-monetary-based authentic experiences including encounters and emotional connections with local people.

As the story of Lucy illustrates, it was difficult for many Northern women to maintain a divide between their erotic life and the so-called "impersonal laws of the market" (Paz 1993: 147).

Lucy

It was at Reggae Beats where Lucy, a Canadian woman in her thirties, met Thomas, a local Afro-Caribbean man in his early forties. She had not expected to go out dancing that night but had befriended some foreign women earlier in the day while eating her lunch of veggie tacos at an open-air café in town. They were friendly and encouraged her to come along with them for reggae night. Traveling on her own through Costa Rica for the summer holiday, Lucy was a schoolteacher back in Canada. Single and an avid outdoor-adventure enthusiast, she had been drawn to Costa Rica for the adventure sports' possibilities. The southern Caribbean region was at the top of her list of places to travel within the country because she wanted to learn to surf and also spend her days walking the long stretches of sandy beaches. When she arrived she had been pleasantly surprised to see all the signs for yoga classes, meditation, and massage therapy – and decided to stay longer in order to partake in these offerings before she had to return to her teaching job back home in rural western Canada.

She had not anticipated becoming involved with a local man. If any romance was to happen, she had figured it would have been with another tourist. Meeting Thomas had caught her off guard and, as she explained to me while she and I were taking a long beach walk at sunrise one morning in July, happened entirely due to what she called "fluky circumstances." When I asked her what she meant by the circumstances, she told me the story of their chance encounter on a rare occasion when she had left her hotel cabina to go out in the evening.

When she arrived at the club, she immediately felt the "vibe" of the place. Candles were lit all along the front of the club, near the beach, casting a magical glimmer to the dark night air. People of all backgrounds were milling around with drinks in their hands on the outdoor patio, while inside bodies were moving on the dance floor to the melodic sounds of reggae music from the DJ box. Local men and older teen boys, dressed in baggy surf shorts and flip flops or bare feet, danced on their own along the edge of the dance floor, their eyes closed as their hips swayed; they seemed completely focused on the music. Lucy hung out with her new acquaintances – an American woman in her twenties who worked at a local restaurant and an Italian woman in town to visit a local boyfriend for a few weeks – and enjoyed the attention the three of them received from the hoards of men crowding around the bar and the dance floor.

She felt really good about herself. Her face and limbs were tanned from a full week of surfing. The short skirt she was wearing, which she had bought at a local shop in town, had a European look to it that she thought made her look cool, and the tank top was sporty yet sexy. Not one to drink very much, she accepted a *mojito* rum drink from one of the girls, and soon felt a warm glow induced by the alcohol and the stimulation from the frenetic but "chill" atmosphere of bodies, chatter, music, and lights around her. When the girls got up to dance, Lucy joined them, at first somewhat reluctantly, self-conscious of her slightly stilted dance moves, but soon she danced without a care in the world, feeling the beats of the music and the energy of the crowd.

In her description of the evening all of its components had affected Lucy's sense of adventure and romance, and had served as a kind of staging ground for what she understood as a romantic transcultural encounter that was a "fluke." At one point she had felt overwhelmed by the throbbing mass of people dancing so closely together and people's bodies rubbing and grinding, so had stepped outside to feel the fresher air. It was when she decided to brave it to go inside again to the sweaty packed dance floor that she spotted Thomas, a handsome tall black man with long dreads, and they had made a connection. She had been struck by his beautiful smile and the way that he had instantly noticed her. As Lucy put it, "Before I knew what was happening I was dancing to some old-style roots reggae music at two in the morning."

She had gone back to his house after the club closed. In her mind it had been a fun and spontaneous casual encounter. Caught up in the moment, she had been excited by the evening's sounds, sights, and the kinetic feeling from dancing close to strangers' bodies. Having sex with a man she had just met was entangled with those erotic and sensuous surroundings and social interactions. So, when only a few minutes after they had finished their love-making in the wee hours Thomas had asked her outright, although in a joking manner, whether she could buy him some soccer gear when she went back to Canada, she was completely taken aback. In her mind, his request to her, especially because of the timing of the request just a few hours after they had met, transformed what she understood as a mutual attraction to one another – which was circumstantial and influenced by the alcohol consumption and stimulation from the evening's heady atmosphere – from a non-monetary social relation to a "fungible" one (Illouz 2007).

Lucy had felt annoyed and confused with the unexpected twist in her holiday fling. As she recounted over several interviews, despite her uncertainty with the pecuniary aspects, she had become more deeply involved with Thomas than she had possibly anticipated at first and she eventually spent a considerable amount of money buying gifts for him and also paying for his food.[6] Over a course of several months, though, she no longer wished to be involved in constant negotiations over cash and items of clothing and electronics, which he at first requested and then began to demand. It was then that she ended the transnational romance that had begun, as many do, in the erotically charged spaces of the discos and bars, imagined as locales for local/global sexual culture and chance encounters.

Time and locale in cross-border erotics

Lucy's story elucidates especially clearly how cross-border encounters were tinged with economic dimensions that caught Northern tourist women unaware. It also shows how her Caribbean holiday experience extended to a lengthier transnational relationship, with attendant sets of expectations from both parties that she had not anticipated. Why did Thomas expect Lucy to give him things? Was it a requirement of being his girlfriend or was it because she was a middle-class Canadian that he felt he could take advantage of her? If she gave him what he seemingly needed and could not afford to purchase himself, she might be helping him out materially but what would these gifts mean symbolically? Also, was it not possible that they could continue a sexual relationship without any financial strings? These were the questions she grappled with, since in relationships and casual sex encounters back home in Canada, money did not normally encroach on the sanctity of erotic life.

Before I address these struggles over the meaning of money that Lucy and other women experienced, I elaborate on two important elements related to how transnational relations transpired in Puerto Viejo – time and locale. These contextual elements provide clues as to how women interpreted the monetary underpinnings of the sexual frisson they felt towards local men.

The length of time that a foreign woman remained in the area or how frequently she returned had a bearing on whether money came into the picture. This is complicated, however, since both short-stay and extended-stay/returnee tourists experienced monetary entanglements with local men of some nature or another.[7] However, amongst the women I knew it was mostly the ones residing temporarily beyond a week or so or, like Lucy, those returning after a romance with a local man sprung up, who were more deeply implicated in the material–erotic exchanges. Recall Zoë (in Chapter 2) and how it was only after she decided to remain behind after her sister returned to the States after their two-week holiday that she began to cover some of Marco's expenses when he spent time with her. Micaela (Chapter 4) was not asked for small loans from Antonio until she became a tourist returnee, returning every few months to Costa Rica when her work schedule allowed. Ember (Chapter 3) felt like she was a continual fund of resources – cigarettes, cash, and beer – immediately after her decision to find work in the local tourism industry. Women I interviewed who were in the community only briefly did not seem to have been exposed to the same appeals – although some were, as Lucy's story illustrates. Certainly it is possible that they had simply not wished to share this information with me, since the social stigma surrounding "payment for sex," as I explain, was palpable in the town's rumor mills.

Another important element of women's subjective experiences of the unexpected negotiations was locale. The nightclubs, specifically the open-air reggae bars or "discos" as women also referred to them, were by far the most frequently cited places where cross-border romances and liaisons began. Repeatedly I heard about chance meetings with local men, exuding an appealing vibe, a wide smile, or a hot way of dancing that took place in one of a smattering of discos; locations that constantly changed as far as being the most popular. Before its demise, Bambu was "the" place for the best nights of fun, exceptionally good music for dancing and a good vibe, and the site of numerous transnational relationships that I have discussed in the book.[8] Yet other places filled in the gap soon afterward (although there was much contestation in town over how well), the main point being that these dance places, noted for their reggae tunes and transnational DJs like the white Rasta from Switzerland and, importantly, the local men who frequented them, were seen by tourist women as culturally distinct and as quintessentially "local" places.

Locale is significant because, as Flowers *et al.* (2000) have pointed out, certain erotic and sexual spaces shape the sexual behaviors that unfold within them, although, I add, the meanings ascribed will not necessarily be shared. While in relatively homogeneous sexual cultures, such as the male gay bars in Glasgow that Flowers *et al.* (2000: 79) studied, it may be the case that "sexual repertoires are shaped by the specifics of certain locations which embody shared expectations of the likelihood and feasibility of certain sexual acts," in the multicultural demographics of a transnational tourist town in Caribbean Costa Rica the likelihood of shared expectations was reduced. For tourist women, the open-air discos were erotically charged places, seemingly intended for what Andrews *et al.* call "the sociable eroticism of the everyday," and as such they were places beyond the reaches of organized tours and the profit-oriented erotics of all-inclusive resorts and were therefore erotic spaces for tourists effectively outside of the market (2007: 248). Other locales where women met the men were the beach and also on tourist activities such as jungle hikes, where men were the guides. These locales, in turn, as I will show, held different meanings for the men with regards to money and borderland erotics.

The intersection of time and locale, then, formed a particular context of sexual excitement and also expectation of what might happen. Spaces such as the discos, and also the beaches and jungles, were imagined through the metanarrative of spontaneity and in women's minds were not associated with sexual commerce but rather with socially sanctioned recreational sex and sexual and romantic spontaneity. A British woman's recollection of how she fornicated in public with a local guy she met in the disco on her first night in town believing that this was "how they did things in Puerto Viejo," and then later, horrified in retrospect with her behavior and naivety, realizing that she had fallen into the trap of acting like a "slutty tourist," illustrates this point. Therefore, I argue, the clubs (and other locales) were spaces in which a complex sexual culture had emerged over the years since the first tourists arrived and more rapidly due to globalization in the 1990s – and foreign women were squarely situated as important social actors in a heterosexuality-based inter-ethnic economic system wherein erotics and money were closely intermingled.

Euro-American women were regarded by local men as "hot for sex" and even as sex addicts, as well as "soft," meaning overly sympathetic and gullible (in contrast to the "toughness" of local women). As my friend, Jackson, explained to me, white foreign women were not nearly as passionate in bed as Latino and Afro-Caribbean women (in fact, he said, they would often "go cold" fairly quickly) but they were the most sexually available women, according to local men's experiences. Often blithely unaware of, or unconcerned about, such stereotyping, tourist women thus interpolated themselves into a local sexual economy characterized by local men's "hunting" practices and hopes of finding generous foreign women to support them. Cross-border erotics were produced within these volatile conditions of economic disparity between two groups of people who exoticized one another and respective poverty or wealth. Power imbalance, as Bhattacharyya puts it, undoubtedly "heightens the sexual hit" (2002: 102). Local men I spoke with acutely recognized this dynamic. I recounted in the Introduction a friend admonishing me for not understanding what he thought was so simple, a reversal of normative heterosexual gender scripts, "Men want money, and women want sex, love and *'una experiencia'*." Racial, national, cultural stereotypes abounded in these locales where foreign women and local men encountered one another, with the role of money a silent specter at first but, as women stayed on or returned for a second or third visit, increasingly audible and impossible to ignore.

In short, for various reasons, which I have touched on, women did not expect "to pay" for their sexual experiences. I now turn to the stigmatizing discourses about gender, sex, and money in which tourist women were mired, before describing "the local system," as explained to me by two male interlocutors, Filipo and Danny.

Women pay, women don't pay: rumors and social stigma

May 2009   Fieldnotes Alex and I had a conversation about this recently. So many different allegations seemed to circulate about women who forked out $200 a night to sleep with a local guy, women who paid for this tract of land, for this vehicle, for this piece of electronic gear, for the bright shiny purple soccer shorts worn by the guy who had only ever been seen in tattered shorts before he got a German girlfriend.

A local man, one of the vendors who sold fruit at the corner, told me once that "land and a house" is "the dream of every man who fucks a foreign woman."

"So what's the scoop, Alex, do you know any women who are paying directly for sex? Or for that matter, men who ask for cash up front?" I asked her, yesterday when we were swimming at Playa Chiquita on her day off from work.

She shook her head, she didn't know. But then she ventured a guess, "I think if there are, it's older women, maybe, or women who aren't very attractive. That's what I've heard. But I've never spoken with anyone who actually has." She told me that she'd ask Simón [her *Tico* boyfriend].

Simón didn't have any concrete information for us either. He told Alex that he didn't think any men in Puerto Viejo had to ask for money: Women just gave the money to them on their own accord. Like guilt money? I wondered.

Today I spoke with Iris about this.

"No, it's not about guilt," she suggested, "but about trying to keep the men with them. It's money to keep men from having another woman. To keep the men around."

Then when I spoke with Zelda, she added another layer to the complicated mess. She said something like, "The foreign women have ruined the local men, teaching them that they don't have to work for anything, that the world owes them a living."

I was curious about cash, whether they gave them cash.

Zelda was adamant: "Of course they give them cash! They give them what they ask for," she had replied before heading off to prune the beautiful bougainvillea in her garden out front of the guesthouse.

February 28, 2006   Interview with Illondra

ILLONDRA: I've been thinking of American sex tourists, friends of mine who come here and [think] "I'm going to get that guy." They're not "little stay-at-home-girls" in the States. They go out and get sex in the States too. I wouldn't say that I'm sluttier than I am there; it's just easier here.

SF: I hear about women who come here and pay for a guy for a week, but I haven't come across them. No one has introduced me to one …

ILLONDRA: Since I've got here people had made fun of the "rent-a-rasta" thing but I've never come across someone who has rented a person. And even then, I have guy friends here who live really, really low [cheaply] and when their girlfriend comes [from abroad] he lives with her and she rents a nice little house. I guess it is about that but she's not coming here to rent a person. I know these girlfriends. She has her boyfriend here and she pays for things when she's here, not while she's gone.

While Afro-Caribbean and *Tica* women were widely accepted as economic providers within local social organization, a diverse combination of female-headed households, nuclear families, extended families, and common-law unions, the role of foreign women in local intimate economies remained a constant source of gossip and speculation.[9] Two of the most popular topics in town were real estate and the scandalous behavior of foreign women, and each of these revolved, in turn, around money. But in getting to know townspeople, I learnt about how different Italian, French, Swiss, Austrian, German, American, and Canadian women held laudable roles as breadwinners in transnational families that had developed out of cross-border encounters, and roles as financiers too, in the lives of some young local men.

While one "type" of tourist girl was denigrated by Afro-Caribbean natives, the "type" of women who contributed to local men's futures, by getting them jobs in France, or helping them get a small business started locally, for instance, were regarded with respect. A long-time resident and local politician, Mr. Duncan, put it this way:

> These foreign ladies, they give them opportunities in other countries, they are willing to spend money and help them. Not only buy things, no! Not only take them to eat, no! Because most of these girls don't come and treat you like an animal, they treat you like people.

Mr. Duncan's view of foreign women stands in contrast, then, to the claim made by the Limónese taxi driver, Mateo, that the majority of solo female travelers are looking for sex-for-cash. Crucially, social stigma accrued to this latter category, and not so much to the former, although, in the eyes of townspeople, the line between "helping" and "ruining" was often very blurry.

Whether foreign women were regarded as "providers" or as "slutty sex tourists," the practice of intermingling economics with cross-border erotics, especially if cold cash was involved, remained obfuscated by rumor and malicious gossip. One reason for secrecy was related to local gender discourses of *machismo* that dictated "real" men want women for sex not money. A conversation with Mateo helped me to see this.

Explaining the norms to me, he insisted, "Latin men wouldn't feel like men if they took money from women, and wouldn't let them buy them drinks [either]. "However," he continued, "if women insist on acting like men, well, then maybe, some rastas might take their money."

When I asked Mateo what he meant by "women acting like men," he replied, "Some foreign women are like men, American women especially, because they are so independent."

Therefore, while it is not solely black Afro-Caribbean men who "sponge" (Brennan 2004b) nor solely white Euro-American foreign women who "give men whatever they want," each of these groups have gained reputations as key actors in transforming erotic frisson into something of potential value.[10]

I want to underscore the very important difference in the way in which stories about women "paying for sex" are circulated as a gendered discourse that contrasts with the open bravado wherein, according to Rivers-Moore (2009), *gringo* sex tourists in San José brag about paying, or how little they paid, for sex with Costa Rican female prostitutes. On the "supply side," men who "sell sex" seemingly compromise the naturalized eroticism of masculinity (and thus mute their sexual labor). Note how Mateo's comment upheld a hierarchy of masculinities so that Latino men were seen as more powerful than "rastas" who, in his eyes, were less manly and thus ranked down a notch or two, because they seemingly had no qualms about "accepting" money from women for sex. Note, too, that in these discourses men never ask for money; money is a gendered currency, where women "give" and men "accept."

On the "demand side," on the other hand, male sex tourists bolster their heteronormative masculinity through male bonding and outspoken bravado about the purchasing of sex. Payment for sex is something men discuss publicly (Rivers-Moore 2009; 2011). Referred to by Gregory as "a homoerotic economy of desire," heterosexual men's sex tourism is as much about relations between men as about sex acts with subordinated women (Gregory 2007) – and therefore having an audience to boast to is part of borderland erotics for men.

In contrast, as my interlocutors confirmed, the act of women paying for sex or erotics is highly stigmatized and regarded as a moral transgression by women themselves, such that shame and concealment rather than forthrightness enveloped the topic.[11] Within the town, they were called names that coded white feminine sexuality in terms of deviancy – sluts, whores, *putas*, fresh meat, "loose" *gringas*, to name a few. Tourist women, the rumor mills went, did not just "give it away," calling up alleged promiscuity, but, worse, they "paid" for "it." As I will explain, this meant that finding ways to negotiate men's requests that fit within acceptable boundaries of feminine heterosexuality, as well as with anti-materialist ideologies about tourism and authenticity, was an exigency for European and North American women.

"Men here eat not when they're hungry but when the food is there"

Mr. Duncan's insights, gained from his years involved in local community economic development, especially for the black community, helped me to understand the complicated ways in which the roles of foreign women within intimate economies were deeply rooted in wider systemic failures. His list included: lack of quality education; lack of well paying jobs; and racial discrimination and corruption that maintained white economic and political dominance in the country. The young men who remained in Puerto Viejo, Mr. Duncan suggested, were those without the family support necessary to afford to "go outside" for education and employment. The generosity and goodwill of foreign women, he argued, supplanted those opportunities that the Costa Rican government had denied the most disenfranchised boys and young men in the community. Put in this light, the expectations placed on foreign women's shoulders, largely completely unaware of these wider historical and political economic circumstances, were huge. Moreover, the contentiousness of transnational sex and romance becomes clearer – tourist women did not see themselves in, nor particularly want, these roles.

Recall the anti-materialism discourses that women deployed as tourist consumers: These discourses, which aligned with spiritual, religious, and racial beliefs, were also used to construct local men as living close to nature, living off the land, and ideologically opposed to consumer culture, which I discuss in Chapter 5. Yet the livelihoods of many local men were actually a mystery to women, unless they worked in the tourist industry, which some men did as self-employed surf instructors and guides, for instance.[12] When I asked them what their boyfriends did to make money, responses such as, "Well, that's a bit sketchy to me" or "I think he does some construction work, occasionally" or "He's a guide of some kind" were common. Many women had some knowledge about the locals who sold marijuana, often because that was how women met their boyfriends. But otherwise, doubts were often cast in women's minds as to how the local men survived. Within this nebulous imagery of personal economics, where men are mysteriously available for leisure time with them and at the same time are clearly not well off and possibly quite poor, tourist women tried to make sense of things. They felt in the dark. Some women were unsure if paying for men's meals was an expectation of them or an insult to a local guy. Yet, if they wanted to go out to a restaurant to eat, which they often did, since they were on vacation, they had to negotiate this transaction. Figuring out the economic dimensions of these new dating practices was often a challenge. As I will show, they vehemently resisted when the role of "sugar mama" was foisted on them.

When I spoke with local men about this issue, a line between "providing for" and "paying" (as different interpretations of foreign women's material–erotic involvement in poorer men's lives) was further blurred. Two men, Filipino and Danny, spoke about the ways in which women, linked to relative and perceived wealth, "liked to give." In their view, foreign tourist women neither "paid" for sex nor "helped" "desperate" men but rather bestowed men, whose company they enjoyed, with gifts.

Filipo

We were flipping through magazines while waiting for our drinks to arrive. The restaurant lounge was quiet. Only a few tourists sat on the tables on the patio, while locals and foreign residents hung out at the lounge area close to the bar and kitchen. Filipo was dressed in his usual impeccable attire. Clean jeans, spotless white cotton V-necked T-shirt, a silver chain around his neck, and expensive leather sandals. We looked at a fashion magazine together, chatting about the hair and clothing styles.

"How do the women pay the men, Filipo?" I ventured, taking advantage of an opportune moment to broach a topic I had wanted to ask him about for some time.

"*Qué?*" he replied, "How do they pay the men? They don't pay, Susan. The women never pay, Susan."

I prodded, "Well, they do give the guys some money, Filipo. I thought you told me that before. How do they do that? Do they just give you a handful of money? And when?"

Filipo smiled back at me, showing his grin. He seemed to be enjoying my questions, for once. Our drinks arrived, delivered by a Canadian woman I had become friends with over the past months. Filipo took a sip of his icy cold minty *mojito* (rum drink) and then patiently explained to me how "the system" worked:

The men meet tourist women through their activities in town, going to the clubs, and their friendships with other foreigners who live here. Afterwards, the women send them money and things that they know they might like. Clothing, soccer gear, electronics sometimes. They find this out after spending lots of time together doing things that they like – going to the beach, nice restaurants, dancing at the reggae clubs. When they return back home to their regular lives some women send wire transfers through Western Union. Personally, he has never asked any woman for money. They want to do it for him because they like him and because they want to keep him around and to show them a good time in Costa Rica. They expect to return. The issue for the men is always a matter of when.

"So," I ask him, "You never ask them for money, even if [the women] are slow at figuring things out?"

"Susan, why would I ask them for money? Men don't do that," Filipo replied, both annoyed, I thought, and amused by my persistence and apparent lack of comprehension.

"Women want to give me things, I tell you," he joked with me, ending the conversation as more people he knew came into the bar.

Danny

I return for a moment to Reggae Beats, where Lucy met Thomas. The nightclubs were spaces for "sociable eroticism of the everyday" for local men too; that is, places where eroticized social relations were outside of the modalities of the market (Andrews *et al.* 2007: 248). Yet the role of material things in erotic exchanges with foreign women in the clubs nevertheless looms as a possibility.

As Lucy's story indicates, young men, and older ones as well, would often be seen dancing off to the side of the main crowd, blissed out on ganga or alcohol and the rhythm of the music. As the evening progressed, the pocket lighters would come out and in synch with particular lyrics the males would press the flames from their lighters in the air, chanting in unison. Danny was one of these young men. A surfer during the day, at night he was a regular in the bars and clubs.

He told me a story of when he was in his late teens and he had decided it was time for him to meet foreign women like the other male youth his age. He was nervous about the prospect but ultimately it was easy for him because one night in the disco a tourist girl approached him. In Danny's words:

> [It was] time to have a girl. And I don't see anybody. And then that girl came. And I see that girl. So many people see that girl right there in the corner down there. And she's dancing in this corner. I see a lot of guys go to her, and she don't want anything with anybody, you know. That's good. I think that she might say hello to me, calling me. So, I just keeping danc- ing. And then I see this girl look at me. And through all these people, I see her face. I see the little face of that girl.

And I see and I say hi. Okay, that is the girl. I go walking through all these people, and I don't take my face from her face. I know she's looking to me. And I go straight through all these people, and she's looking at me. Then I am really close to her face. My face is really close to her. My hair is crazy. I know that. She pulls me head-to-head, and she takes my hand and we start to dance.

Really slow, really soft, very nice. You know, it was the perfect moment. In that moment. And we dance, and you know, like. And I start to [say to her], "Come baby, you are mine now." She puts her arms around my body and this and that. And I get too horny and already that moment, and boom. And then I ask her, "You wanna come with me?" And she takes me hand and we walk outside. We walk and walk. I think she really wanted to. But she was special, that one. That night we start to be together.

For Danny, the "dance floor moment" was imbued with significance. He had set out to meet a foreign woman and knew that the club was the place to go. He too (like Lucy in her story) was caught up in the moment, where the atmosphere and also the tactile, proximate relations with this one tourist woman were intense and dynamic sensual experiences for him. Danny fell for this particular woman and they were together for a few months. His heart was broken when she returned to France. He told me that he had not wanted any money from her nor, for that matter, from any of the other foreign women that he now regularly hooks up with. "Sometimes, though," Danny added, to qualify the economic underpinnings, "they give me money or they buy me things."

Here we see how gendered discourses – where women "give" things to men and men "do not ask" for money – shape both men's stories. While one man, well traveled and cosmopolitan in his coolness and vibe, more squarely fits the conventional definition of a hustler or gigolo, even, and the other so utterly fits the image of Mr. Duncan's disenfranchised black youth, their sexual interactions with foreign women are entangled with stories of exchange, of one kind or another.

Many different people explained "the system" to me. Filipo, above, but also Mariella (in Chapter 3), and Jackson, too (this chapter). Over time, the notion of women "paying for sex," the simplistic stereotype I arrived at in 2004, gave way to a much more complicated picture. "The system" entails a historical relationship between foreign women, local men, money, commodities, desires, sex, intimacy, procreation, and wider local and global markets in which both parties were complexly situated.

As part of the storied presence of foreign women constituting the vibe of the place, which I explain in Chapter 3, there were abundant and varied accounts of their hugely significant economic roles. Recall Juan's imaginative and figurative explanation, in Chapter 1, of local men's sexual interest in foreign women. His words, "Men here, they eat not when they're hungry but when the food is there," invokes the ways in which foreign women have "fed" men, metaphorically and literally, for decades. People told stories of who started "the whole system," tracing it back to Norwegian women who received subsidies from their government

Figure 6.2 Transnational, interracial, heterosexual couples leisurely stroll and cycle down the main street of Puerto Viejo, where foreign women are key actors as consumers, income earners, and producers in the town's daily life. Photo by author.

to have babies and raise them while living in Puerto Viejo, supporting the fathers of their children. Another story pinpointed the origins to an American woman who paid a teen boy, in dire circumstances, who had sold her drugs to spend the night with her, and she then returned the next year with several female friends. These stories of lascivious, procreative Northern women contrast with Mr. Duncan's story of altruistic white women as salvation, but in other ways are congruent. "Food," as both a metaphor for sex and nutritional sustenance, is closely linked with what has become the typified gender performance of Euro-American women (as generous, giving women).

Negotiating heterosexual erotics: learning to "give"

It is not surprising that Euro-American women such as Lucy and many others are perplexed when local men they sleep with, after meeting them in a place they associate with "erotic exploration," turn out to place monetary expectations on them. The reason Lucy had been upset when Thomas prodded her about the soccer gear back in Canada was not because he had tainted an idyllic romantic moment that in her mind had been a fun, spontaneous sexual adventure. She was bothered because what she took to be a mutual relationship, of no strings attached recreational sex with an equal partner, transformed into a relationship where the inequalities were strikingly apparent.

Suddenly she saw herself as a potential target, to be taken advantage of, because of wealth she did not otherwise see herself as possessing, which was a feeling she did not like. Moreover, her eyes were opened to the material impoverishment around her, which meant the touristic fantasy of the Caribbean as a naturalized hedonistic place was ruptured by Thomas's benign requests. First for soccer gear, later for cash so he could afford to eat rice and beans in the sodas at night, with each request Lucy felt the metanarrative of spontaneity loosen its hold. Eventually, she decided that economic equality was imperative in an intimate relationship, and she ended things with Thomas because, in her words, "It just never felt right to give him money."

Lucy, like many other tourist women, was naïve, another sanctioned element of contemporary travel and tourism. Cross-border erotics in Latin America have long been structured by global inequality and political economic asymmetry between the global North and South. Bhattacharyya draws a distinction between the "limp vanilla pleasures of equality and reciprocality in intimate life" and "the theatre of power imbalance ... [that serves] to heighten the sexual hit" (2002: 102). She argues, "The more worldly pleasures of the body," accessible via travel south of the border "require recognition that social equity may not feel sexy ... [and instead] power relations can be solidified for erotic ends" (Bhattacharyya 2002: 102). Yet, I argue, in return, women had naively under-estimated, or were blind to, and vehemently resisted the economic underpinnings of North–South erotics, or at least in certain configurations, as I will show.

Bhattacharyya's claim that increased commodification of transnational sex is an evitable outcome of global capital because "the internationalized sex trade is a response to the buying power and movement of those who travel" (2002: 121) is worth pondering. As more and more women travel do they, too, envisage "the adventure of sex as a far-from-home experience" where "the stock icons of eroticism – a stranger's glance, an unfamiliar place, an escape from norm and convention, the rush into hair, skin, breath, sweat, loss of self and the touch of the other" are theirs to realize via their supposed "buying power"? This question is at the center of a key debate in literature on female sex tourism encapsulated in the title of Jeffreys' (2003) article, "Sex Tourism: Do Women Do It Too?" (e.g. Hernández 2005; Herold *et al.* 2001; Sánchez Taylor 2001).

Yet these claims prove to be too over-determining, for what goes on in Puerto Viejo is not nearly as unfettered and naturalized as these provocative images suggest. While Euro-American women undoubtedly brought a battery of racialized fantasies with them, fresh out of trashy novels it sometimes seemed to me, they did not engage in the fantasy of economic power at all in the way that the stereotype of "the sex tourist" conjures up. The exotic to them was absolutely hot, sexy, and arousing; the economic imbalances, however, proved to be entirely unsexy.

Men's poverty was romanticized in the sense that women arrived as humanitarian tourists and as New Age yoga tourists with liberal notions of development aid, for instance, insisting that, as Heron (2007) has pointed out in her research on Canadian development workers in Africa, they were "the 'good guys' of the world." But most of my interlocutors were uncomfortable with being situated as an "aid" donor in their intimate lives and definitely not in eroticism either. Money to a beggar outside the *Buen Precio* supermarket, maybe, but, to put it crassly, a beggar in the bedroom was an entirely different, and uneasy, kind of "buying power." International travel engenders eroticism through exoticism, yet locality and actual corporeal gendered beings shape the outcomes of sexual exchange.

Rarely in straight sexual culture are women placed in the position of wanting or needing to "pay" for sex. Heterosexuality and hegemonic masculinity, in Western and Latino cultures, uphold the gender-dimorphic discourse that "men sow their seeds" – and women "contain" their sexual desire to legitimate relationships. As I explain in Chapter 3, casual sex is a vexed practice according to discourses of proper femininity. In the West, heteronormativity dictates that both money and erotics are bracketed out of the institutionalized heterosexual relations of marriage and legitimate (reproductive) unions. Because of its naturalization, as queer theory and feminist theory argues, heterosexuality is considered an erotically muted sexuality, while at the same time heteronormativity marks what is regarded as "normal" and "acceptable" sexual practice (Richardson 1996: 6). On the one hand, heterosexuality is "the most idealized of economic relations" because of its gendered division of labor and double workload for women (Rich 1980: 659); on the other hand, heterosexual intimacies have become synonymous with "pure" intimacies unhinged from the "cold" arena of capitalism (Illouz 2007) and "hostile worlds" of corporations and business transactions (Zelizer 2007). This is the messiness of heterosexual material–erotics that tourist women I knew were situated within as sexual actors and subjects.

By Thomas (or Danny) calculating what he might gain from the tourist women he met in the club, Lucy, in turn, was compelled to think too about a commensurable "exchange" for the gifts she eventually brought back from Canada for him. In this way, a fusing of economics with erotics were brought to the fore much more quickly and acutely, and in ways that she had never experienced before. Did she want to continue having sex with him or did the "gift-giving" in actuality dull the erotic tension between them to the point where she would prefer to be friends or "*una patrocinadora*" (a sponsor)?

The cross-border erotics that women engage in through contemporary travel thus expose tourist women to different erotic cultures that are enmeshed in and influenced by a wider political economy and formal and informal tourism markets within local economies. Travel shapes heterosexualities in complex ways. But this does not mean that heterosexualities "at home" are not also enmeshed in various modalities of the market.

In the West, in the age of high divorce rates and consumer culture, through new forms of casual sex arrangements including hook ups, "friends with benefits," internet-mediated dating, and cyber-sex, straight women are subjected to different "markets" in which their sexual identities and performances of heterosexual femininity are continually produced and judged (Frohick and Migliardi 2011; Kalish and Kimmel 2011). The *negotiation* of heterosexual relations is thus an increasingly imperative and quotidian aspect of normative sexualities and "ordinary life," as Jackson (2008) persuasively argues. Illouz (2007: 36) traces what she refers to as the "fungible" underpinnings of contemporary intimate relationships back to the mid-twentieth century. Due to the increasing influence of "market-based repertoires" on interpersonal and intimate relations in late capitalism, as Illouz (2007: 05) suggests, relationships become interchangeable entities that require work, continual reflection, and cost–benefit assessments, in other words, "objects that can be traded and exchanged."

The concept of "exchange" applied to seemingly "market-free" erotically charged spontaneous encounters in the borderland thus asks us to consider the valuation in terms of what was given and received in exchange. This, in turn, prompts a second look at the meanings that Euro-American women gave to spending practices and money more generally as tourists in Puerto Viejo.

Ember talked explicitly about how she tricked her local boyfriend into believing she was giving him all the cash she had on her by tucking a "*rojo*" (2,000 colone note, worth about US$5) in her wallet to offer him, when he inevitably asked her for some money. Kelly did not feel it was appropriate to pay for her boyfriend's passport application fees (about US$100) but, on the other hand, beers and weed were fine. Other women felt that small loans to help pay for medicine or other medical needs for family members, or schooling costs for younger siblings, were appropriate. Electronics, such as cell phones, were sometimes offered as "special" presents, when women wanted to make their boyfriends feel particularly happy; for instance, after a long absence back home in England or the United States. Cash for restaurant meals, as Lucy indicated, was out of the question ultimately because it was too visible, too public a statement about the man's "sponging" off a foreign woman. Authenticity mattered insofar as my interlocutors strove to forge "rewarding relationships with those living in tourist destinations," which implicated them in continual negotiations over the meanings and politics of money (Desforges 2001: 362).

This brief glimpse into the material nature of what Euro-American women were willing to exchange for erotic adventures in Costa Rica with local men who were relatively much poorer than they were illuminates the gendered practices of sexual exchange. Returning to Bhattacharyya's seductive claims, above, about the "stock icons of eroticism" being enacted by the exotic stranger, I suggest now that such claims reveal how eroticism associated with travel as antithetical to intimacy and domesticity, as I explained in Chapter 4, is rooted in masculinist understandings of both travel and erotics. Turning to a wider picture of transnational sex through contemporary travel for a moment allows us to see that gender shapes borderland erotics in participatory ways.

On a wide scale, according to a number of recent studies involving large sample sizes, the numbers of male travelers to report having sex with local residents in foreign countries such as Peru and Thailand are much higher than for women. Studies with youth backpackers and international travelers underscore the gendered dimensions of travel sex, where significantly fewer numbers of female tourists compared to male tourists engage in sex with a new partner while on holiday (Cabada *et al*. 2003; Egan 2001), although the numbers are higher for long-term travelers compared to short-term travelers (McNulty *et al*. 2010) and depend on the specific country and context (Bauer 2009). A crucial point raised by researchers looking at women's sexual behavior on holiday relates to the issue of gender dynamics and (hetero)sexual negotiation. In other words, given the gender power relations in which heterosexuality is played out wherein dominance and the subordination of women accrues to hegemonic masculinity, whether at home or away from home heterosexual (and bisexual) women are confronted with risk issues (condom use, personal safety) in their pleasure seeking and negotiation of sexual gratification (Thomas 2000).

In qualitative research with Australian and British women solo travelers, researchers found that, while women actively sought out sexual gratification when traveling abroad, at the same time they reported difficulties in negotiating sexual encounters with new male sexual partners "in a way that resulted in pleasure for them" (Thomas 2000: 205). Related to the temporal and spatial organization of tourism, when relationships are likely to proceed at a more rapid pace than in a non-holiday environment, for instance, and also the alcohol use associated with holidaying and *macho* masculinities (found throughout the world), women found it challenging to negotiate condom use and also to find safe and private spaces for encounters (Puccia 2009; Thomas 2000, 2005; Wilson and Little 2008). Solo women travelers, too, reported a sense of constant self-consciousness about being female and about being white, about who they were with, and what they were doing, such that they felt "that their bodies were not meant to be in certain places" (Wilson and Little 2008: 181), themes I explored in Chapter 3. Feminist analyses of travel thus underscore the ways in which "travel spaces are not innocuous and objectively defined images reflective of the travel guides. Rather, such spaces are politicized, sexualized, subjective, and gendered" (Wilson and Little 2008: 182). Gender dynamics are part-and-parcel of negotiations underway in cross-border erotics; these include the place of money (a touchy subject), as well as when and where kissing, fondling, undressing, and putting on the condom (or not) might occur, and if oral sex (another touchy subject) is a cultural taboo or not, and how to say no (or yes) to anal sex, for instance. Lucy's story reveals how the excitement of a one-night encounter and erotic experimentation with a sexy black Costa Rican man gave way ever so quickly to the rather tawdry and much less erotic necessity of negotiating power dynamics in all kinds of ways. Many of my interlocutors had to deal with similar issues and multiple concerns. As much as they did not expect to, or hoped that they would not, they were compelled to come to terms with their concerns over being emotionally manipulated, over giving too much in the way of presents or giving too little, over the realities of STIs and HIV, concerns that did not disappear even within a place where "make love!" was a touristic imperative. Learning "to give," in material ways, became a requirement wedded to the gender scripts for Euro-American female tourists.

Another important story warrants being told if we are to understand more fully the ways in which heterosexual subjectivity was shaped by material–erotic exchange in Costa Rica for some women. Sexual subjectivity refers to more than sexual identity and orientation, as I explain in Chapter 1, and more than inner processes. Drawing from feminist and anthropological conceptualizations, sexual subjectivity refers to the ways in which people come to understand themselves as sexual beings through subjective experiences of embodiment, affect, cognition, and also how they are constructed by others as subjects (because these processes are not separate). Therefore, as Biehl *et al.* offer, "attending to subjectivity in ethnographic terms" requires that we "encounter the concrete constellations in which people forge and foreclose their lives around what is most at stake" (2007: 05). Here, then, I turn to Rayne's answer to the question of what heterosexual subjectivity feels like …

"Sugar mama"

Rayne was one of the few women I interviewed who did not shy away from the topic of money. She met Sebastian while on a working holiday on a farm located in the jungle south of Puerto Viejo, as I explain in Chapter 5. (Lucy, Ember, Illondra, Alex, and another woman, Helena, were also forthright with me.[13]) One late afternoon in August 2007 Rayne and I sat on the beach together to enjoy the last few minutes of sun before the sudden dusk would make us feel cold and ready to run for our bikes.

I asked her, "So, how did the money thing work out for you?"

Rayne answered:

> It was a mystery to me how he survived. Sure, he could eat and stay at the farm for free, and he could stay as long as he liked. He was often away, though. It was amazing to see how easy it was for him to travel without money through all these impoverished towns, and always get by. But, you know what, he must have taken food or money somewhere. I don't know how. To tell you the truth, I never took track of my cash. Had little bits gone missing, I would have never noticed. I have never seen him steal things and sell things.

"Was it an issue for you guys?" I prodded further.

"Always," Rayne responded immediately, wrapping her sarong closer to her body. She continued:

> The whole stigma of white woman and black men from the coast is that they are in it for the cash, and the women are in it for the romance and the sex, the sex. I think that is one of the things that destroyed us or my ability to feel connected with him. I could never go anywhere with him and feel okay. There was always someone looking at me as though I was a crazy, stupid whore. There was always someone looking at him as though he were a manipulative player that was false, selling himself for sex, kind of thing. The dynamic was everywhere.

Plus, he didn't have any money. So, if I wanted to go to dinner, I'd have to pay for him. If I wanted to go somewhere, I'd have to pay for him. It was so strange for me to be on the other side of that stick. In Canada, I was always making less than the poverty level, now all of a sudden I was the "fat cat sugar mama." It really bothered me.

We sat in silence for a few minutes, watching the waves break over the coral reef just a few hundred meters away. Then Rayne told me a story about how Sebastian and her were in a restaurant in a small rural town outside of Limón. A young girl, maybe seven years old, pointed at Rayne and whispered something to her mother about the ugly black man with the white woman. Rayne felt sick to her stomach.

It was in a redneck farming region of Costa Rica, and that's the mentality. That black men are ugly and that white women pay them to have sex. It was awful. Even still, when I want to pay the tab, I see the waitress look at me like that [too]. I don't know if it's me imagining her looking at me like that or if it's there. The vibe is always there. I hate it.

Conclusion

Euro-American women's desires for a Caribbean experience resulted in new confrontations for them, as they were drawn, with much resistance, into what I call "material–erotic" exchanges. This participation in material–erotic exchanges, or the negotiation of material goods for erotic experiences, in turn, affected their sexual self-understandings. While a Caribbean experience, such as a chance meeting with a sexy local man in an erotically charged reggae club, was a titillating prospect, as Lucy's story demonstrated, at the same time, women contested and felt ambivalent about being treated as a "sugar mama." They were not the only ones in the relationships to give, in that their local boyfriends provided them sometimes with food such as rondon soup or small gifts of a ripe starfruit or papaya, or herbal remedies such as bush tea when a tourist girlfriend had dengue fever or a cold. Sometimes, too, men's material contributions were more than token gestures. One local man, a divorced *Tico*, told me how he had lent money to his Canadian ex-wife when they were married to pay off her credit card and he never did see any of the money returned to him. But, yet again, Ember told me how she became "tired of men not bringing her anything." The relentless expectations placed on her by local suitors caused her, ultimately, to end her extended holiday in the place she called "the twilight zone" and head back North. These are complex transactions that women do not expect to happen.

Histories of "what happen[ed]" (Palmer 2005) before individual tourists arrived are obfuscated in processes of tourism, masqueraded under the language of hospitality. Tourists are "guests" and local people are "hosts" in the parlance used throughout the tourism development industries (Wright 1992). Yet, as local politicians, the parents of sons involved in transnational relations, and other townspeople in Puerto Viejo indicated, a history of foreign women "giving" had started decades ago and continued over the years, changing with the ebb and flow of the global economy (in the 2008 recession foreign businesses closed down and foreign-owned land was put up for sale – and foreign women were amongst those who suffered economically). Women arrived with ideals of sexual spontaneity and at the same time were confronted with economic realities that changed them; they found themselves as key actors within local erotic economies, situated between contradictory discourses of "ruining" and "helping" local men.

The affects of material–erotic exchanges and being on the "giving" end, or what feels like the giving end, were articulated in the expression, "sugar mama." In this regard, the price of what was regarded as "mind blowing sex" was ultimately overshadowed by the feelings of denigration and racist stereotyping. The glaring of waitresses in restaurants. The antagonistic stares from *Ticas* and Afro-Caribbean women watching a white woman walking into any kind of store with a local black guy. Lucy said, "We white woman think we are practicing 'free love' but it costs us terribly." Heterosexuality shifted, from the assumption of an ideal of gender equality and a "market-free" zone of authentic connection and playful erotics, to a sense of sexual self that required decision-making about soccer shoes, mobile phones, and other commodities that did not align with an anti-materialist travel ethos. Another woman expressed this shift in erotic terms – she wanted to "be fucked" without being "fucked over."

While "female sex tourism" scholarship has critically drawn attention to the political economic inequities in which Northern women have been consumers in sexual economies for decades now, particularly in the Caribbean (Kempadoo 2004; O'Connell *et al.* 2005; Phillips 1999, 2002; Sánchez Taylor 2001) but also in the Gambia (Ebron 1997; Ware 1997), there is much more to say about these exchanges. More generally, as Donnan and Magowan have argued, analyses of sex tourism tend to oversimplify the "force" of the political economic at the expense of ignoring "the diversity of the relationships between money and sex" (2010: 91). They argue for recognition of the "diverse ways in which sex is embedded in the economy without being wholly subsumed by it and to understand the influence which this has on sexual agency and subjectivity" (Donnan and Magowan 2010: 91). Reality is much more complex than white Euro-American women paying for fantasies of being desired by, and desiring, poor black Costa Rican men. Moreover, as Cabezas and others whose aims are to bring nuance to understandings of sexual exchange show, affective–sexual transcultural relationships in Third World tourism destinations are linked to, not separate from, "heteronormativity in other contexts deemed more legitimate" (2009: 137).

Cross-border erotics were entangled in contestations over money and its multiple and culturally diverse meanings (Bloch and Parry 1989). Many of the women I interviewed and spend time with in the bars, beaches, and cosmopolitan cafés and Caribbean eateries, came to realize, all too personally, how tourist places are sites where gender politics, class, and racial politics and inequities are struggled over in very material ways – and that sexual spontaneity in the borderland, as my interlocutor put it, "comes with a price."

Conclusion

Departures

"Who's using who?"

May 26, 2007 *Fieldnotes* Yesterday, I was sitting in Helena's kitchen hanging out with some foreign women, a mix of residents and recent arrivals. Helena was sharing her thoughts about a book she is currently reading by the Buddhist author, Thich Nhat Hanh, which is influencing her aspiration for more equitable relationships with men in the town. Someone changed the subject and then we were talking about how foreign women can't handle the infidelity that is inevitably the headwall they come into. They talk about one [European] woman who had accepted her [local] boyfriend completely as he is without any expectations whatsoever that he'll change…. At some point, Maddy (an American woman living in Puerto Viejo) wanders into the kitchen. I ask her how she's doing. She is in a "new relationship," she tells me.

As soon as she says that she corrects herself, "Well, it's hardly 'a relationship.' I barely look at him. He barely looks at me. We don't kiss. When the sex is over, there's nothing else, he just leaves." Then she continues, "Come to think of it. I haven't had an orgasm with any of these guys. Well, maybe one in a year, maybe."

Maddy and Helena both laugh.

"It's such a myth [that these guys are good lovers]," Maddy offers.

I ask them why they bother then, if the sex isn't any good. Neither of them come up with an answer to appease the persistent anthropologist, although they continue talking about sex. They change topics to a favorite one of which guys in the town are the hottest. Helena says that she has not been with many men over the age of twenty-four when Maddy mentions that she went out with a "man" (she emphasized) who was about thirty. But she tells a story about how he gave a different name than his actual name, so that, it turned out, he could refuse her phone call.

Helena laughed when she heard that, "Yeah, he knows that if he comes into town and gives you a call, you'll be right there!"

The constant flow of women.

While many tourist women return home or move on to their next destination (such as Bluefields in Nicaragua or the Bay Islands in Honduras along the Caribbean corridor in Central America, popular with many female tourists), taking with them their special memories such as Josie's magical sexual adventure at the seashore with Michael (in Chapter 3), some Euro-American women remain in Puerto Viejo – for several months or more, often until their money runs out or they have a fight with their boyfriend. When they do stay on, they find that the fantasies they arrived with, which were mediated through myriad media representations and tourism discourses, transmute into rather tawdry and quotidian negotiations of heterosexual social relations. The excitement and pleasure in being sought after and showered with attention by a local man gave way to the constant vigilance over condom use or to feelings of jealousy because of his flirtations with other tourist women. The enjoyment in the unexpected "instant relationship" with a local man shifted to acute awareness of gendered social organization and gender double standards. Many women told me how they found themselves acting like "an insane jealous girlfriend," behavior that they did not normally identify with. In the scenario above, derived from participant observation after being in the field for three years, in their quotidian activities as heterosexual women spending time together and talking about men and sex, Euro-American women discuss the influx-ness of heterosexual culture and normativity within a transnational tourist town: Will they succumb to the accepted local practices of (barely) tolerated male infidelity?[1] Equitable relationships may be an aspiration, mediated by New Age philosophy, but the age gap creates sexual frisson. Chasing men is possible, but it is still a matter of waiting for the man to call the woman. Penetrative sex is good but yet the eroticism of kissing is lacking. These are the choices, decisions, and issues entailed in the making of heteronormativity in a tropical paradise.

Yet as much as the point in this book is that these quotidian negotiations do occur, that is, that tourist spaces are important contexts in the production of "mundane heterosexuality" (Hockey *et al.* 2007), it is equally important for me to stress the asymmetry that structures, although it does not over-determine, the meanings of transnational (heterosexual) sex in borderland places like Puerto Viejo, Limón, Costa Rica.

Multiple dimensions of power undoubtedly underpin the heterosexual cross-border relations, as I have discussed throughout the book. Political economic asymmetry places tourist women in positions of relative power over local men, with regards to their money and resources and also, crucially, their mobility – related to their passports and citizenship in First World countries that grant them the access to go almost anywhere in the world they can afford to go. Yet at the same time, gender discourses that assign power to masculinity (regardless of socio-economic standing) enable local men, as they control the town's public and semi-public spaces of leisure and informal economies and engage in performances of hyper-masculinity, to use physical and symbolic power over heterosexual (and bisexual) tourist women for whom being desired by men is highly seductive and valued. One day when I was discussing this conundrum of two-way power dynamics between local men and foreign women with a friend and local resident, Milo, he articulated this fundamental tension to me by raising the question, "Who's using who?"

Milo's question is useful for drawing out the multifaceted power dynamics in cross-border sex – as well as demonstrating the self-awareness that local men show about their own instrumentality and the micro-politics underpinning their awareness that tourism places them in positions of exploitation in many different ways. Transnational romance and sex is one arena but it is linked with economic and social marginalization on the national level by the government and growing disparities between the working poor and middle-class elites within Costa Rica. His question invokes local men's feelings that tourists take advantage of them, for sex and for the good times that men, like no other townspeople, are in unique social positions to show the heterosexual female tourists. It is stressful for local men to withhold their emotions constantly or run the risk of being hurt and emotionally distraught when it is time for the tourist to return home. On the other hand, Milo's question reflects his knowledge that tourist women feel that the local men (the players and hustlers) take advantage of them, using them for their money and casting them aside quickly for the next new tourist woman who arrives on the next bus, or by retaining multiple girlfriends and thus access to sex and potentially more resources through the deployment of "tactical sex" (Cabezas 2009). All in all, my interlocutor's grappling with and his analysis of the plight and peril of both social groups – the foreign women and the local men – as a mix of exploitation and instrumentality on both sides is the framework that I, too, put forward.

With regards to what other scholars have said about the asymmetries of borderland erotics, unfortunately a predominant political economic framework has tended to view the matter as a unidimensional exertion of power where, in their pursuit of racialized exotica and erotic experiences, heterosexual Western women (often stereotyped as older, unattractive, and desperate women) are seen to wield, in my mind, extraordinary economic power over disenfranchised non-Western men (also see Campbell 2007). This image does not resonate with what I saw taking place in Puerto Viejo. As I explain in Chapter 6, the women I interviewed and spent time with resented and contested the "sugar mama" identity. I found that their realization of economic disparity, while naïve, did not become a rationale for them to feel justified in, or to embrace the possibilities of, exploiting poor men or boys. Instead, tourist women chose to withdraw from the entanglements of money and sex, not harness the inequities to pursue sexual fantasies. Some scholars have recognized how gender complicates any oversimplification of one-way power via geo-economic inequities (e.g. Jeffreys 2003; Meisch 1995 ; Pruitt and LaFont 1995). A body of literature has analyzed the contentiousness of the subjectivity of "female sex tourist," largely centering on the issue of whether women access transnational sex through the masculinized practices of sexual commerce, and hence are the female counterparts to "male sex tourists," or whether by virtue of norms of femininity and gender difference women cannot exert masculinized power and thus are subordinated in transnational encounters without the agency to be exploitative, at least not the same way that male sex tourists are (e.g. de Albuquerque 1998; Herold *et al.* 2001; Jeffreys 2003; Sánchez Taylor 2006).[2] My work builds on and challenges this literature, aiming for new analytical directions and more nuanced accounts.

What I have demonstrated in the book is that realities for Euro-American women and Costa Rican men are more complicated than any unidimensional framework of power suggests. Moreover, and this is a key contribution, my interlocutor's question, "Who's using who?" encourages an examination of cross-border sex beyond individuals' exertions of gender, or economic-based power or manipulations, to look at the "force" of tourism on both social groups as generative (and not simply destructive or deleterious). How does tourism "use" both groups in the pursuit of profits? (Both groups are subject to flexible labor markets, for instance.) How do tourism markets, condoned by the state, allow certain sexual actors and not others? Heterosexual tourism – what I refer to as "straight tourism" (Frohlick and Johnston 2011) – warrants a closer investigation of heteronormative and non-normative forms of sociality that occur between tourists and local people (as well as between tourists) (Frank 2007). In particular, given the ever-increasing salience of international travel to the lives and identity formations of North American and European youth and young adults (Amit 2007; Desforges 1998) it behooves anthropologists and tourism scholars to pay attention to how tourism travel, more specifically, affects the production of heterosexual subjectivities, which, as I have previously stated, are fluid and in process (Curtis 2004; LaMarre 2011; Richardson 1996). Rather than a complete rupture or "escape" from their everyday lives into a realm of liminality, transgression or carnivalesque, as tourism is sometimes conceptualized, I contend that the travel experiences sought by the Euro-American women I came to know in Costa Rica were given meaning in the context of desires for transformations related to their life course, such as youth and mid-life changes, and ideologies of personal growth and environmentalism. In other words, a trip to Costa Rica was about the start of a new life post-divorce or post-university, or carrying out work as a yoga teacher in a different locale, rather than a break from absolutely everything left behind at home. In addition, as Franklin and Crang (2001: 9) reminded us a decade ago, the practice of tourism by necessity consists of "a succession of mundane activities" punctuated by a very few out-of-the-ordinary moments; therefore, the boundary between "the extraordinary" and "the everyday" in reality is actually very blurred for tourists (as well as for locals) – as I saw time and time again.

With this view of tourism as a "de-exoticized activity" (Franklin and Crang 2001), white Western women's heterosexual subjectivities, and attendant power dynamics, can be seen to be intertwined with ongoing formations of self, body, and identity through travel. The gender politics of heterosexual hook ups, relationships, and marriages were played out in a complex multicultural site rapidly changing due to globalization and tourism development. Men, as Milo pointed out, used foreign women to chase their own dreams, just as women's fantasies were expected to be fulfilled by men; both parties were, in different ways, naïve about a mutuality of these dreams and aspirations, which, as it became clearly evident over time, were not shared. Both parties' dreams were situated in the machinations of globalization and late capitalism, such as consumer culture, new media technologies, unstable economies, and social anxieties over dating, marriage, and family.

"Have sex, will travel"[3]

In telling stories of how cross-border sex "just happens" for specific women in a particular time and place (the basic premise of ethnography), I have aimed to show the complications and nuances of their relationships. Locale, physical sensations, palpable "senses of place" (the vibe), the presence of foreign women, and other factors intersect to produce a space that has become understood as a "twilight zone"; that is, for the expression of women's heterosexual interracial desires. In writing about women's experiences I have also told stories of how women's sexuality shapes travel practices and the wider social processes of tourism too. Simply put, heterosexuality, as "a complex of institution, practice, and experience, all which intersect with gender" (Jackson 2005: 26), was an embodied means by which white Euro-American women's travel practices in Costa Rica were given meaning and contingently unfolded. International travel was a space and set of relations through which heterosexuality was performed, embodied, and produced.

As feminist scholars posit, heterosexuality does not only order sexual lives, in that heterosexuality encompasses more than erotic desire and more than "the sexual" and therefore serves to structure the "domestic and extra-domestic" aspects of heterosexual women's lives. Heterosexuality is a (unmarked) status that, according to Hockey *et al.* (2007: 136, 143), "must be both negotiated and sustained" and involves "the proximity of bodies ... the materialities of shared eating, sleeping, and washing." In other words, it is through "everyday sexual and social practices" that heterosexuality is reaffirmed (Jackson 2005: 32), not only as an institution but also as a sense of sexual being and subjective experience (of privilege and normativity as well as surveillance and non-normativity). I return to the opening epigraph in the Introduction where I recall a conversation where someone had asked me why I was making the situation of women's transnational sex so complicated. I replied that heterosexual sexual relations "don't just happen." Although heterosexuality is naturalized and given meaning as the "fallback for all other sexual experiences ... the sex that just is" (Bhattacharyya 2002: 18), in actuality, heterosexuality is historically and socially variable, and has changed over time and place just as other forms of sexual expression have changed, and continue to change (Katz 2007). Transnational sex, enabled through travel mobilities and a societal valuation of travel, is one such historical expression – and I am interested in how women have performed and also negotiated heterosexuality as everyday practices in the context of these cross-border mobilities.

As I have demonstrated, in Puerto Viejo, women arrived with notions of sexual spontaneity that aligned with gender norms of proper heterosexual femininity and they distanced themselves (at least at first) from "slut" categories. Women interpreted encounters with local men through notions of heterosexuality naturalized as sexual impulse, linked to romance and passion and to external forces, including men's power over women's sexual agency. Heterosexual femininity, bound up with whiteness, with fit and shapely bodies, with youth and cosmopolitanism, included ways of being and subject positions that enabled Euro-American straight women in Puerto Viejo a freedom and privilege of mobility not realized by all women. Moreover, as they moved through the town's spaces (the bus stop, the beaches, the night clubs, and the streets) their sexualities shaped whom they interacted with, whom they did not, and the access they gained to local culture through the sexual relations they formed with local men. These were complex encounters, and entailed constraint as much as freedom. Women were marked and watched by local men and by gendered practices of homosocial relations, male camaraderie, and emphasized heterosexuality. Women's sexualities affected their physical mobility within the town too; for instance, being restricted to legitimate spaces for tourists within the town but also being allowed into the social worlds, and sometimes dwelling spaces, as in the scenario above, of foreign women who lived and worked in Puerto Viejo. In sum, they "deployed" sexuality in their travel mobilities at the same time as they actively participated in the fluidity of heterosexuality as historically and culturally situated "ways of being straight" (Ward 2010: 31). Through the lens of tourism we have been able to see in sharp relief the micro-processes of embodiment, bodily practices, intimacies, domesticity, eroticism, and material exchanges entailed in women's heterosexual subjectivities.

Contemporary travel, gender, and sexuality

> It's just about adventure.
>
> (An anthropology student, January 2011)

In a class I taught last fall, I was discussing with my students how global tourism affects interracial sexual relations and changing attitudes towards them. For the Canadian university students, the notion of cultural taboo in mixed relationships was resonant for some students but not others. When a female student in her early twenties explained to the class that because of international travel it was now "pretty normal" for women (or men) to want to experiment across cultures, she offered the rationale, "It's just about adventure." This normalization of international travel as something that every young person participates in, as well as the normalization of cross-border desire as an "adventure" that is therefore fueled by an underlying frisson of frontier crossing and the like, serves as an entry point for a wider discussion of sexuality through contemporary travel. It is easy to forget, for instance, the complicated relationship that women as a social group have with adventure as a historically masculinized form of rationalized travel. Notions of sex as an adventure, especially crossing racial/ethnic/national lines, obfuscates the gendered politics of both international travel and transnational sex, which warrants a discussion.

A large body of scholarship has addressed the history of travel as a masculine practice, which I do not go into detail here (see Kaplan 1996; Mills 1991; Smith

2001). Decades ago, Enloe underscored the gendered differences in travel practices in many societies where "masculinity has been the passport to travel" and in contrast "femininity has been defined as sticking close to home" (2000: 21). Travel was conducted by men and also, more importantly, the cultural logic of travel has been historically and widely rooted in discourses about masculinity (Smith 2001). This "ideological gendering of travel (as male)" has carried with it profound implications for women, as Wolff (1993: 234) has observed, both as an impediment to female travel and also as problematic to "the self-definition of (and response to) women who *do* travel."

Since the late nineteenth century, travel has been associated with modernity and the "freeing" of women from inequalities, including the unshackling of femininity from the home, etc. According to Smith (2001: 19), bourgeois women who traveled eschewed romance and sexually explicit behaviors to uphold social respectability and also because "the centrality of heterosexual romance" was founded upon a "degraded form of femininity." The valuation of travel as a means to "an enhanced authority experience" (Kaplan 2001: 220) is thus situated within a concomitant valuation of the palpably "masculine subject" (Rojek and Urry 1997). As Kaplan (2001: 223) contends, "traveling alone, seeking adventure, without the baggage of home or family is the preferred modus operandi for the modern Western [male] traveller." Zooming forward to the twenty-first century when the number of females traveling is equal to, if not greater than, males (Harris and Wilson 2007), it is claimed, in particular within global feminist discourses, that women's travel is therefore an inherent form of empowerment (Kaplan 1995). The problem, however, is that in viewing transnational sex as "an adventure" the geopolitics of race, nation and gender are completely erased; townspeople in Puerto Viejo made derisive comments about foreign women who used the local men to fulfill their "*aventuras*," because of the unlikelihood that the men would benefit in the long run for the sake of short-term pleasure. Not to diminish the men's experiences of enjoyment, satisfaction, and realization of their own dreams that they too gain from transnational encounters with foreign women, the undeniable reality is the relative lack of social and geographical mobility they have access to in comparison to their foreign girlfriends.

International travel, as significant a modality of selfhood, identity, and social capital as it is today for youth (Desforges 1998) and adults, is not only a "liminal space" where gender and sexuality result in an increased risk of sexual diseases for women travelers (Thomas 2005) and risks of sexual harassment (Jordan and Aitchison 2008; Lozanksi 2007; Wilson and Little 2008), although it is that too. Instead, as I have tried to show throughout the book, contemporary travel as a set of disjunctures and a highly meaningful activity is a social practice in which heterosexual desires are not "unleashed" as repressed impulses but are negotiated. By "negotiate" I mean that heterosexual desires and ways of being heterosexual (subjectivities) are brought about as well as managed and relationally derived in social relations between people. Amit (2007: 2) aptly describes contemporary travel as "various modalities of movement between locals" – in other words, people travel for work, study, and to relocate, as well as strictly for pleasure. It is the asymmetry between those who engage in these "modalities of movement" and those who do not that creates the very premise of contemporary travel – the basic fact is that for all the hundreds of millions of people moving across international boundaries, "the majority of the world's population is either not moving at all or not very far" (Amit 2007: 6). With regards to the local men with whom my interlocutors had relations, they held their own fantasies about traveling and living elsewhere too, but issues related to finances and visa restrictions meant that few of them traveled on their own accord and even with foreign girlfriends trying to facilitate trips to Germany and England, it was not always possible. These fundamental asymmetries between people who travel and people who cannot are the mechanisms by which potenti-alities for more exciting lives, more "pure" and nature-oriented lifestyles, more healthy and bodily-transformative experiences, or more adventuresome sex were, in the sense that Amit (2007) means, "unleashed."

Women's sexualities were negotiated within these intractable contexts and thus were shaped by micro- and macro-processes of global tourism in myriad ways. To think of tourism as transformative, I do not mean in the sense of magical properties of tourism as restorative and ritualistic. Rather I mean that tourism entails a constant transformation, where domesticity and "the everyday" influ-enced what women did and who they interacted with (and how) as much as, if not more than, the extraordinary or "liminal" elements of tourism. As I have shown, bodies came into being in the processes of tourism and new subjectivities arose.

Babies, "*violencia tres*," half-built homes

While this book has focused on the subjective experiences of Euro-American women, as they have encountered Costa Rica and Puerto Viejo as particular and idealized places and as sites where bodies, intimacies, and sexualities were trans-formed in small ways at least, the influence of foreign women as a social group and external "force" on the community has been hinted at but not foregrounded. Communities of foreign women who own property and small businesses have formed throughout the area. Foreign women are involved in recycling programs, in the development of after-school programs for children, and in hiring local tour guides and restaurant employees. In other words, the material implications of transnational sexual relations have not been discussed in the book yet play a cen-tral part in the contemporary social history of tourism in Puerto Viejo. Three domains of social life stood out for me – bicultural babies born to foreign women out of relationships with local men that began as "spontaneous" encounters, domestic violence that occurred within transnational couples, and the real estate (land and housing) owned by foreign women as an outcome of relationships with local men. I touch on these briefly here to suggest the profound ways in which tourism creates desires for many things, in which erotics and sexuality are deeply implicated but that have a much longer lasting presence within the community and local spaces than a casual fling during a holiday.

While a few of the women I interviewed at the beginning of my fieldwork had babies with local men, by the end of my research in 2009 it seemed a baby boom was taking place. Women who had arrived as tourists when I first interviewed them had returned to Costa Rica to live temporarily or to relocate permanently. I noticed women with babies strapped in baby seats on their bicycles and pushing their babies in strollers down the bumpy roads in town. During one visit when I stayed in a hotel in town with a swimming pool that Breck could enjoy while I worked, on a warm afternoon we found ourselves surrounded by several new moms and their infants. While we shared the pool with them, a Swiss woman I knew, with a splashing baby in tow, explained to me that her pregnancy had been a surprise to her. She told me that she had read somewhere that "nearly 80 percent of pregnancies in the world" are "unplanned," which provided me with a rich metaphor to think about the linkage between sexual spontaneity and procreation in the context of tourism. Women spoke of their desires for "brown babies" and "mixed race" babies, desires that they traced back to their girlhoods back home in Europe or the United States. Babies, in this regard, were part of wider tourist imaginations of the Caribbean and of a tropical paradise. Such understandings were not lost on townspeople who were acutely aware of the social implications of tourists' dreams for what one Afro-Caribbean woman referred to as "souvenir babies," children borne out of relationships with local men who were the sons and nephews of local women for whom kin relations and cultural identity were paramount (Frohlick 2011). I see these babies and children therefore as mediators of new relationships formed in the interstices of global tourism and borderland erotics, genealogical connections between local women and foreign women, and therefore yet another reconfiguration of intimacy and relatedness.

Violence perpetuated by their local boyfriends was a theme in several women's interviews. One woman referred to two separate incidents, each one occurring in a distinct time and place in her recollection as "*violencia uno*," and "*dos*," where her boyfriend struck her, once, and nearly strangled her another time, out of what she regarded as anger and frustration. The second incident occurred when she was getting ready to leave him and return home, and she saw his lashing out related to psychological trauma caused by the women in his life leaving him over and over again. Women mentioned incidents of confrontations when their boyfriend wanted money from them, or had accused the woman of trying to control them or spy on them. In addition to numerous references to incidences of domestic violence between couples (and women admitted to hitting their boyfriends too, so the aggression was not completely one sided), there were several incidents over the five years of my fieldwork of men's physical assaults against tourist women in public spaces. A woman I knew quite well had been accosted on her bicycle one night riding back home from the village along the coastal road and had been badly hurt; ostensibly she had been robbed but valuables in her possession had not been taken. Additional assaults occurred where the female victims, apparently unknown to the assailants, had been badly beaten. One woman died from her injuries. I have not kept track of these incidents, so here I write about them as the vague bits of news I would hear when I was back in Canada in telephone and email conversations with friends living in Puerto Viejo. Yet violence touched all of the women I came to know well, either through their own experiences or those of their friends.

Like all violence against women the incidences require careful contextualization and unraveling. Mental health issues, familial violence, poverty, drug addictions, rapid social change, increasing economic disparity within Costa Rica, in addition to the power struggles pertaining to gendered mobility (that is, the foreign women's ability to leave whenever they want to), are all pieces of the very complex puzzle that the local practices of men's violence towards tourist women warrants. Here, I raise the question of the mutual construction of desire and the impossibility of attaining things that are played out in tourism economies – and the impossible, and treacherous, position in which foreign women are mired as potential sponsors, on the one hand, and the despised "enemy," on the other. I cannot help but think of a man I spoke with only once who, in the short time we spoke together, told me how badly he wanted to meet a foreign women to buy him land and a house and how he, as I would find out later, had a reputation for beating up women and had served time in prison for doing so. A fuller account of cross-border desire would look more closely at these skirmishes, for they are as much a part of the sociality and physical landscape as the "*se vende*" signs that litter the coastal road.

The mention of "for sale" signs is important too, for land deals and the selling of tracts of jungle for the development of vacation and residential housing are also an important economic context to, and the material tracings of, cross-border desire in Puerto Viejo. What I found fascinating was the way in which dreams to own land and to build a small house were aspirations that many foreign women developed over the course of their holiday visits (as I did too). Friends inspired friends to spend relatively small amounts of money in relation to the cost of land in the United States, Europe, or Canada to carve out a piece of Costa Rica for themselves. In hearing women talk about real estate (and in looking around myself), it became apparent to me how, once again, desires for one thing were linked to other desires sparked by tourism capitalism and consumption. After awhile it seemed as though having a local boyfriend and a tract of land to build a house went completely hand in hand. Rumors circulated that foreign women bought land to "lure" local men and to "keep" them. When a friend of a friend started to build a house and got as far as the cement foundation and cinder block walls, and abandoned the project when she returned to the United States (with a baby in tow), the site reminded me of the semi-permanence of the flows of tourist women in and out of Puerto Viejo. Weeds took over quickly, turning grey cement into a blaze of bright green – forming a kind of monument to the social relations that formed so instantly and yet were ultimately very fragile. This half-built house is a physical manifestation of the flux and fluidity of cross-border desires that goes well beyond erotic acts to acts of support, of hope, and relatedness that have yet to be fully worked out.

Ethnographic failings ...

> Hence, to situate ethnography as a ruin/rune is to foreground the limits and necessary misfirings of its project.
>
> (Lather 2001: 202).

> Something is always said. The question remains – what is the relation between these representations, suggestions, rumours, and fictions and the actual acts of sex in any time.
>
> (Bhattacharyya 2002: 54)

On a visit to Puerto Viejo in August 2009 as this project was wrapping up, I write in my fieldnotes about how tired I am and that I have to remind myself how tiring fieldwork is, especially in the tropical climate. (August is very humid, with high temperatures, on the Atlantic coast.) Following the note to myself about needing time to readjust to the weather, I write:

> Enough guilt. Enough excuses. This is fieldwork: The incessant feeling of never doing it right, either enjoying it too much or not enough, of not talking to the right people, or of wanting to talk to more of the right people as the right person is talking to you at the present moment … on it goes. The other project now [is] taking more of my efforts than the last one, and the other project [a third project] takes a back seat to both of those.

That same day, I spend several hours in the afternoon with Alex. She shows me the land she has bought at a reduced price in 2009 (after the recession in 2008) where she hopes to build a small house in the coming years. We get a bit lost on our way to the property because I am unfamiliar with these new streets carved in the dense jungle to accommodate the demand for land; Alex gets out of the jeep and walks the last bit, directing me where to park so that my daughter and I can get out to take some photographs. Later in the afternoon, I spent another hour or more with another friend, Salina, a woman I interviewed in 2006, now the mother of a beautiful little girl, whose father is a local resident. She, too, is buying some property. Although she does not know his role exactly in her and her daughter's lives – we discussed the pros and cons of having his name on her birth certificate – my friend is happy to have made a family for herself in Costa Rica.

I discussed with both women my interest in researching "the next phase" of transnational romances, the children borne out of cross-border relations between foreign women and local men, and they agree with me that it is a great idea. Alex told me that what was really interesting "about 'the baby thing' was because," in her words, "having a baby with a local man was the ultimate last commitment sort of thing, that you can have your fling with a local guy, feel like you're in love, but to have a child with him is a relationship forever with him." Salina disagrees that this is the most interesting aspect. For her, already a mother, it is not the conception part but rather what happens after the baby is born and the mother is trying to raise them here in Costa Rica that she thinks I should research.

Later again during that same fieldwork visit, another friend, Iris, is lending me her support in writing the book (this book). I am surprised to hear her version of the book, that it should tell the story of white women exploiting black men, with a legacy of slavery and colonialism, by treating them as hypersexual objects. We engage in an intense conversation about this. "Really?" I ask her, pressing her to remember our first conversations several years ago when her opinion suggested the opposite, that local men were oppressing white tourist women who were relatively powerless against the men's physical strength and emotional cunning. She looks puzzled for a second, then her face grimaces. "True, yes, that is also true. I did say that!" Iris offered, and we went on to discuss the complexities, once again, as we had before. That night I had a difficult time sleeping, as thoughts raced through my mind. Someone in the room below me, another hotel guest, had left their television on, and the sound of muffled voices, incomprehensible but audible, further disturbed the quietude I was seeking. I went outside to the balcony of the guesthouse room. The outside noises were easier on my ears. I could hear the waves crashing in the front of the town, a few blocks away. Probably Salsa Brava, I reasoned.[4] At the back of the town, I heard the cicadas, crickets, and the occasional sound of a dog barking.

While I have set out to "capture the lived experiences of women," the fundamental project of feminist ethnography, as noted in the Introduction, I have accomplished this task partially and with partiality. In the excerpts and transcriptions from my fieldnotes throughout, I have indicated the personal limitations of ethnography as a fully embodied methodology and also the interested manner in which I sought knowledge about the "field." In previous chapters I have articulated the role of fatigue, stress, and the limited capabilities of observation and embodied participation that played out for me in my fieldwork. These are important limitations to point out for they clarify to the reader the impossibility, and the arrogance, of a "fully knowing" ethnographer (Coffey 1999; Lather 2001). Yet there is another related and equally important point that I wish to make about feminist ethnography as a productive rather than apologetic "failure" (Visweswaren 1994). This concerns the strategies that provide compensation, although only partially satisfactory, to what has been referred to as the "violent act" of representation that characterizes ethnography by its very nature (Behar 1993).[5]

Since the 1980s, feminist ethnography has grappled with multiple tensions in telling women's stories, especially in light of postcolonial critiques of white supremacy within feminist scholarship. Productive debates about the failure of ethnography, not only as method but also as epistemology, have ensued (e.g.

Ahmed 2000; Lather 2001). I share concerns with the inescapable politics entailed in formulating accounts about other women's lives, even when the women are white, privileged, and relatively elite, as I am. Yet it remains the case that spending time with women over durations of time as they go about their day and in seeing the contradictions in their actions and words, while recognizing all of it as a mere "tip of the iceberg" in terms of what is not seen, or heard, or known, results in a view of women's sexual lives that is situated in the everyday. This, in turn, facilitated my own emergent conceptualization of heterosexuality as that which goes beyond sexual desires and practices to thinking about straight culture and women's agentive roles in its production and reproduction. A feminist ethnography of Euro-American women based on the indeterminacies of complex lives is thus, I argue, an important corrective to the polemical and thinly researched accounts of a rather contentious figure in the sexist social imagination where, more generally, women's sexuality, no matter what race, ethnicity, nationality, or sexual preference, remains subjected to scrutiny.

Within the current assemblage of global imagery, women's cross-border sexual relations are often either romanticized or demonized. Popular representations and academic scholarship reflect a kind of polemical reaction to the apparent behaviors of women who have sex with local men in Third-World destinations. As I argue elsewhere, the advent of "female sex tourism" has piqued somewhat of an abject fascination in the public imagination (Frohlick 2010: 54). A phenomenon traced to about the late 1970s when women began to engage in international tourism en masse influenced by "sexual liberation" movements and second wave feminism in North America and Western Europe, a new social category emerged – the female sex tourist. Movies, books, plays, and other popular culture reflect a kind of public anxiety over the potentially wider and farther reach of women's sexual desire as women gain economic power and independence from work and home to travel. As Aston has suggested, "Socially and culturally the figure of the female sex tourist attracts a range of hotly debated views" (2008: 181).

At one end of the spectrum of representation of women's cross-border sex are what I call "romanticizations," which are representations that construct and celebrate a heroic salacious female sexual subject. The book, *Romance on the Road* (Belliveau 2006), that purports to depict "traveling women who love foreign men," is a prime example of liberal feminist discourses that uphold and applaud the sexual conduct of women pleasure seekers as liberating. On the other hand, scholarship that addresses women's sex tourism in terms of heinous sexual exploitation of beach boys and hustlers in Jamaica, the Dominican Republic, and other Caribbean destinations, made possible due to vast political economic and racial disparities, tends to construct a view of white feminine heterosexual sexualities as particularly disdainful and, even, despicable (notably, O'Connell Davidson and Sánchez Taylor 2005). Yet another kind of what I have referred to elsewhere as "despicable sexuality" (Frohlick 2010) can be seen in online forums, print media, and films where "the female sex tourist" is represented as a despised and pathetic figure, "where her longings for sexual conquest in tropical poverty-stricken countries like Haiti or Jamaica hinge on failure to win a man back home in Canada or Britain or failure to embody the aesthetics of normative feminine beauty" (Frohlick 2010: 55). In Aston's commentary on the phenomenon of "the staging of female sex tourism" (about two plays in Britain about female sex tourists) she writes about this sort of derision. An article appearing in the British newspaper *Guardian* states, "the female sex traveler in the twenty first century is ... someone who both deludes herself (paying for sex masquerading as holiday romance) at the same time exploiting men from poorer, developing, tourist destinations" (Aston 2008: 181).

This book hopes to challenge these polemical and sensationalistic accounts by providing specificity to how transnational sex happens from the perspectives of women involved in the relationships and also by humanizing them so that the line between "us" and "them," and between "sex tourism" and "ordinary sex" (Jackson 2008), is ruptured. Many women I interviewed would tell me in one breath that local men were like prostitutes and in the next breathe that what was happening was not "sex tourism." I relate this disjuncture in part to the promise of international travel and tourism to provide the ultimate in "unique" experiences, linked to the metanarrative of authenticity and spontaneity. It cannot be sex tourism if I am having my own unique experience ... but the whole point of the book has been to respectfully tear away at that illusion as well as to argue that so much more is happening than any notion of a simple sexual exchange, if such a relationship exists. When we were discussing female sex tourism in one of my classes recently, a young woman articulated this kind of de-exoticization of sex tourism very well when she explained to another student (who simply refused to imagine any "smart enough woman" falling for a beach boy type guy), "You have to experience it yourself because once you meet these guys you can imagine that it is possible." Through the stories of women's experiences, I hope that I have said less about the "actual acts of sex" at the historical moment in time (Bhattacharyya 2002: 54) and more about the social relations and social processes that give rise to them and to the rumors and representations that exoticize them and make them a source of outrage.

Imagining tourist places

May 21, 2010: Fieldnotes People seem to be watching me. Cherise, a local woman who is often standing at the corner of the bridge at the edge of town, reputedly sells herself for sex, walked up to Alex today and told her, "I see that friend of yours in [one of the local bars]. That's not a good place. Don't worry," she assured Alex, "I watching her for you." Later in the evening, I was at another friend's who had a small gathering of foreign and local residents. A young Costa Rican man I met at least three years ago recognized me. "You're writing that book, right?" he asked me.

A story that I heard early on in my fieldwork has always stuck with me. It is about a town resident, a young Afro-Caribbean man, who traveled to Germany to spend time with his girlfriend, and discovered that she lived in a very small apartment in a large building without any access to the outdoors and with very few windows. He spent his days inside waiting for her to get home from work because he found the city streets frightening on his own. When he returned to Puerto Viejo, he told his friends that he would never return to Europe because he didn't want to be stuck in a box. While this is a fascinating allegory to tame the effervescent love of international travel that foreign women project onto the people they meet in Puerto Viejo (how incredulous is it that someone might not want to travel?), I borrow it here for another purpose. My own concern with sticking people in boxes has to do with my interest in not writing people into boxes in my representation of the town. On a visit in 2010, long after the manuscript had been started, a foreign resident asked me, "When will your book be done?" I replied with my usual answer, "Oh, it's taking me awhile. It's tough to write about these things." He was nonplussed about the apparent difficulties I was grappling with over the ethical issues of representation. He replied very matter-of-factly with this advice, "Don't judge anyone, just tell the truth."

Feminist ethnography is attentive to the politics of representation as I outline above, to the point of self-abjection at times, as Lather (2001: 222) describes. She writes about how feminist ethnography proceeds in spite of the anxieties on which it is based. In a similar way, I urge that tourism scholars write from the tension between the politics of representation and the impossibilities of not writing, despite anxieties of doing so. Adams writes about "the unique ethical quandaries that anthropologists face when conducting research in touristic milieus" and how ethical dilemmas can "ensue once we have left the field and are at home constructing theoretically informed anthropological portraits of the toured communities we study" (2005: 46). She goes on to say how we are expected to "present captivating, entertaining, and tantalizing accounts of the cultures being toured," which presents dilemmas since our own theories often "collide" with local perceptions and tourism-generating activities (Adams 2005: 47, 57). I, too, see this space of potential immobilization as "an ethically murky zone" (Adams 2005: 57), and my own concern is that I may represent a small community dependent on tourism revenue in an unfavorable light. Many townspeople did not like me speaking about sex and sexuality, let alone writing about what are for religious folks taboo topics and in a country where the Catholic Church wields influence over any public sexual discourse. I am also concerned about writing about illegal activities undertaken by tourists and foreign and local residents (foreigners staying past their tourist visas, working without papers in restaurants, locals selling marijuana, foreigners having sex with underage minors). I weigh out these concerns with the proliferation of media that circulates, including state-funded media campaigns, as I describe in Chapter 2, which constructs and perpetuates the double-edged secret. The first secret is the mythology that paradise is paradise, and the second is that of sexual secrecy. *Escondido*. Nobody is having sex, yet everyone talks about it. As Bolton (1995) has very clearly articulated, sexual secrecy is a means by which hypocrisy, abuse, the spread of sexual disease, and even rape, are enabled. The trope of paradise and the normative practice of sexual secrecy are powerful and intertwined stories in Puerto Viejo. My interest in writ-ing, amidst a myriad of anxieties, is in both drawing attention to and disrupting the taken-for-granted assumptions entailed in contemporary travel to a place imagined in a particular way. Women imagined things one way, and the reality was very different. That, for me, is the crux.

In the words of my interlocutor, Nadine, an American woman in her mid-twenties who had arrived as a fresh tourist girl a year before I met her, and returned every few months to visit her local boyfriend:

> I think a lot of girls leave here broken. You see that a lot. I see that a lot. You know, they come here thinking that all their dreams are gonna be fulfilled in Puerto Viejo and they leave, you know, disappointed I guess.

Notes

Introduction

1 I use "rasta" rather than the capitalized "Rasta" to reflect a generalized category of black counterculture male identity, which had been adopted by a range of men by 2004, when I arrived for fieldwork, and which had already become globalized – performed by men in Indonesia and Thailand, for instance, and therefore not associated exclusively with blackness. See Anderson (2004) for a history of Rastafarianism in the southern Caribbean of Costa Rica where it is closely linked to tourism. Many townspeople as well as several Rastafari-tourists told me that in Puerto Viejo there were no "real" "Rastas," that is, those who ascribed to Rastafari principles, nor did any local men tell me that they wished to be taken as Rastafarian. Rather, they found that foreign women liked the looks of dreadlocked hair, the sounds of reggae music, anti-materialism ideology, and also the resonance of "nature" that aligns with both ecotourism discourses and Rastafarian beliefs as a source of power and healing, including marijuana (ganja) and herbal medicinal cures (Chevannes 2010.

2 "*Tico*" (or *tica*, for females) is a term for any native of Costa Rica but in Puerto Viejo often reserved for ethnically "white" Costa Ricans with European ancestry.

3 To clarify a confusing situation, there are three towns in Costa Rica that have the name "Puerto Viejo," which means "Old Harbor." To further complicate things, Puerto Viejo on the Atlantic coast is known by different names too, including "Puerto Viejo de Limón" and Puerto Viejo de Talamanca (its official name). Throughout the book I use "Puerto Viejo" to refer not only to the town proper but also the surrounding area about ten kilometers to the south of the town, which includes several small hamlets and communities. After weighing out the advantages and disadvantages, I decided to use the actual name of the town rather than a pseudonym in this book. The use of false names for places in anthropological writing is a contested convention (see Finnegan 2003) as much as it can be an important strategy to ensure anonymity of a small population (Hopkins 1993). My decision was pragmatic insofar as researchers before me have used the actual name in important published literature that I cite, although I have argued elsewhere that there are no easy answers to ethical issues especially when the research topic is controversial (Frohlick 2008a).

4 This name is a pseudonym, as are all the people's names throughout the book. I have altered real names and identifying characteristics of research participants in order to protect their anonymity while retaining as much accuracy as possible. The false names I use, to the best of my ability, reflect the ethnicity, gender, and generation of the participant and, to some degree, their actual name. I consulted with research participants for options, and some chose their own pseudonym and others provided me with a list of suitable names.

I apologize to anyone who feels I ultimately did not succeed in getting the balance quite right. Scores of details of people's experiences and stories told to me in interviews are purposely left out of the book to protect the privacy of my participants and also the privacy of the men whose lives became part of the women's stories. The dignity of my research participants and of the community at large was a primary concern in my writing strategies.

5 "*Gringo*" is used in Costa Rica mostly to refer to American men, and "*gringa*" to refer to American women. "*Gringos*" can be a neutral term for "tourists" but it also carries negative meanings, often associated with amoral sexual behavior of Western foreigners, and often specifically Americans, as Rivers-Moore (2009) discusses in her thesis on transnational sex tourism in Costa Rica.

6 "Foreign women" was a category used locally that signified women from countries in the global North (rather than women from Nicaragua or Panama, for instance), regardless of racial identity – although whiteness was predominant. I use "foreign" in this local sense, as a relational category. I use "Euro-American" as an imperfect analytical category to refer broadly to women from Europe, Canada, the United States, New Zealand, and Australia and thus to emphasize nationality and citizenship, which are especially salient markers of identification in tourist communities. I do not use the term to refer to North Americans of European ancestry, which is sometimes how the term is used elsewhere. Because it is less misleading in this regard, I prefer the longer phrase, "European and North American," although it is more cumbersome. The way all of these terms homogenize a diverse group of people and obfuscate important socio-cultural and historical-political differences between nationalities as well as ethnic, racial, and cultural differences within national citizenship is important to the understanding of global tourism and associated homogenizing processes.

7 This gravel road has since been paved.

8 Eddie Ryan wrote a handmade pamphlet in 2004 that was locally distributed, outlining the diversity of the local population, where he coins the expression "ethno-cultural rondon." Ryan writes about how the ethno-cultural "rondon" (a local stew made with whatever one can "rundown") was on the rise from about the 1920s onwards. His characterization of the town's heterogeneity is a positive one, echoing a discourse common within transnational Euro-American-Costa Rican families in the community: "The stew is now rich and thick with an exotic, provocative flavor. These are the children of the rainbow, Caribbean youth, young Talamancans, multi-lingual Costa Ricans – the future! On the recipe the directions tell us to cook it with love, stirring it gently, with the final product a new identity, a community that promotes and defends the common interest."

9 The Central Valley refers to the central highlands where the capital city, San José, is located along with other towns related to the central administration and commerce of the country. The Talamanca region as the home of the country's racial minorities has a long complex history in its relations with the Central Valley, and this continues in the era of the region's tourism development.

10 Costa Rica is divided into seven provinces, which are sub-divided into "cantons" (counties). The country is also divided into six regions, mostly related to public health administration. With respect to human geography, Puerto Viejo is located in the Limón province, the Huetar Atlántica district, and the canton of Talamanca.

11 Thanks to Miss Siannie Palmer for giving me this wonderfully picturesque phrase.

12 I plan to carry out future research on the sexual health implications of the sexual behaviors of tourists in this area of Costa Rica. See Freidus and Romero-Daza (2009) and Romero-Daza and Freidus (2008) for discussion on HIV implications for female tourists in other regions of Costa Rica.

13 This figure is from the World Tourism Organization website.

1 Desiring Costa Rica

1 From the pamphlet *CifraTurísticas*, Edicíon 1, Noviembre 2010, published by the *Instituto Costarricense de Turismo*. The exact figure for 2008 international tourist arrivals is 2,089,174. The numbers decreased the following year to 1,922,579.

2 These are taken from the same source as above.

3 In the late 1990s estimates of 3,000 sex workers in San José alone with over 11,000 sex workers in the entire country were reported by Downe (1997: 1575).

4 End Child Prostitution and Child Pornography and Trafficking of Children for Sexual Purposes (ECPAT) is an international network of non-government organizations against child sex trafficking, which has been subject to its own share of criticisms.

5 http://thefastertimes.com/travelnews/2010/01/06/thriving-sex-tourism-industry-bumps-costa-rica-from-list-of-worlds-most-ethical-destinations/ (accessed 22 June 2010).

6 http://www.zoomvacations.com/prcostarica.htm (accessed 24 June 2010).

7 These posters can be seen on the following website for the ICT's 2004 International Campaign: http://www.visitcostarica.com/ict/paginas/en_afiches_portada.asp.

8 A plethora of discourses circulate globally about the apparent "happiness factor" of Costa Rican society, based on a ranking put out in 2009 by The New Economics Foundation (NEF) called "The Happy Planet Index." For instance, see http://edition.cnn.com/2009/WORLD/americas/07/05/costa.rica.happy.nation/ (accessed 2 February 2012). Although no interviewees mentioned this specific designation, several women referred more generally to how Costa Rica "is known" as a "happy place."

9 http://pocketcultures.com/2010/01/26/costa-rica-is-"pura-vida"/ (accessed 2 February 2012).

10 More specifically, Costa Rica was being held up to global scrutiny for its role as a "staging ground" for the American imperialist power and their support of the US-backed Contras as well as a "testing ground for US free trade and privatization policies" (Honey 2004: 407).

11 http://www.usatoday.com/travel/deals/inside/2006-07-26-safe-womens-travel_x.htm (accessed 22 February 2008).

12 See *Tico Times*, 18 August 2006, p. 52.

13 http://www.smartertravel.com/travel-advice/the-best-and-worst-destinations-for-women-worldwide.html?id=1266033&page=4 (accessed 2 February 2012).

14 Statistics on tourist arrivals into Costa Rica by gender are non-existence; however it is based on the 1.7 million arrival figure in 2005 and the 2 million arrival figure in 2008 that I am making this claim. See http://costarica-information.com/about-costa-rica/economy/economic-sectors-industries/tourism/tourism-statistics (accessed 2 February 2012).

15 The main fieldwork trips included August 2005, January to April 2006, August 2006, December 2006, April and May 2007, September 2008, and August 2009. Shorter follow-up trips took place in 2010 and 2011 (September).

16 The University of Manitoba Joint Faculty Research Ethics Board Research approved the research protocol. Informed consent was an ongoing process, and participants were informed that I was writing a book and other publications. Most interviewees were given the opportunity to read their transcripts and make comments or changes. Only one woman retracted her initial interview and subsequently volunteered for a second interview so that I could use the material. A few women made slight corrections or changes but the majority did not make any. Also, post-fieldwork correspondence with participants was not always possible or successful (emails that were not answered, for instance) even though I had hoped it would be.

17 Approximately 50 percent of the women I interviewed were from Canada and the United States while the remaining 50 percent were from Europe and Australia/New Zealand. Two women were from Costa Rica and were included because they were daughters of Euro-American mothers.

18 Ten women were full-time residents who first came to Costa Rica as tourists; most of them had babies or older children fathered by local men, a main reason they had relocated. While this latter group more accurately fit other categories including "expatriates" or "immigrants" their stories to me focused on when they first arrived in Costa Rica as tourists. I have written elsewhere about how love, sex, and cross-border intimacies have shaped tourism-related migration for these women (Frohlick 2009). In this book, I foreground the stories of women who were not permanent residents. However, in their interviews the women who had been in Puerto Viejo for several years provided absolutely crucial wider historical context to the current situation, and some of these women's stories are interwoven in the book.

19 See   http://pub.unwto.org/WebRoot/Store/Shops/Infoshop/Products/1034/1034-1.pdf (accessed 4 February 2011).

20 "Because they are dogs."

21 See Maksymowicz (2010) for an analysis of competing masculinities between foreign men and local men in Puerto Viejo.

22 Men's experiences remain to be examined in a future study.

2 Sexuality

1 The resistance to condom use by men in Costa Rica as reported by foreign women is widespread (Freidus and Romero-Daza 2009; Ragsdale *et al.* 2006; Romero-Daza and Freidus 2008). Factors include a constrained public discourse around sexuality and sexual health in Costa Rica, the cost and unavailability of condoms in the rural areas, and gender dynamics in heterosexual relations. In Puerto Viejo, condoms were available for sale in the pharmacy but free condoms were not readily available as in the larger cities, partly because prior to 2009 there were no sexual health clinics or sex education non-government organizations. In 2007, a local physician expressed his concern about the high risk of HIV related to what he referred to as "a highly sexual community" and, in his words, "a lot of promiscuity in the town [where] one mix with the other, the other mix with the other ... without any type of protection" (interview, August 2007).

2 "Sport fucking" refers broadly to casual sex. Kipnis (2006) draws out its masculinist connotations when used by women that implies the achievement of sexual empowerment by acting "like one of the guys," where masculinity, sports, competition with other men, and sex overlap. Josie's usage invokes this gendered meaning as well as the contextual meaning where sex is akin to entertainment in a place where tourist mobility determines sexual sociality for local people.

3 Throughout the book I include fieldnote excerpts for a variety of reasons. Fieldnotes are meant to describe observed cultural realities (Clifford 1990: 51) and to generate "thick descriptions" (Geertz 1973). But fieldnotes are necessarily partial and perspectival as they are based on "experiences, thoughts, hunches, dreams, interactions, and observations" of the researcher; thus, they are "part of the larger story of who you [the researcher] is, "where you've been, what you read and talked about and argued over, what you believe in and value, what you feel compelled to name as significant" (Goodall 2000: 87). I use fieldnotes both to evoke a sense of what happened in the field and to allow

readers to recognize the creative process that is entailed in the process of selecting field-notes and transforming experience into theory and representation (Hastrup 1995: 21). My fieldnotes consist mostly of semi-regular jottings, usually at the end of a fieldwork day, on my laptop computer, in narrative and sometimes point form. I preferred narrative form because I wanted to capture the events as stories unfolding before me.

4　Colones are the national currency in Costa Rica. In 2006, 200 colones were worth about 40 US cents US (or 50 Canadian cents or 30 Euro cents).

3　Embodiment

1　Local women occupy these spaces too, such as the woman who sells grilled chicken to late-night revelers and women who hustle tourists for cash, cigarettes, food, drugs, or sex. Between 2005 and 2008, a few local women went to the discos to dance. The gendered dynamics of public spaces of leisure and consumption were changing, however, as I noticed more local women and younger girls out when I was there in 2010 and 2011.

2　Consumption of drugs and marijuana were central to some women. Drug practices of their boyfriends were recurrent themes in many women's interviews, and undoubtedly substance abuse issues were present in many different groups in the community including foreign residents. The role of foreigners in the local history of illicit drugs was hinted at in stories that circulated about several notorious drug-trafficking tourists and vagabonds who made their way to Puerto Viejo in the 1980s and 1990s. The complexity of the linkages of drugs (ingesting, selling, suffering effects of) and transnational sex and intimate relations remains to be seen, however, in further research. Recreational drug use is important to mention here as one particularly obfuscated aspect of bodily practices in tourism and also as a contravening factor in discourses of "nature" and "pure" that permeate the branding of Costa Rica and the narratives of tourist women.

3　He was referring to the Gandoca-Manzanillo National Wildlife Refuge, a 13,000-acre protected area of coastal rainforest and mangrove that is a popular tourist attraction, and was the impetus for a paved road down to the southernmost region of Atlantic Costa Rica.

4　The "vibe" of the town's atmosphere was heterosexualized in many ways, including the religious sanctions against same-sex relations, the Caribbean community's disavowal of homosexuality, the lack of a lesbian tourism industry, and the surfing atmosphere. This was not an area for lesbian tourists the way that it was a place for heterosexual and straight tourist women, in other words. See also note 8.

5　Not only European and North America but also Japanese women took part in new gendered travel mobilities during the growth of women's international travel, although not to Costa Rica.

6　I have altered aspects of Gretta's life story, leaving out identifying features to protect her anonymity.

7　Only three years later, in 2008, the global recession had resulted in closed real estate offices.

8　Kelly's observation was not far off the mark. Although the notion of Caribbean culture as homophobic is problematic in its stereotyping, at the same time the degree of intolerance for same-sex sexualities in the town due to religious, cultural, national, and transnational influences was markedly strong. Scholars point to the entrenched homophobia in Costa Rican society as a "key field of national identification" performed in soccer (Sandoval-Garciá 2005: 228), and to the queer bashing that proliferates in reggae lyrics and Rastafarism in Jamaica and throughout the Caribbean that links being gay with "Babylon" and white, Western, liberal sexual ideology (Lewis 2003). What seems true in Puerto Viejo is that "in-your-face heterosexuality" and "hatred of LGBT-people" (lesbian, gay, bisexual and transgender individuals) appear to be "two sides of the same coin," as La Font (2009: 109) claims about Jamaica. Yet recognition of such attitudes should not obscure the homosexual practices and gay, lesbian, and other so-called non-normative sexualities occurring in everyday life in the community including the very visible gay (men's) tourism that was developing in 2010. Kelly's visit took place within this changing social landscape where levels of tolerance for gay men may have been increasing, at least publicly, but social stigma for lesbians was unmistakable.

9 I would like to acknowledge Liz Millward for pointing this out to me.

10 Kantsa's work on the spatial transformation of the beach town, Skala Eresos, on the Greek island of Lesvos to "a 'lesbian' place" is pertinent here (2002: 39). She shows how its history as the birthplace of Sappho has led to the town's transformation since the 1970s as a "place with a 'different' energy" by lesbian tourists and Greek lesbians attracted to the possibility of shared lesbian space and free expression of erotic feelings (2002: 51). This is a useful analogy to thinking about Puerto Viejo as a place with a special vibe, and a place that attracts heterosexual women insofar as "tourism plays a significant role in the production of sexualized spaces" (Kantsa 2002: 36).

4 Intimacy

1 This refers to the notion that anthropologists gauge the depth of their knowledge about people's lives by various measures, including, in Wolcott's (2005: 71) view, what they know about their informants' "sleeping arrangements," meaning sleeping practices and also sexual partners. While sleeping arrangements, along with laundry habits and people's grandmothers, are only one "litmus test" anthropologists might use, according to Wolcott, I found it telling that these measures were salient for tourist women, too, in their own assessments of intimacies they formed with local boyfriends in Puerto Viejo. For instance, being introduced to men's family members, especially a grandmother, carried social currency. This reflects the sort of cultural immersion travel experience they were seeking, which has gendered underpinnings.

2 In an earlier article about Alex and Fernando (Frohlick 2009), I wrote that he had moved in to her rented *cabina* when they first met and that she paid all of the bills. This was incorrect. Since then, Alex has set the record straight by explaining that Fernando actually had been the "provider" in the beginning and insisted that she not work at all. This is an important corrective to my own assumption about the role of foreign women's financial contributions to cross-border relationships, which is much more dynamic and two-way than stereotypes and also scholarship on female sex tourism suggest.

3 My interlocutors often used "*machismo*" and "*macho*" to index the negative aspects of local masculine gender identities and performances of masculinity including sexual promiscuity, "cheating," and aggression but they also used it to ridicule the men for what seemed like ridiculous behavior to the foreign women, such as needing to be the person to ride the bicycle or ATV with the women as the passengers. Just as in Mexico where the image of macho "is a complex one with multiple and shifting meanings" (Gutmann in Wade 2009: 226), so too is it in Costa Rica. The central point is that tourist women constantly were puzzled by, contested, made fun of, and yet also held up hegemonic meanings of macho in their desires for local men.

4 Researchers conducting studies on transnational sex in other tourist areas in Costa Rica observe a similar desire by Northern tourists for "direct and regular interactions with locals" (Freidus and Romero-Daza 2009; Romero-Daza and Freidus 2008). Enrolling in Spanish language study, participating in university field schools, or opening up small businesses such as youth hostels are activities foreign women find appealing in the region of Monteverde and that allow them to participate in long-stay tourism (Freidus and Romero-Daza 2009: 687, 688; Romero-Daza and Freidus 2008). Freidus and Romero-Daza point out how such particularly intimate "global flows" of people influence "the structuring of social and sexual relations," including the increased likelihood of sexually transmitted infections and HIV/AIDS, which is the focus of their research (2009: 684).

5 "*Novia*" means girlfriend but does not signify a sexually exclusive relationship the way that "girlfriend" does in sexual cultures in Northern societies. "*Mujer*," meaning "woman," was a new term for many of my interlocutors, and they struggled with trying to understand the implications of this category that often implied a much stronger commitment to the local man than Euro-American women at first realized. At the same time, some women considered being a local man's "*mujer*" was a supreme compliment and they liked being referred to as such-and-such's *mujer*, which was common practice. Misunderstandings occurred frequently, as women indicated to me in interviews and conversations, and cross-cultural clashes over different categories of intimacy and relatedness resulted in many emotional upsets on the part of women I knew.

5 Difference

1 This brand of rubber sandal, made in Brazil, is popular with tourists and local surfers. It serves as one of many signs of transnationalism and globalization in Puerto Viejo.

2 I use the anthropological kinship term, "endogamous," here to conceptualize sex between tourists as akin to sexual relations within cultural groups.

3 Indigeneity was less visible to tourists partly because of the spatial social organization of indigenous people in the area; that is, they lived in communities that were located in the hills and forests rather than in the beach towns. A nearby town, much larger than Puerto Viejo, BriBri, named after the local indigenous group and the region's administrative centre, would be where indigenous people would be seen by tourists, on their way to various tours, such as to see banana plantations or waterfalls or to go kayaking in the Sixaola River. None of my interlocutors expressed an attraction to indigenous masculinities, although a couple of foreign resident women I knew had been involved with indigenous men. One woman, Gretta, (whose story appears in Chapter 3) once told me that she thought indigenous men were on the brink of becoming the new "fashion" for tourist women's aesthetic appeal. However, in her view, it was still "black men and the Caribbean adventure" that was most attractive to most foreign women.

4 Lancaster (1992) uses this term specifically for how racial difference is played out relationally, according to color lines of black, brown, and white, in Nicaragua. His point, that discrimination in Nicaragua based on shifting readings of people's skin is part of the *mestizo* culture rather than directed at "black" people as an absolute category, which is why he uses "colorism" rather than "racism," sheds light on how Euro-North American women were so confused by this system of "colorism" that does not exist in the same way in their home countries.

5 On a tourist website called "The Talamanca Region," the author of a guidebook for Costa Rica writes, "Talamanca is Costa Rica's southeastern frontier region." See http://www.infocostarica.com/places/talamanca_hp.html (accessed December 26, 2011).

6 See http://www.gadventures.com/trips/costa-rica-on-a-shoestring/CRRS/2012/?aff=18424 (accessed December 26, 2011).

7 See http://www.discovercr.com/zone_south_caribbean.htm (accessed December 26, 2011).

8 *Rough Guides*, a guidebook series owned by the Penguin publishing company in the UK, are endorsed by Bill Bryson, a prominent literary figure in contemporary travel writing, who claims the guidebooks to be "consistently readable, informed, and most crucially, reliable" (McNeil 2001: front cover).

9 The images for this campaign can be found on the Internet. See http://visitcostarica.com/ict/paginas/en_afiches_portada.asp

10 See Frohlick (2008b) for a longer and slightly different analysis of Linda's experiences, in which I focus on how tourist women's erotic subjectivities were constructed through racializing discourses of fixed-in-place black men and mobile white women.

11 This is a paraphrase. His actual words may have been even more offensive.

6 Erotics

1 The remaining list of recommended activities went like this (and hints at the relatively inexpensive scale and also bodily and health-oriented tourism that is popular in this area): "Learn to surf ... eat good food ... watch a movie ... massage and spa ... read and write ... whitewater raft ... yoga ... drink ... and ... make the rain your friend."

2 As I explain in Chapter 3, a study in 2006 established that only 15 percent of small businesses were owned by Afro-Caribbean townspeople compared to the predominance of businesses owned by wealthy Costa Ricans from San Jose and foreigners, a number of local business people that had drastically declined from 30 percent five years earlier (Vandegrift 2007).

3 See Anderson for an illuminating discussion of how particular images of the "Caribbean" put forth by foreigners have been contested by local residents in southern Caribbean communities over the past two decades, notably the struggles over transnationalized and localized versions "enacted through the politics of aesthetics, food and body" (2004: 25).

4 There were some larger and more expensive European-owned resorts further south of the village, and by 2010 more expensive private home rentals had begun to emerge on the local/global market. The women I interviewed did not stay in such places, although a few of them worked in them as massage therapists, yoga instructors, or front office staff.

5 See Vandegrift (2007) for an excellent discussion of the opposing aims of the Costa Rican government and big business with those of local people and small business in the southern Caribbean as mobilized in protests spanning decades now.

6 I extend this discussion of the gendered meanings and politics of foreign women paying for local men's food in a forthcoming article (Frohlick 2013). In Lucy's situation, Thomas had insisted she give him cash to support his food consumption, which was based on gender discourses of femininity as source of nurturance and sustenance.

7 A form of monetary relationship that I do not address here is that of sponsorship, which entailed foreign women expatriates taking on financial responsibility for a local man and/ or his family. I discuss this in a forthcoming article (Frohlick 2013) but leave it aside here because my emphasis is on tourist encounters and therefore touristic contexts. However, such relationships, although muted in the community, warrant further investigation because of the gender power dynamics at play, as well as national structural realities of

deep economic marginalization, poverty, and mental health issues in the Talamancan region that give rise to them.

8 I use the actual name of the club since it no longer exists and also because it played such a central role in the vexed transnational social influences in the community, not only transnational romances but also cocaine trafficking, criminality, and, in the eyes of many townspeople, the moral decay brought on by open sexual and erotic behavior. It represented "Babylon" to many.

9 Distinctions between the Afro-Caribbean and white Costa Rican communities as far as family structure is concerned were apparent in Puerto Viejo; like elsewhere in Limón province and the rest of the Caribbean, Afro-Caribbean women in female-headed extended households and in serial common-law unions and as economic providers was a predominant pattern (McIllwaine 1997; Madrigal 2006)

10 Brennan shows how global tourism has shaped gender norms in the Dominican Republic where, contrary to myths that men are the breadwinners, Dominican men who "siphon money from their Dominican girlfriends – even from women who have sex with other men for a living – are not see as any less macho" (2004b: 719). She suggests that due to the sex economy, financial dependence on girlfriends and wives involved in transnational sex work is now seen as *macho*. A similar recasting of masculinity, refracted through complex racial underpinnings, has taken place in contexts of female sexual tourism in Costa Rica.

11 In her fascinating study of "host clubs" in Japan catering to affluent Japanese women who wish to escape into fantasy worlds of romance and sex with attractive young men, Takeyama notes that, in contrast to the hundreds of "hostess clubs" for Japanese male clients lining the streets of Tokyo and other cities, the host clubs are underground and "largely invisible to the public" (2005: 200).

12 Local men were also kept out of the tourist industry, especially foreign-owned businesses that preferred to hire foreigners with skills acquired in Western countries.

13 Their stories appear in a forthcoming journal article (Frohlick 2013).

Conclusion

1 I refer here to how Euro-American women understood local masculine heterosexuality within the gender category of *machismo*, which implies a naturalized and thereby socially accepted need for sex outside of a primary relationship. Women talked about how they might begrudgingly "accept" their boyfriend's infidelity if that was part of the culture, since local women seemed to. However, the degree to which local women actually accept men's extra-marital sexual practices is contestable.

2 See Frohlick (2007) and Jacobs (2009, 2010) for a discussion of this debate.

3 I borrow this apt phrase from Jessica Jacobs in her article entitled "Have Sex will Travel: Romantic 'Sex Tourism' and Women Negotiating Modernity in the Sinai" (Jacobs 2009).

4 Salsa Brava is the name of the town's infamous big wave that draws surfers from all over the world during December and March when at its strongest.

5 Behar (1993: 13) states: "It worries me that one does violence to the life history as a story by turning it into the disposable commodity of information." I share her concerns as well as her solution, in that we seek to write with what she calls "vulnerability."

References

Ackerman, S. (2010) "Plastic Paradise: Transforming Bodies and Selves in Costa Rica's Cosmetic Surgery Tourism Industry," *Medical Anthropology* 29(4): 403–423.

Adams, K. (2003) "Global Cities, Terror, and Tourism: The Ambivalent Allure of the Urban Jungle," in R. Bishop, J. Phillips, and W. W. Yeo (eds) *Postcolonial Urbanism: Southeast Asian Cities and Global Processes*. New York: Routledge, pp. 37–62.

Adams, K. (2005) "Generating Theory, Tourism and "World Heritage" in Indonesia: Ethical Quandaries for Anthropologists in an Era of Tourism Mania," *NAPA Bulletin* 23: 45-59.

Ahmed, S. (2000) "Who Knows? Knowing Strangers and Strangeness," *Australian Feminist Studies* 15(31): 49–68.

Alexander, J. (1994) "Not Just (Any)Body can be a Citizen: The Politics of Law, Sexuality and Postcoloniality in Trinidad and Tobago and the Bahamas," *Feminist Review* 48 (Autumn): 5–23.

Alexeyeff, K. (2008) "'Are You Being Served?' Sex, Humour and Globalization in the Cook Islands," *Anthropological Forum* 18(3): 287–293.

Alsop, R., Fitzsimons, A., and Lennon, K. (2002) *Theorizing Gender*. Cambridge: Polity Press.

Amit, V. (ed.) (2000) *Constructing the Field: Ethnographic Fieldwork in the Contemporary World*. New York: Routledge.

Amit, V. (2007) "Structures and Dispositions of Travel and Movement," in V. Amit (ed.) *Going First Class? New Approaches to Privileged Travel and Movement*. New York: Berghahn, pp. 1–14.

Anderson, M. (2004) "Arguing Over the 'Caribbean:' Tourism on Costa Rica's Caribbean Coast. *Caribbean Quarterly* 50(3): 25–46.

Andrews, H., Roberts, L., and Selwyn, T. (2007) "Hospitality and Eroticism," *International Journal of Culture, Tourism, and Hospitality Research* 1(3): 247–262.

Appadurai, A. (1988) "Putting Hierarchy in its Place," *Cultural Anthropology* 3(1): 36–49.

Appadurai, A. (1996) *Modernity at Large: Cultural Dimensions of Globalization*. Minneapolis, MN: University of Minnesota Press.

Appadurai, A. (1997) "Discussion: Fieldwork in the Era of Globalization," *Anthropology and Humanism* 22(1): 115–118.

Arroba, A. (2001) "New View of Women's Sexuality: The Case of Costa Rica," in E. Kaschak, and L. Tiefer (eds) *A New View of Women's Sexual Problems*. New York: Routledge, pp. 53–58.

Aston, E. (2008) "A Fair Trade? Staging Female Sex Tourism in Sugar Mummies and Trade," *Contemporary Theatre Review* 18(2): 180–192.

Bauer, I. (2009) "Relationships between Female Tourists and Male Locals in Cuzco, Peru: Implications for Travel Health Education," *Travel Medicine and Infectious Disease* 7: 350–358.

Beasley, C. (2011) "Libidinous Politics: Heterosex, 'Transgression,' and Social Change," *Australian Feminist Studies* 26(67): 25–40.

Beatty, A. (1999) "On Ethnographic Experience: Formative and Informative (Nias, Indonesia)," in C. W. Watson (ed.) *Being There: Fieldwork in Anthropology*. London: Pluto Press, pp. 74–97.

Behar, R. (1993) *Translated Woman: Crossing the Border with Esperanza's Story*. Boston, MA: Beacon Press.

Behar, R. (1995) "Introduction: Out of Exile," in R. Behar and D. Gordon (eds) *Women Writing Culture*. Berkeley, CA: University of California Press, pp. 1–32.

Belliveau, J. (2006) *Romance on the Road: Traveling Women Who Love Foreign Men*. Baltimore, MD: Beau Monde Press.

Beres, M. and Farvid, P. (2010) "Sexual Ethics and Young Women's Accounts of Heterosexual Casual Sex," *Sexualities* 13(3): 377–393.

Berlant, L. (2000) "Intimacy: A Special Issue," in L. Berlant (ed.) *Intimacy*. Chicago, IL: University of Chicago Press, pp. 1–8.

Bhattacharyya, G. (2002) *Sexuality and Society: An Introduction*. New York: Routledge.

Bhattacharyya, G. (2009) "Introduction: Ethnicities, Values, and Old-Fashioned Racism," in G. Bhattacharyya (ed.) *Ethnicities and Values in a Changing World*. Farnham, Surrey: Ashgate, pp. 1–34.

Biehl, J., Good, B., and Kleinman, A. (eds) (2007) *Subjectivity: Ethnographic Investigations*. Berkeley, CA: University of California Press.

Bishop, R. and Robinson, L. (2002) "Travellers' Tails: Sex Diaries of Tourists Returning from Thailand," in S. Thorbek and B. Pattanaik (eds) *Transnational Prostitution: Changing Patterns in a Global Context*. London: Zed Books, pp. 13–23.

Bloch, M. and Parry, J. (1989) "Introduction: Money and the Morality of Exchange," in J. Parry and M. Bloch (eds) *Money and the Morality of Exchange*. Cambridge: University of Cambridge Press, pp. 1–32.

Bloor, M., Thomas, M., Abeni, D., Goujon, C., Hausser, D., Hubert, M., Kleiber, D., and Nieto, J. (2000) "Sexual Risk Behaviour in a Sample of 5676 Young, Unaccompanied Travellers," in S. Clift and S. Page (eds) *Tourism and Sex: Culture, Commerce and Coercion*. London: Pinter, pp. 157–167.

Blunt, A. (1994) *Travel, Gender, and Imperialism: Mary Kingsley and West Africa*. New York: Guilford Press.

Boellstorff, T. (2007) "Queer Studies in the House of Anthropology," *Annual Review of Anthropology* 36: 17–35.

Bolton, R. (1995) "Tricks, Friends, and Lovers: Erotic Encounters in the Field," in D. Kulick and M. Willson (eds) *Taboo: Sex, Identity and Erotic Subjectivity in Anthropological Fieldwork*. New York: Routledge, pp. 140–167.

Bordo, S. (1993) *Unbearable Weight: Feminism, Western Culture, and the Body*. Berkeley, CA: University of California Press.

Bourgois, P. (1986) "The Black Diaspora in Costa Rica: Upward Mobility and Ethnic Discrimination," *New West Indian Guide* (3/4): 149–165.

Bowen, D. and Schouten, A. (2008) "Tourist Satisfaction and Beyond: Tourist Migrants in Mallorca," *International Journal of Tourism Research* 10(2): 141–153.

Brennan, D. (2004a) *What's Love Got to do With It? Transnational Desires and Sex Tourism in the Dominican Republic*. Durham, NC: Duke University Press.

Brennan, D. (2004b) "Women Work, Men Sponge, and Everyone Gossips: Macho Men and Stigmatized/ing Work in a Sex Tourist Town," *Anthropological Quarterly* 77(4): 705–733.

Bruner, E. (1989) "Of Cannibals, Tourists, and Ethnographers," *Cultural Anthropology* 4(4): 438–445.

Bruner, E. (1995) "The Ethnographer/Tourist in Indonesia," in M. F. Lanfant, J. Allcock, and E. Bruner (eds) *International Tourism: Identity and Change*. New York: CAB International, pp. 224–241.

Bruner, E. (1996) "Tourism in the Balinese Borderzone," in S. Lavie and T. Swedenburg (eds) *Displacement, Diaspora and Geographies of Identity*. Durham, NC: Duke University Press, pp. 157–180.

Bruner, E. (2005) *Culture on Tour: Ethnographies of Travel*. Chicago, IL: University of Chicago Press.

Budgeon, S. (2008) "Couple Culture and the Production of Singleness," *Sexualities* 11(3): 301–325.

Burns, P. (1999) *An Introduction to Tourism and Anthropology*. New York: Routledge.

Butcher, J. (2003) *The Moralisation of Tourism: Sun, Sand ... and Saving the World?* New York: Routledge.

Butler, J. (1993) *Bodies Don't Matter: On the Discursive Limit of "Sex."* New York: Routledge.

Cabada, M., Montoya, M., Echevarria, J., Verdonck, K., Seas, C., and Gotuzzo, E. (2003) "Sexual Behavior in Travelers Visiting Cuzco," *Journal of Travel Medicine* 10(4): 214–216.

Cabezas, A. (2009) *Economies of Desire: Sex and Tourism in Cuba and the Dominican Republic*. Philadelphia, PA: Temple University Press.

Cameron, D. and Kulick, D. (2003) *Language and Sexuality*. Cambridge: Cambridge University Press.

Campbell, H. (2007) "Cultural Seduction: American Men, Mexican Women, Cross-Border Attraction", *Critique of Anthropology* 27(3): 261–283.

Cantet, L. (2005) *Heading South (Vers le Sud)*. Film. Shadow Distribution.

Cantú, L. (2009) *The Sexuality of Migration: Border Crossings and Mexican Immigrant Men*. New York: New York University Press.

Cartier, C. (2005) "Introduction: Touristed Landscapes/Seductions of Place," in C. Cartier and A. Low (eds) *Seductions of Place: Geographical Perspectives on Globalization and Touristed Landscapes*. London: Routledge, pp. 1–19.

Chambers, E. (2000) *Native Tours: The Anthropology of Travel and Tourism*. Prospect Heights, IL: Waveland Press.

Chevannes, B. (2010) "Selection from *Rastafari and Other African-Caribbean Worldviews*," in P. Scher (ed.) *Perspectives on the Caribbean: A Reader in Culture, History, and Representation*. West Sussex: Wiley-Blackwell, pp. 2007–2226.

Clifford, J. (1990) "Notes on (Field) Notes," in R. Sanjek (ed.) *Fieldnotes: The Making of Anthropology*. New York: Cornell University Press, pp. 47–70.

Clifford, J. (1997) *Routes: Travel and Translation in the Late Twentieth Century*. Cambridge, MA: Harvard University Press.

Coffey, A. (1999) *The Ethnographic Self: Fieldwork and the Representation of Identity*. London: Sage.

Cole, S. and Phillips, L. (1995) "The Work and Politics of Feminist Ethnography: An Introduction," in S. Cole and L. Phillips (eds) *Ethnographic Feminisms: Essays in Anthropology*. Ottawa: Carleton University Press, pp. 1–17.

Coleman, S. and Crang, M. (2002) "Grounded Tourists, Travelling Theory," in S. Coleman and M. Crang (eds) *Tourism: Between Place and Performance*. Oxford: Berghahn, pp. 1–20.

Constable, N. (2009) "The Commodification of Intimacy: Marriage, Sex, and Reproductive Labour," *Annual Review of Anthropology* 38: 49–64.

Cornwall, A. and Lindisfarne, N. (eds) (1994) *Dislocating Masculinities: Comparative Ethnographies*. New York: Routledge.

Crouch, D. (2002) "Surrounded by Place: Embodied Encounters," in S. Coleman and M. Crang (eds) *Tourism: Between Place and Performance*. Oxford: Berghahn, pp. 207–218.

Crouch, D. and Desforges, L. (2003) "The Sensuous in the Tourist Encounter: Introduction: The Power of the Body in Tourist Studies," *Tourist Studies* 3(1): 5–22

Crouch, D., Jackson, R., and Thompson, F. (2005) "Introduction: The Media and the Tourist Imagination," in D. Crouch, R. Jackson, and F. Thompson (eds) *The Media and the Tourist Imagination: Converging Cultures*. New York: Routledge, pp. 1–13.

Curtis, D. (2004) "Commodities and Sexual Subjectivities: A Look at Capitalism and Its Desires," *Cultural Anthropology* 19(1): 95–121.

Curtis, D. (2009) *Pleasures and Perils: Girls' Sexuality in a Caribbean Consumer Culture*. New Brunswick, NJ: Rutgers University Press.

de Albuquerque, K. (1998) "In Search of the Big Bamboo," *Transition* 77: 48–57.

Deliovsky, K. (2006) "Elsewhere from Here: Remapping the Territories of 'White' Femininity," unpublished PhD dissertation. McMaster University, Hamilton, Ontario.

Deliovsky, K. (2010) *White Femininity: Race, Gender and Power*. Winnipeg: Fernwood Publishing.

de Regil, A. (2009) "'Like It or Not, Here We Are:' Exploring Xenophobia towards Nicaraguan Immigrants in Costa Rica," unpublished MA thesis. University of British Columbia, Vancouver.

Desforges, L. (1998) "'Checking out the Planet:' Representations/Local Identities and Youth Travel," in T. Skelton and G. Valentine (eds) *Cool Places: Geographies of Youth Cultures*. New York: Routledge, pp. 175–192.

Desforges, L. (2001) "Tourist Consumption and the Imagination of Money," *Transactions of the British Geographers* 26(3): 353–364.

Desmarais, F. (2007) "Advertisements as Tourism Space: 'Learning' Masculinity and Femininity from New Zealand Television," in A. Pritchard, N. Morgan, I. Ateljevic, and C. Harris (eds) *Tourism and Gender: Embodiment, Sensuality and Experience*. Wallingford, UK: CAB International, pp. 207–218.

Desmond, J. (1999) *Staging Tourism: Bodies on Display from Waikiki to Sea World*. Chicago, IL: University of Chicago Press.

DeWalt, K. and DeWalt, B. (2002) *Participant Observation: A Guide for Fieldworkers*. Lanham, MD: Rowman & Littlefield.

di Leonardo, M. (1997) "White Lies, Black Myths: Rape, Race, and the Black 'Underclass'," in R. Lancaster and M. di Leonardo (eds) *The Gender/Sexuality Reader*. New York: Routledge, pp. 53–70.

Donnan, H. and Magowan, F. (2010) *The Anthropology of Sex*. New York: Berg.

Downe, P. (1997) "Constructing a Complex of Contagion: The Perceptions of AIDS among Working Prostitutes in Costa Rica," *Social Science Medicine* 44(10): 1575–1583.

Dragojlovic, A. (2008) "Dutch Women and Balinese Men: Intimacies, Popular Discourses and Citizenship Rights," *The Asia Pacific Journal of Anthropology* 9(4): 332–345.

Ebron, P. (1997) "Traffic in Men," in M. Grosz-Ngate and O. Kokole (eds) *Gendered Encounters: Challenging Cultural Boundaries and Social Hierarchies in Africa*. New York: Routledge, pp. 223–244.

Echtner, C. and Prasad, P. (2003) "The Context of Third World Tourism Marketing," *Annals of Tourism Research* 30(3): 660–682.

Egan, C. (2001) "Sexual Behaviours, Condom Use and Factors Influencing Casual Sex Among Backpackers and International Travellers," *Canadian Journal of Human Sexuality* 10(1/2): 41–58.

Enloe, C. (2000) *Bananas, Beaches, and Bases: Making Feminist Sense of International Politics*. Berkeley, CA: University of California Press [1st edition 1989].

Errington, F. and Gewertz, D. (2004) "Tourism and Anthropology in a Postmodern World," in S. B. Gmelch (ed.) *Tourists and Tourism: A Reader*. Long Grove, IL: Waveland Press, pp. 195–218.

Ewing, K. (1994) "Dreams from a Saint: Anthropological Atheism and the Temptation to Believe," *American Anthropologist* 96(3): 571–583.

Farquhar, J. and Lock, M. (2007) "Introduction," in M. Lock and J. Farquhar (eds) *Beyond the Body Proper: Reading the Anthropology of Material Life*. Durham, NC: Duke University Press, pp. 1–16.

Finnegan, R. (2003) "Anonymity and Pseudonyms," *Anthropology Today* 19(2): 22.

Flowers, P., Marriott, C., and Hart, G. (2000) "'The Bars, the Bogs, and the Bushes:' The Impact of Locales on Sexual Cultures," *Culture, Health, and Sexuality* 2(1): 69–86.

Foucault, M. (1977) *Discipline and Punish: The Birth of the Prison*. London: Allen Lane.

Frank, K. (2007) "Playcouples in Paradise: Touristic Sexuality and Lifestyle Travel," in M. Padilla *et al.* (eds) *Love and Globalization: Transformations of Intimacy in the Contemporary World*. Austin, TX: Vanderbilt University Press, pp. 163–185.

Frankenberg, R. (1993) *White Women, Race Matters: The Social Construction of Whiteness*. Minneapolis, MN: University of Minnesota Press.

Franklin, A. and Crang, M. (2001) "The Trouble with Tourism and Travel Theory?" *Tourist Studies* 1(1): 5–22.

Freidus, N. and Romero-Daza, A. (2009) "The Space Between: Globalization, Liminal Spaces and Personal Relations in Rural Costa Rica," *Gender, Place and Culture* 16(6): 683–702.

Frohlick, S. (2006) "'Wanting the Children and Wanting K2:' The Incommensurability of Motherhood and Mountaineering in Britain and North America in the Late Twentieth Century," *Gender, Place, and Culture* 13(5): 477–490.

Frohlick, S. (2007) "Fluid Exchanges: The Negotiation of Intimacy between Tourist Women and Local Men in a Transnational Town in Caribbean Costa Rica," *City & Society* 19(1): 139–168.

Frohlick, S. (2008a) "Negotiating the Public Secrecy of Sex in a Transnational Tourist Town in Caribbean Costa Rica," *Tourist Studies* 8(1): 19–39.

Frohlick, S. (2008b) "'I'm More Sexy Here:' Erotic Subjectivities of Female Tourists in the 'Sexual Paradise' of the Costa Rican Caribbean," in T. P. Uteng and T. Cresswell (eds) *Gendered Mobilities*. Aldershot: Ashgate, pp. 129–142.

Frohlick, S. (2009) "Pathos of Love in Puerto Viejo, Costa Rica: Emotion, Travel, and Migration," *Mobilities* 4(3): 389–405.

Frohlick, S. (2010) "The Sex of Tourism? Bodies Under Suspicion in Paradise," in. J. Scott and T. Selwyn (eds) *Thinking through Tourism*, Oxford: Berg, pp. 51–70.

Frohlick, S. (2011) "'Souvenir Babies' from Costa Rica: Moral Economies of Conception, Commodification, and Mobility," paper presented at the Canadian Anthropology Society in Fredericton, Canada, May.

Frohlick, S. (2013) "Intimate Tourism Markets: Money, Gender, and the Complexity of Erotic Exchange in a Costa Rican Caribbean Town," *Anthropological Quarterly* 86(1).

Frohlick, S. and Harrison, J. (2008) "Engaging Ethnography in Tourist Research: An Introduction," *Tourist Studies* 8(1): 5–18.

Frohlick, S. and Johnston, L. (2011) "Naturalizing Bodies and Places: Tourism Media Campaigns and Heterosexualities in Costa Rica and New Zealand," *Annals of Tourism Research* 38(3): 1090–1109.

Frohlick, S. and Migliardi, P. (2011) "Heterosexual Profiling: Online Dating and 'Becoming' Heterosexualities for Women Aged 30 and Older in the Digital Era," *Australian Feminist Studies* 26(67): 73–88.

Fullagar, S. (2002) "Narratives of Travel: Desire and the Movement of Female Subjectivity," *Leisure Studies* 21(1): 57–74.

Gagnon, J. (2004) *An Interpretation of Desire: Essays in the Study of Sexuality.* Chicago, IL: University of Chicago Press.

Geertz, C. (1973) *The Interpretation of Culture: Selected Essays.* New York: Basic Books.

Ghose, I. (1998) *Women Travellers in Colonial India: The Power of the Female Gaze.* New York: Oxford University Press.

Giddens, A. (1990) *The Consequences of Modernity.* Cambridge: Polity Press.

Gmelch, S. B. (2004) "Why Tourism Matters," in S. B. Gmelch (ed.) *Tourists and Tourism: A Reader.* Long Grove, IL: Waveland Press, pp. 3–22.

Goodall, H. L. (2000) *Writing the New Ethnography.* Walnut Creek, CA: AltaMira Press.

Goodfellow, A. and Mulla, S. (2008) "Compelling Intimacies: Domesticity, Sexuality, Agency," *Home Cultures* 5(3): 257–269.

Goss, J. (1993) "Placing the Market and Marketing Place: Tourist Advertising of the Hawaiian islands, 1972–1992," *Environment and Planning D: Society and Space* 11: 663–388.

Graburn, N. (2002) "The Ethnographic Tourist," in G. Dann (ed.) *The Tourist as a Metaphor of the Social World.* New York: CAB International, pp. 19–39.

Gregory, S. (2007) *The Devil Behind the Mirror: Globalization and Politics in the Dominican Republic.* Berkeley, CA: University of California Press.

Grewal, I. (1996) *Home and Harem: Nation, Gender, Empire and the Cultures of Travel.* Durham, NC: Duke University Press.

Grewal, I. and Kaplan, C. (2001) "Global Identities: Theorizing Transnational Studies of Sexuality," *GLQ: A Journal of Lesbian and Gay Studies* 7(4): 663–679.

Grosz, E. (1994) *Volatile Bodies: Towards a Corporeal Feminism.* Bloomington, IN: Indiana University Press.

Gutmann, M. (2003) "Introduction: Discarding Manly Dichotomies in Latin America," in M. Gutmann (ed.) *Changing Men and Masculinities in Latin America.* Durham, NC: Duke University Press, pp. 1–23.

Harpelle, R. (1993) "The Social and Political Integration of West Indians in Costa Rica: 1930–50," *Journal of Latin American Studies* 25(1): 103–120.

Harpelle, R. (2000) "Bananas and Business: West Indians and United Fruit in Costa Rica," *Race and Class* 42(1): 57–72.

Harpelle, R. (2001) *The West Indians of Costa Rica: Race, Class, and the Integration of an Ethnic Minority.* Montreal: McGill–Queen's University Press.

Harris, C. and Wilson, E. (2007) "Traveling beyond the Boundaries of Constraint," in Pritchard, A., Morgan, N., Ateljevic, I., and Harris, C. (eds) *Tourism and Gender: Embodiment, Sensuality, and Experience.* New York: CAB International, pp. 235–250.

Harrison, J. (2003) *Being a Tourist: Finding Meaning in Pleasure Travel.* Vancouver: UBC Press.

Hastrup, K. (1995) *A Passage to Anthropology: Between Experience and Theory.* New York: Routledge.

Hastrup, K. and Hervik, P. (eds) (1994) *Social Experience and Anthropological Knowledge.* New York: Routledge.

Hemmings, C. (2002) *Bisexual Spaces: A Geography of Sexuality and Gender*. New York: Routledge.

Hepburn, S. (2002) "Touristic Forms of Life in Nepal," *Annals of Tourism Research* 29(3): 611–630.

Hernández, T. (2005) "'Sex in the [Foreign] City:' Commodification and the Female Sex Tourist," in M. Ertman and J. Williams (eds) *Rethinking Commodification: Case Readings in Law and Culture*. New York: New York University Press, pp. 222–242.

Herold, E., Garcia, R., and DeMoya, T. (2001) "Female Tourists and Beach Boys: Romance or Sex Tourism?" *Annals of Tourism Research* 28(4): 978–997.

Heron, B. (2007) *Desire for Development: Whiteness, Gender, and the Helping Imperative*. Waterloo: Wilfred Laurier University Press.

Ho, P. and Tsang, A. (2000) "Negotiating Anal Intercourse in Inter-racial Gay Relationships in Hong Kong," *Sexualities* 3(3): 299–323.

Hockey, J., Meah, A., and Robinson, V. (2007) *Mundane Heterosexualities: From Theory to Practice*. Basingstoke: Palgrave Macmillan.

Holland, J., Ramazanoglu, C., Sharpe, S., and Thomson, R. (1994) "Power and Desire: The Embodiment of Female Sexuality," *Feminist Review* 46 (Spring): 21–38.

Honey, M. (2004) "Giving a Grade to Costa Rica's Green Tourism," in S. B. Gmelch (ed.) *Tourists and Tourism: A Reader*. Long Grove, IL:Waveland Press, pp. 407–418.

hooks, bell (1992) *Black Looks: Race and Representation*. Cambridge: South End Press.

Hopkins, M. (1993) "Is Anonymity Possible? Writing about Refugees in the United States," C. Brettell (ed.) *When They Read What We Write: The Politics of Ethnography*. Westport, CT: Bergin and Garvey, pp. 121–129.

Howe, A. C. (2001) "Queer Pilgrimage: The San Francisco Homeland and Identity Tourism," *Cultural Anthropology* 16(1): 35–61.

Hume, L. and Mulcock, J. (eds) (2004) *Anthropologists in the Field: Cases in Participant Observation*. New York: Columbia University Press.

Illouz, E. (2007) *Cold Intimacies: The Making of Emotional Capitalism*. Cambridge: Polity Press.

Ingraham, C. (1996) "The Heterosexual Imaginary: Feminist Sociology and Theories of Gender," in S. Steidman (ed.) *Queer Theory/Sociology*. Cambridge: Blackwell, pp. 168–193.

Jackson, S. (1999) *Heterosexuality in Question*. London: Sage.

Jackson, S. (2005) "Sexuality, Heterosexuality, and Gender Hierarchy: Getting Our Priorities Straight," in C. Ingraham (ed.) *Thinking Straight: The Power, the Promise, and the Paradox of Heterosexuality*. New York: Routledge, pp. 15–38.

Jackson, S. (2008) Ordinary Sex, *Sexualities* 11(1/2): 33–37.

Jacobs, J. (2009) "Have Sex Will Travel: Romantic 'Sex Tourism' and Women Negotiating Modernity in the Sinai," *Gender, Place, and Culture* 16(1): 43–61.

Jacobs, J. (2010) *Sex, Tourism, and the Postcolonial Encounter: Landscapes of Longing in Egypt*. Farnham, Surrey: Ashgate.

Jeffreys, S. (2003) "Sex Tourism: Do Women Do it Too?" *Leisure Studies* 22(3): 223–238.

Johnston, L. (2001) "(Other) Bodies and Tourism Studies," *Annals of Tourism Research* 28(1): 180–201.

Johnston, L. (2005) *Queering Tourism: Paradoxical Performances at Gay Pride Parades*. New York: Routledge.

Jolly, M. and Manderson, L. (eds) (1997) *Sites of Desire, Economies of Pleasure: Sexualities in Asia and the Pacific*. Chicago, IL: University of Chicago Press.

Jordan, F. and Aitchison, C. (2008) "Tourism and the Sexualization of the Gaze: Solo Female Tourists' Experiences of Gendered Power, Surveillance and Embodiment," *Leisure Studies* 27(3): 329–349.

Kalish, R. and Kimmel, M. (2011) "Hooking Up: Hot Hetero Sex or the New Numb Narrative?" *Australian Feminist Studies* 26(67): 137-151.

Kantsa, V. (2002) "'Certain Places have Different Energy:' Spatial Transformations in Eresos, Lesvos," *GLQ: A Journal of Lesbian and Gay Studies* 8(1/2): 35–55.

Kaplan, C. (1995) "'A World without Boundaries:' The Body Shop's Trans/National Geographics," *Social Text* (43): 45–66.

Kaplan, C. (1996) *Questions of Travel: Postmodern Discourses of Displacement*. Durham, NC: Duke University Press.

Kaplan, C. (2001) "Hilary Rodham Clinton's Orient: Cosmopolitan Travel and Global Feminist Subjects," *Meridians* 2(1): 219–240.

Katz, J. (2007) *The Invention of Heterosexuality*. Chicago, IL: University of Chicago Press. [1st edition 1995]

Kelsky, K. (2001) *Women on the Verge: Japanese Women, Western Dreams*. Durham, NC: Duke University Press.

Kempadoo, K. (2004) *Sexing the Caribbean: Gender, Race, and Sexual Labour*. New York: Routledge.

Kipnis, L. (2000) "Adultery," in L. Berlant (ed.) *Intimacy*. Chicago, IL: University of Chicago Press, pp. 9–47.

Kipnis, L. (2006) "Something's Missing," *WSQ: Women's Studies Quarterly* 34(3/4): 22–42.

Kitossa, T. and Deliovsky, K. (2010) "Interracial Unions with White Partners and Racial Profiling: Experiences and Perspectives," *International Journal of Criminology and Sociological Theory* 3(2): 512–530.

Kitzinger, C. (2005) "'Speaking as a Heterosexual:' (How) Does Sexuality Matter for Talk-in-Interaction," in D. Cameron and D. Kulick (eds) *The Language and Sexuality Reader*. New York: Routledge, pp. 169–188.

Koutnik, J. (2005) *Costa Rica: A Quick Guide to Customs and Etiquette*. San José, Costa Rica: Ediciones Jadine.

Kulick, D. (1995) "Introduction: The Sexual Life of Anthropologists: Erotic Subjectivity and Ethnographic Work," in D. Kulick and M. Wilson (eds) *Taboo: Sex, Identity, and Erotic Subjectivity in Anthropological Fieldwork*. London: Routledge, pp. 1–28.

LaFont, S. (2003) *Constructing Sexualities: Readings in Sexuality, Gender, and Culture*. Englewood Cliffs, NJ: Prentice Hall.

LaFont, S. (2009) "Not Quite Redemption Song: LGBT-Hate in Jamaica," in D. Murray (ed.) *Homophobias: Lust and Loathing across Time and Space*. Durham, NC: Duke University Press, pp. 105–122.

Lake, O. (1998) *Rastafari Women: Subordination in the Midst of Liberation Theology*. Durham, NC: Carolina Academic Press.

LaMarre, N. (2011) "Sexual Narratives of 'Straight' Women," in S. Seidman, N. Fischer, and C. Meeks (eds) *New Sexuality Studies* (2nd edition). New York: Routledge, pp. 253–259.

Lambevski, S. (2005) "Bodies, Schizo Vibes and Hallucinatory Desires – Sexualities in Movement," *Sexualities* 8(5): 570–586.

Lancaster, R. (1992) *Life is Hard: Machismo, Danger, and the Intimacy of Power in Nicaragua*. Berkeley, CA: University of California Press.

Lancaster, R. (2003) *The Trouble with Nature: Sex in Science and Popular Culture*. Berkeley, CA: University of California Press.

Lather, P. (2001) "Postbook: Working the Ruins of Feminist Ethnography," *Signs: Journal of Women in Culture and Society* 27(1): 199–227.

Lefever, H. (1992) *Turtle Bogue: Afro-Caribbean Life and Culture in a Costa Rican Village*. London: Associated University Press.

Levin, M. (2002) "Flow and Place: Transnationalism in Four Cases," *Anthropologica* 44(1): 3–12.

Lewis, L. (2003) "Caribbean Masculinity: Unpacking the Narrative," in L. Lewis (ed.) *The Culture of Gender and Sexuality in the Caribbean*. Gainesville, FL: The University Press of Florida, pp. 94–128.

Lock, M. and Farquhar, J. (2007) "Introduction," in M. Lock and J. Farquhar (eds) *Beyond the Body Proper: Reading the Anthropology of Material Life*. Durham, NC: Duke University Press, pp. 1–16.

Löfgren, O. (1999) *On Holiday: A History of Vacationing*. Berkeley, CA: University of California Press.

Lovell, N. (2007) "When Things Get Personal: Secrecy, Intimacy, and the Production of Experience in Fieldwork," in A. McLean and A. Leibing (eds) *Shadow Side of Fieldwork: Exploring the Blurred Borders between Ethnography and Life*. Malden, MA: Blackwell Publishing, pp. 56–80.

Lozanksi, K. (2007) "Violence in Independent Travel to India," *Tourist Studies* 7(3): 295–315.

Lyons, A. and Lyons, H. (2004) *Irregular Connections: A History of Anthropology and Sexuality*. Lincoln, NE: University of Nebraska Press.

Lyons, A. and Lyons, H. (2011) "Introduction: Sex, Race, and Gender in Anthropological History," in A. Lyons and H. Lyons (eds) *Sexualities in Anthropology: A Reader*. Oxford: Wiley-Blackwell, pp. 29–34.

MacCannell, D. (1992) *Empty Meeting Grounds: The Tourist Papers*. New York: Routledge.

McGlotten, S. (2007) "Virtual Intimacies: Love, Addiction, and Identity @ the Matrix," in K. O'Riordan and D. Phillips (eds) *Queer Online: Media, Technology, and Sexuality*. New York: Peter Lang, pp. 123–138.

McIlwaine, C. (1997) "Vulnerable or Poor? A Study of Ethnic and Gender Disadvantage Among Afro-Caribbeans in Limón, Costa Rica," *The European Journal of Development Research* 9(2): 35–61.

McNeil, J. (2001) *The Rough Guide to Costa Rica*. London: Penguin.

McNulty, A., Egan, C., Wand, H., and Donovan, B. (2010) "The Behaviour and Sexual Health of Young International Travellers (Backpackers) in Australia," *Sexually Transmitted Infections* 86: 247–250.

Madden, R. (2010) *Being Ethnographic: A Guide to the Theory and Practice of Ethnography*. London: Sage.

Madison, D. S. (2005) *Critical Ethnography: Method, Ethics, and Performance*. Newbury Park, CA: Sage.

Madrigal, L. (2006) *Human Biology of Afro-Caribbean Populations*. Cambridge: Cambridge University Press.

Maksymowicz, K. (2010) "Masculinities and Intimacies: Performances and Negotiation in a Transnational Tourist Town in Caribbean Costa Rica," unpublished MA thesis. University of Manitoba, Winnipeg.

Manderson, L. (1992) "Public Sex Performances in Patpong and Explorations of the Edges of the Imagination," *Journal of Sex Research* 29(4): 451–475.

Marcus, G. (1998) *Ethnography through Thick and Thin*. Princeton, NJ: Princeton University Press.

Mascia-Lees, F. (2010) *Gender and Difference in a Globalizing World: Twenty-First Century Anthropology.* Long Grove, IL: Waveland Press.

Maticka-Tyndale, E. and Herold, E. (1997) "The Scripting of Sexual Behaviour: Canadian University Students on Spring Break in Florida," *Canadian Journal of Human Sexuality* 6(4): 317–332.

Mauss, M. (1950) "Les Techniques du Corps," in M. Mauss (ed.) *Sociologie et Anthropologie.* Paris: Presses universitaires de France, pp. 363–386.

Meisch, L. (1995) "Gringas and Otavaleños: Changing Tourist Relations," *Annals of Tourism Research* 22(2): 441–462.

Mellom, P. J. (2006) "Code-switching at a Bilingual School in Costa Rica," unpublished MA thesis. University of Georgia, Athens.

Metcalf, P. (2002) *They Lie, We Lie: Getting on With Anthropology.* New York: Routledge.

Mills, S. (1991) *Discourses of Difference: An Analysis of Women's Travel Writing and Colonialism.* New York: Routledge.

Molz, J. G. (2006) "Cosmopolitan Bodies: Fit to Travel," *Body and Society* 12(3): 1–21.

Momsen, J. (2005) "Uncertain Images: Tourism Development and Seascapes of the Caribbean," in C. Cartier and A. Lew (eds) *Seductions of Place: Geographical Perspectives on Globalization and Touristed Landscapes.* New York: CAB International, pp. 209–221.

Murray, D. (2007) "The Civilized Homosexual: Travel Talk and the Project of Gay Identity," *Sexualities* 10(1): 49–60.

Nagel, J. (2003) *Intimate Intersections, Forbidden Frontiers: Race, Ethnicity, and Sexuality.* Oxford: Oxford University Press.

Nash, D. (1981) "Tourism as an Anthropological Subject," *Current Anthropology* 22(5): 461–468.

Nava, M. (2007) *Visceral Cosmopolitanism: Gender, Culture, and the Normalisation of Difference.* London: Berg.

O'Connell Davidson, J. and Sánchez Taylor, J. (2005) "Travel and Taboo: Heterosexual Sex Tourism to the Caribbean," in E. Bernstein and L. Schaffner (eds) *Regulating Sex: The Politics of Intimacy and Identity.* New York: Routledge, pp. 83–99.

Olsen, K. (2002) "Authenticity as a Concept in Tourism Research: The Social Organization of the Experience of Authenticity," *Tourist Studies* 2(5): 159–182.

Ortner, S. (1996) *Making Gender: The Politics and Erotics of Culture.* Boston, MA: Beacon Press.

Padilla, M. (2007) *The Pleasure Industry: Tourism, Sexuality, and AIDS in the Dominican Republic.* Chicago, IL: University of Chicago Press.

Padilla, M., Hirsch, J., Muñoz-Laboy, M., Sember, R., and Parker, R. (eds) (2007) *Love and Globalization: Transformations of Intimacy in the Contemporary World.* Nashville, TN: University of Vanderbilt Press.

Palmer, P. (2005) *What Happen': A Folk History of Costa Rica's Talamanca Coast.* San José, Costa Rica: Publications in English SA. [1st edition 1993]

Palmer, S. and Molina, I. (eds) (2004) *The Costa Rica Reader: History, Culture, Politics.* Durham, NC: Duke University Press.

Papatheodorou, A. (2001) "Why People Travel to Different Places," *Annals of Tourism Research* 28(1): 164–179.

Paz, O. (1993) *The Double Flame: Love and Eroticism.* London: Harcourt. Translated by H. Lane.

Phillips, J. (1999) "Tourist-Oriented Prostitution in Barbados: The Case of the Beach Boy and the White Female Tourist," in K. Kempadoo (ed.) *Sun, Sex, and Gold: Tourism and Sex Work in the Caribbean.* Lanham, MD: Rowman & Littlefield, pp. 183–200.

Phillips, J. (2002) "The Beach Boy of Barbados: The Post-Colonial Entrepreneur," in S. Thorbek and B. Pattanaik (eds) *Transnational Prostitution: Changing Patterns in a Global Context.* London: Zed Books, pp. 42–56.

Piscitelli, A. (2001) "On 'Gringos' and 'Natives:' Gender and Sexuality in the Context of International Sex Tourism in Fortaleza, Brazil," paper presented at the Latin American Studies Association meeting in Washington, DC, August.

Plummer, K. (1995) *Telling Sexual Stories: Power, Change, and Social W*orlds. New York: Routledge.

Poovey, M. (2000) "No Sex in America," in L. Berlant (ed.) *Intimacy.* Chicago: University of Chicago Press, pp. 86-112.

Povinelli, E. and Chauncey, G. (1999) "Thinking Sexuality Transnationally: An Introduction," *GLQ: A Journal of Gay and Lesbian Studies* 5(4): 439–449.

Pratt, M.L (1992) *Imperial Eyes: Travel Writing and Transmigration.* London: Routledge.

Pritchard, A. and Morgan, N. (1996) "Sex still Sells to Generation X: Promotional Practice and the Youth Package Holiday Market," *Journal of Vacation Marketing* 3(1): 69–80.

Pritchard, A., Morgan, N., Ateljevic, I., and Harris, C. (2007) (eds) *Tourism and Gender: Embodiment, Sensuality, and Experience.* New York: CAB International.

Pruitt, D. and LaFont, S. (1995) "For Love and Money: Romance Tourism in Jamaica," *Annals of Tourism Research* 22(2): 422–440.

Puar, J. (2002a) "Circuits of Queer Mobility: Tourism, Travel, and Globalization," *GLQ: A Journal of Gay and Lesbian Studies* 8(1/2): 103–139.

Puar, J. (2002b) "A Transnational Feminist Critique of Queer Tourism," *Antipode* 34(5): 934–946.

Puccia, E. (2009) "For Neither Love nor Money: Gender, Sexuality, and Tourism in Costa Rica," unpublished PhD dissertation. University of South Florida, Tampa, FL.

Purcell, T. (1993) *Banana Fallout: Class, Color, and Culture among West Indians in Costa Rica.* Los Angeles, CA: Center for Afro-American Studies, University of California Press.

Ragsdale, K., DiFranceisco, W., and Pinkerton, S. (2006) "Where the Boys Are: Sexual Expectations and Behaviour among Young Women on Holiday," *Culture, Health and Sexuality* 8(2): 85–98.

Raventos, P. (2006) "The Internet Strategy of the Costa Rican Tourism Board," *Journal of Business Research* 59: 375–386.

Rich, A. (1980) "Compulsory Heterosexuality and Lesbian Existence," *Signs: Journal of Women, Culture and Society* 5(4): 631–660.

Richardson, D. (1996) "Heterosexuality and Social Theory," in D. Richardson (ed.) *Theorizing Heterosexuality.* Buckingham: Open University Press, pp. 1–20.

Ringer, G. (ed.) (1998) *Destinations: Cultural Landscapes of Tourism.* New York: Routledge.

Rivers-Moore, M. (2007) "No Artificial Ingredients? Gender, Race and Nation in Costa Rica's International Tourism Campaign," *Journal of Latin American Cultural Studies* 16(3): 341–357.

Rivers-Moore, M. (2009) "Getting Ahead in Gringo Gulch: Transnational Sex Tourism in Costa Rica," unpublished PhD thesis. University of Cambridge.

Rivers-Moore, M. (2011) "Imagining Others: Sex, Race, and Power in Transnational Sex Tourism," *ACME: An International E-Journal for Critical Geographies* 10(3): 392–411.

Robertson, J. (2005) *Same-Sex Cultures and Sexualities: An Anthropological Reader.* Malden, MA: Blackwell.

Rodman, M. (1992) "Empowering Place: Multilocality and Multivocality," *American Anthropologist* 94(3): 640–656.

Rojek, C. and Urry, J. (1997) "Transformations of Travel and Theory," in C. Rojek and J. Urry (eds) *Touring Cultures: Transformations of Travel and Theory*. New York: Routledge, pp. 1–22.

Romero-Daza, N. and Freidus, A. (2008) "Female Tourists, Casual Sex, and HIV Risk in Costa Rica", *Qualitative Sociology* 31: 169–187.

Rosaldo, R. (1989) *Culture and Truth: The Remaking of Social Analysis*. Boston, MA: Beacon Press.

Rosenfeld, M. and Soo, B. S. (2005) "The Independence of Young Adults and the Rise of Interracial and Same-Sex Unions," *American Sociological Review* 70(4): 541–562.

Ross, E. and Rapp, R. (1997) "Sex and Society: A Research Note from Social History and Anthropology," in R. Lancaster and M. di Leonardo (eds) *The Gender/Sexuality Reader*. New York: Routledge, pp. 153–168.

Rubin, G. (1984) "Thinking Sex: Notes for a Radical Theory of the Politics of Sexuality," in C. Vance (ed.) *Pleasure and Danger: Exploring Female Sexuality*. Boston, MA: Routledge and Kegan Paul, pp. 267–319.

Rushbrook, D. (2002). "Cities, Queer Space, and the Cosmopolitan Tourist," *GLQ: The Journal of Gay and Lesbian Studies* 8(1–2):183–206.

Russell, M. (1994) *The Blessings of a Good Thick Skirt*. London: UK General Books.

Ryan, C. and Hall, M. (2001) *Sex Tourism: Marginal People and Liminalities*. New York: Routledge.

Sánchez Taylor, J. (2001) "Dollars are a Girl's Best Friend? Female Tourists' Sexual Behaviour in the Caribbean," *Sociology* 35(3): 749–764.

Sánchez Taylor, J. (2006) "Female Sex Tourism: A Contradiction in Terms?" *Feminist Review* 83: 43–59.

Sandoval-García, C. (2004) *Threatening Others: Nicaraguans and the Formation of National Identities in Costa Rica*. Athens, OH: Ohio University Press.

Sandoval-García, C. (2005) "Football: Forging Masculinities and Nationhood in Costa Rica," *International Journal of the History of Sport* 22(2): 212–230.

Schifter, J. (2000) *Public Sex in a Latin Society*. New York: Routledge.

Scott, J. (1991) "The Evidence of Experience," *Critical Inquiry* 17(4): 773–797.

Seigworth, G. and Gregg, M. (2010) "An Inventory of Shimmers," in M. Gregg and G. Seigworth (eds) *The Affect Theory Reader*. Durham, NC: Duke University Press, pp. 1–28.

Shaffer, K. (1996) "Tico and Gringa Relationships: A Study of Acculturation," *Tourism and Its Consequences: Case Studies from Quepos/Manuel Antonio*. Report published by the North Carolina State University Ethnographic Field School in Costa Rica.

Sharman, R. L. (2001) "The Caribbean *Carretera*: Race, Space, and Social Liminality in Costa Rica," *Bulletin of Latin American Research* 20(1): 46–62.

Sheller, M. (2004a) "Demobilizing and Remobilizing Caribbean Paradise," in M. Sheller and J. Urry (eds) *Tourism Mobilities: Places to Play, Places in Play*. New York: Routledge, pp. 13–21.

Sheller, M. (2004b) "Natural Hedonism: The Invention of the Caribbean Islands as Tropical Playgrounds," in D. Duvall (ed.) *Tourism in the Caribbean: Trends, Development, Prospects*. New York: Routledge, pp. 23– 38.

Sheller, M. and Urry, J. (2004) "Places to Play, Places in Play," in M. Sheller and J. Urry (eds) *Tourism Mobilities: Places to Play, Places in Play*. New York: Routledge, pp. 1–10.

Small, J. (2007) "The Emergence of the Body in Holiday Accounts of Women and Girls," in A. Pritchard, N. Morgan, I. Ateljevic, and C. Harris (eds) *Tourism and Gender: Embodiment, Sexuality, and Experience*. New York: CAB International, pp. 73–91.

Smith, S. (2001) *Moving Lives: Twentieth-Century Women's Travel Writing*. Minneapolis, MN: University of Minnesota Press.

Smith, V. (ed.) (1989) *Hosts and Guests: The Anthropology of Tourism*. Philadelphia, PA: University of Pennsylvania Press.

Stoler, A. (1997) "Desire in Colonial Southeast Asia," in L. Manderson and M. Jolly (eds) *Sites of Desire, Economies of Pleasure: Sexualities in Asia and the Pacific*. Chicago, IL: University of Chicago Press, pp. 27–47.

Takeyama, A. (2005) "Commodified Romance in a Tokyo Host Club," in M. McLelland and R. Dasgupta (eds) *Genders, Transgenders, and Sexualities in Japan*. New York: Routledge, pp. 200–215.

Taussig, M. (1992) *The Nervous System*. New York: Routledge.

Taussig, M. (1999) *Defacement: Public Secrecy and the Labor of the Negative*. Stanford, CA: Stanford University Press.

Thomas, M. (2000) "Exploring the Contexts and Meanings of Women's Experiences of Sexual Intercourse on Holiday," in S. Clift and S. Page (eds) *Tourism and Sex: Culture, Commerce and Coercion*. London: Pinter, pp. 200–220.

Thomas, M. (2005) "'What Happens in Tenerife Stays in Tenerife:' Understanding Women's Sexual Behaviour on Holiday," *Culture, Health, and Sexuality* 7(6): 571–584.

Thomas, M., Bloor, M., and Crosier, S. (1997) *Young People and International Travel: HIV-Prevention and Health Promotion*. London: Health Education Authority.

Tolman, D. (2002) *Dilemmas of Desire: Teenage Girls Talk about Sexuality*. Cambridge, MA: Harvard University Press.

Tsing, A. (1996) "Alien Romance," in L. J. Sears (ed.) *Fantasizing the Feminine in Indonesia*. Durham, NC: Duke University Press, pp. 295–318.

Tucker, H. (2003) *Living with Tourism: Negotiating Identities in a Turkish Village*. New York: Routledge.

Turner, T. (1995) "Social Body and Embodied Subject: Bodiliness, Subjectivity, and Sociality among the Kayapo," *Cultural Anthropology* 10(2): 143–170.

Urry, J. (1990) *The Tourist Gaze: Leisure and Travel in Contemporary Society*. London: Sage.

Vance, C. (ed.) (1984) *Pleasure and Danger: Exploring Female Sexuality*. Boston, MA: Routledge and Kegan Paul.

Vandegrift, D. (2007) "Global Tourism and Racialized Citizenship Claims: Citizen-Subjects and the State in Costa Rica," *Race/Ethnicity* 1(1): 121–143.

Vandegrift, D. (2008) "'This isn't Paradise—I Work Here:' Global Restructuring, the Tourism Industry, and Women Workers in Caribbean Costa Rica," *Gender & Society* 22(6): 778–798.

VanEvery, J. (1996) "Heterosexuality and Domestic Life," in D. Richardson (ed.) *Theorizing Heterosexuality: Telling It Straight*. Buckingham: Open University, pp. 39–54.

Veijola, S. and Jokinen, E. (1994) "The Body in Tourism," *Theory, Culture, and Society* 11(3): 125–151.

Virmani, A. (2010) *Cowboys in Paradise*. Film. Coup Productions.

Visweswaren, K. (1994) *Fictions of Feminist Ethnography*. Minneapolis, MN: University of Minnesota Press.

Wade, P. (2009) *Race and Sex in Latin America*. London: Pluto Press.

Waitt, G., Markwell, K., and Gorman-Murray, A. (2008) "Challenging Heteronormativity in Tourism Studies: Locating Progress," *Progress in Human Geography* 32(6): 781–800.

Ward, J. (2010) "Straight Dude Seeks Same: Mapping the Relationship between Sexual Identities, Practices, and Cultures," in M. Strombler, D. Baunach, E. Burgess, D. Donnelly,

W. Simonds, and E. Windsor (eds) *Sex Matters: The Sexuality and Society Reader* (3rd edition). New York: Allyn & Bacon, pp. 27–32.

Ware, V. (1997) "Purity and Danger: Race, Gender, and Tales of Sex Tourism," in A. McRobbie (ed.) *Back to Reality? Social Experience and Cultural Studies.* Manchester: Manchester University Press, pp. 133–151.

Watson, C. W. (1999) "Introduction: The Quality of Being There," in C.W. Watson (ed.) *Being There: Fieldwork in Anthropology.* London: Pluto Press, pp. 1–24.

Whitaker, R. (2011) "The Politics of Friendship in Feminist Anthropology," *Anthropology in Action* 18(1): 56–66.

Wilson, E. and Little, D. (2008) "The Solo Female Travel Experience: Exploring the Geography of Women's Fear," *Current Issues in Tourism* 11(2): 167–186.

Wolcott, H. (2005) *The Art of Fieldwork.* Walnut Creek, CA: AltaMira Press.

Wolff, J. (1993) "On the Road Again: Metaphors of Travel in Cultural Criticism," *Cultural Studies* 7(2): 224–239.

Wosick-Correa, K. (2007) "Contemporary Fidelities: Sex, Love, and Commitment in Romantic Relationships," unpublished PhD dissertation. University of California, Irvine.

Wright, J. P. (1992) *The Toured: The Other Side of Tourism in Barbados.* Film. Berkeley: University of California Extension Center for Media and Independent Learning.

Yamaga, C. (2006) "Japanese Girl Meets Nepali Boy: Mutual Fantasy and Desire in 'Asian' Vacationscapes of Nepal," unpublished MA thesis. University of Manitoba, Winnipeg.

Zelizer, V. (2007) *The Purchase of Intimacy.* Princeton, NJ: Princeton University Press.

Index